GANG LAND

Also by Tony Thompson

Gangland Britain
The Infiltrators (with Philip Etienne and Martin Maynard)
Blogs 19
Gangs
Reefer Men

GANG LAND

From footsoldiers to kingpins – the search for Mr Big

TONY THOMPSON

HODDER &
STOUGHTON

First published in Great Britain in 2010 by Hodder & Stoughton
An Hachette UK company

1

Copyright © Tony Thompson 2010

A CIP catalogue record for this title is available from the British Library.

Hardback ISBN 978 0 340 92006 0
Trade paperback ISBN 978 1 444 70685 7

Typeset in Sabon by Hewer Text UK Ltd, Edinburgh
Printed and bound in the UK by Clays Ltd, St Ives plc

Hodder & Stoughton policy is to use papers that are natural, renewable
and recyclable products and made from wood grown in sustainable
forests. The logging and manufacturing processes are expected to conform
to the environmental regulations of the country of origin.

Hodder & Stoughton Ltd
338 Euston Road
London NW1 3BH

www.hodder.co.uk

For Harriet

CONTENTS

INTRODUCTION

He made the prediction just moments before they shoved him unceremoniously into the back of the waiting van. For months the twenty-something leader of the notorious drugs gang had lived like a king while spreading fear and misery among the residents of the inner-city estate where he was based. His reign, and that of his gang of dealers, finally came to an end when a team of police officers in full riot gear smashed through his front door and, after a brief scuffle, dragged him out in handcuffs for the start of a journey that would ultimately end with a long spell in prison.

Half the neighbourhood turned out to see him taken away, hopeful that now, at last, life on the estate could start to improve. The gangster scowled as he surveyed the onlookers before uttering the words that would leave them in no doubt that their dream of a brighter future was destined to turn to dust. 'You think we're bad?' he bellowed. 'Just wait till you see what's coming next.'

It is a sentiment that has been repeated all across the country many times since, but only recently has the hard evidence emerged to back it up: gang members are getting younger, more violent and are resorting to lethal force much more swiftly than they would have a generation earlier.

Crime in all its many forms is rarely out of the headlines of the national press, but for many it is the rise of youth gang culture that is by far the most worrying aspect of the underworld. Such gangs have always existed and, to some degree, have always been associated with violence, but as little as fifteen years ago they were still considered a phase that teenagers went through, a simple rite of passage.

Today, however, those in youth gangs find themselves on the edge of the world of grown-up organised crime. Children in their early teens have the opportunity to earn vast sums of money through armed robbery and drug dealing. They can look to older or former members of the gang and see the success and material wealth they have gained and set themselves goals of achieving the same. Rather than a phase, gang membership for many is now the first step on the criminal career ladder.

Since the publication of my first book on Britain's underworld landscape more than fifteen years ago, that career ladder has changed beyond all recognition. When writing *Gangland Britain* I split the chapters along ethnic lines because at that time there was little interaction between the different factions. Ten years later in *Gangs*, the lines between the different groups had become far more blurred. Yardies from Jamaica still dominated the crack trade, but dozens of other groups were also involved. Furthermore, many of the so-called 'Yardies' weren't Jamaican at all; the Jamaicans had been usurped by gangs of home-grown Yardies.

In the space of a few short years, the picture has changed once again. A recent study by the Association of Chief Police Officers (ACPO) found that the underworld economy is worth around £40 billion and that some 15,000 individuals are thought to be involved in organised crime, split among at least 1,000 separate criminal networks. Of the hundreds of crime bosses the researchers identified, twenty-seven were believed to be running their organisations from behind bars.

Some of Britain's criminal networks have sophisticated hierarchies and use a management structure almost identical to that of a FTSE 500 corporation; others are little more than loose-knit groups. Some are involved in well-known rivalries such as that between the Longsight Crew and the Gooch Close Gang in Manchester or the Burger Bar Boys and the Johnson Crew in Birmingham. Others are intimately associated with the names of particular families such as the Adams in London or the Gunns in Nottingham.

INTRODUCTION

Despite an influx of syndicates from Eastern Europe and South East Asia, crime continues to be dominated by home-grown groups. There are, of course, occasional turf-wars but most of the time these groups manage to exist in relative harmony. In fact, if the opportunity presents itself, these groups will come together and form loose coalitions, sharing their specialist skills and contacts in pursuit of the highest possible profit with the lowest possible risk.

The drug trade remains by far the most popular area of operations, today's gangs will deal in any commodity and turn their hand to any activity they believe will make them money. This new blending of criminal interests has had a dramatic effect on gang structure. 'They are quite unlike the Italian mafia model or the Turkish groups,' says the author of the ACPO report. 'There are no set ranks, rules and structures. They are more fluid, flexible and opportunist. There are Mr Bigs, but the person you start out thinking of as the Mr Big is quite often not. These are people who are flying below the radar and you may not realise who they are for a long time.'

Gang Land is an account of a journey in search of those shadowy, elusive characters who sit at the very top of their respective organisations, the de-facto CEOs of modern-day organised crime. It is a journey that begins with the street gangs, low-level dealers and hired thugs that make up the ranks of the foot soldiers, that passes through the world of the smarter, wealthier middlemen and continues on to the place where the kingpins and godfathers reside.

Along the way I hope to shed light not only on exactly who is coming next, but also on where this new generation of criminals that are working their way up through the ranks might ultimately end up.

Tony Thompson
London 2010

3

PART ONE
FOOT SOLDIERS

1
STREET DEALERS

The rush is fast, furious and almost unbelievably intense.

My heart is pounding inside my chest so hard it feels like I'm going to crack a rib. My mouth is bone dry; my palms slick with sweat and my mind is racing. I can breathe only in rapid, shallow bursts. Each and every one of my senses – touch, smell, sight, hearing, even taste – has become heightened to the extreme. A heady mix of fear, euphoria and adrenalin is coursing through my veins at the speed of light. A full-body high.

I'm tingling all over. I feel energised, somehow bigger, more powerful than before. The world has become a very different place and I sense that my position within it is for ever changed. But like most highs, this one is ultimately short-lived. Almost as quickly as they began the feelings start to fade and reality kicks back in. All I can do is wait for the next time and contemplate the realisation that it's true what they say: the buzz you get from selling drugs is every bit as powerful as the one you get from taking them.

It's a little after 12.45 a.m. and I'm one of a handful of dealers working north London's most infamous 'front line', the twenty-four-hour-a-day, seven-day-a-week crack, heroin, cocaine and cannabis bazaar that stretches from just outside Camden Town tube station all the way up past the Regent's Canal and on towards Chalk Farm, encompassing most of the side streets along the way.

The drugs market here is 'open', meaning the dealers will sell to pretty much anyone and everyone, just so long as they have enough money and look the part. The customer base varies according to the time of day but is mostly made up of thrill-seeking clubbers and adventurous tourists, as well as a significant number of students, hopeless addicts and desperate sex workers. But there are huge risks to all those involved. Buyers regularly get ripped-off or robbed while sellers are all too likely to find themselves being relieved of their entire stashes at gunpoint or dealing to under-cover police officers.

Dealers treat such incidents as inevitable occupational hazards. The nature of the work demands that they be out on the street and highly visible to the public for as long as they can, which means they are always horribly exposed. Whenever police launch their periodic clampdowns on drug activity in the area, it is the street dealers who are most likely to be arrested. They are also by far the most easily replaceable part of the distribution pyramid.

Street dealers occupy not only the very bottom of that same pyramid but also sit on the lowest possible rung of the entire organised-crime career ladder. Many are the most junior members of youth gangs desperate to build up their credibility, some are heavy users who sell drugs only to support their own habits; others have run up huge debts and have been forced to shift gear by way of repayment.

While money is the key motivation for almost everyone who gets involved in this kind of work, the amounts that can be earned at this level are often surprisingly low. Prior to my stint in Camden I spent time touring courts all around the country, listening in on the stories of those working in various open markets who had subsequently been caught in the act.

It soon became clear that the life of a low-level street dealer is a world away from the jet-set image of fast-cars, fancy restaurants and endless parties seen in countless TV programmes and films. The men and women whose cases I followed were inevitably found to be in possession of only a handful of wraps and a relatively small amount of cash with at best only a little more of each back home. Most were living with their parents or in shared accommodation. A significant number were technically homeless and none displayed any trappings of wealth in any aspect of their day-to-day existence.

A 2005 study conducted jointly by the Joseph Rowntree

Foundation and King's College London questioned twenty-two low-level dealers about their weekly earnings and found the average was £500. However, the individual income reported varied between a paltry £22 per week and an astonishing £20,000. 'Selling drugs can be profitable and for some highly lucrative,' says the report. 'However, it can also be about economic survival.'

Similarly, a controversial study by the London Borough of Lambeth in 2007 found street dealers working in the area earned an average of £18,800 per year. A few made far more but the majority made a good deal less.

Among dealers, working in an open market is considered only marginally less risky than playing hopscotch on a motorway while wearing a blindfold. The drugs they trade are usually obtained on credit meaning that they retain only a small proportion of the money they make. An arrest can be absolutely devastating.

'The last time I got caught, I'd been doing the business for about four months,' says Lee, a former addict and user–dealer from north London. 'They took everything I had. About three hundred quid and twelve wraps. That was my whole stash. Then they sent me away for three years. The minute I got out I started dealing again. What else was I going to do? I still owed my fucking supplier.'

The best-selling book *Freakonomics* by Steven D. Levitt and Stephen J. Dubner includes a chapter about the economics of the drug business based on the actual financial records of a Chicago gang called the Black Disciples. The figures showed that the vast majority of the gang's foot soldiers were earning less than the minimum wage, despite the considerable risks of being shot or arrested. In a chapter titled: 'Why Do Drug Dealers Still Live with Their Moms?' the authors showed that for every crack dealer rolling in cash, there are hundreds more only barely scraping a living.

Other than desperation, what keeps them on the street is the same thing that keeps millions buying lottery tickets – the hope that they just might strike it lucky. But there is also, in the early days at least, the sheer thrill of doing the deal.

I'm standing just beyond the pool of light that emerges from Camden Town tube station a few feet beyond the field of view of the British Transport Police officers stationed inside and just out of range of the CCTV cameras covering the surrounding area. Huge crowds pour out of the station every few minutes as new trains disgorge more and more revellers eager to partake in the vibrant nightlife.

My elbows are resting against the railing behind me and my right foot is casually tucked up underneath, the flat of my shoe pressing against the metal bar. Both hands are jammed deep into the pockets of my dark blue hooded sports top. To all intents and purposes I look as though I'm waiting for a friend but in reality I've chosen my territory with care.

To my left there are two dealers – a black woman in her mid-twenties and, a little further up on the opposite side of the road, a fifty-something mixed-race man with short dreadlocks. To my right there are two more, one short, one tall, both with deep Mediterranean complexions and pockmarked faces who appear to be working together. I'm hoping that I'm far enough away from the other dealers for them to leave me alone.

I keep one eye on my rivals and use the other to scan the crowd as it passes in front of me. I'm trying hard to look like the kind of guy who might be able to sort someone out with a little something but not the kind of guy who wants to drag them down an alley and steal their worldly goods. I run through a range of expressions, none of which seem to have the desired effect. In the meantime, I see that the dealers to my right have made yet another sale.

Their technique, relatively common in the area, involves the shorter man holding a number of printed flyers for local clubs. Anyone emerging from the station has to run the gauntlet of bored, scruffy students handing these things out so he blends in perfectly.

The only giveaway is that, unlike the others, his pile of leaflets never gets any smaller. Moving swiftly up and down a short strip of pavement at the end of the street he approaches people and holds out one of the leaflets towards them. Once he has their attention he makes his pitch, leaning forward and whispering in their ears, 'You need something? Coke? Weed?'

Most people shake their heads and move on, a few recoil in shock but the man clearly knows what he is doing and picks his targets carefully so that every once in a while, someone will nod their head. While I'm watching, a heavyset black man with baggy jeans and a pale sweatshirt does just that. The short man goes over to the tall man who is several feet away and points out the customer. The tall man then meets up with the black man on the other side of the road to make the deal.

As they walk side by side they carry out a move practised so many times it has become completely natural to them. Their hands flutter together at hip height for just a second and just like that, the drugs and the money have been exchanged. They continue walking together for just a few more steps until, both satisfied, they part and continue on their separate ways.

I'm so caught up in the moment, watching the deal unfold over my shoulder with something akin to rapt admiration, that I completely forget where I am and what I'm doing. By the time I turn my attention back to what's going on in front, the short man is staring directly at me, scowling.

I know I should hold his stare, front this out, but I've been caught off guard and immediately look away, cursing myself when I realise what I've done. Out of the corner of my eye I see the tall man return and the short man beckon him over. They exchange a few words and he nods in my direction. The taller one has that scary wide-eyed, haunted look of someone who just doesn't give a fuck while the short guy, narrowing his eyes to peer at me more clearly, looks as fierce as a pit bull terrier.

I assume they're trying to decide if I'm another dealer, a potential buyer or an undercover police officer so I decide to put their minds at rest by taking a leaf from their own book and becoming a little more proactive. Instead of kicking back and waiting for customers to search me out, I break the ice and give them an opening. As people pass me I give them a quick nod followed by a swift 'All right?'

It leaves those 'in-the-know' in little doubt what's on offer but this catch-all approach also vastly increases my chances of drawing the wrong kind of attention to myself. A few years ago a dealer on Brixton's front line had the misfortune to offer drugs to the local chief superintendent who was in plain clothes and on his way home. The officer declined but when the eager dealer insisted, he found himself under arrest. The man was later dubbed Britain's stupidest drug dealer by the local press.

While my new persona is at least attracting a few half-interested looks, and seems to have successfully seen off the two dealers to my right, I'm getting increasingly anxious and decide to cool off a little, relying on actions rather than words to spell out the fact that I'm a dealer. It's an enormous relief a few minutes later when, despite this, I finally get my first customer of the night.

A young couple have emerged from the station. He wears jeans and a pale short-sleeved top, she a dark green backless dress that finishes just above her knees. Their arms are affectionately wrapped around each other's shoulders but instead of gazing at one another, their eyes are darting around as if they are looking for someone. Or something.

When the man's eyes meet mine I stare back intently, slowly raising my eyebrows as if to silently say 'What do you want?' I hold his gaze just long enough for it to become uncomfortable, which is all the reassurance he needs that he has found the right person. I feel my pulse start to quicken as he approaches me.

Many say that scoring their drugs from strangers has a weird kind of rush of its own. Users in rehabilitation are taught that their addiction covers all aspects of their lifestyle, not just the taking of the drugs themselves. For many, the greater the risk they take to acquire their next fix, the better the high that follows.

It's all to do with dealing with the unknown, breaking the law, the thrill of the chase, the massive build-up of stress, the gut-wrenching worry and finally the huge sense of blissful relief when it all goes smoothly. And it's exactly the same for many dealers, except that the ultimate buzz comes from feeling the bundle of notes in your pocket grow larger.

The man is only a few steps away when his left arm slips out of his jeans pocket and hangs loosely down by his side. In the yellow glow of the street lights, curled beneath his thumb I can just make out a crinkle of orange and white paper, a ten-pound note. I push off the railing and take a few slow steps to my left so that all three of us are moving in unison. To anyone watching we are just a group of friends who have met up at the station.

His girlfriend's face is flushed with excitement. She slips her arm off his shoulder and falls back a little to allow him to lean in towards me. He is brimming with confidence but I can't work out whether it's because he's done this a thousand times before or because he's trying to impress her. He speaks softly. 'You got any white?'

Drug slang, in fact underworld slang in general, varies enormously around the country but 'brown' and 'white' are by far the most universal. Heroin is 'brown' because more often than not it's a bit brownish, but while 'white' normally means cocaine, it can also refer to crack, especially in this part of London so I need to clarify exactly which one my customer is looking for.

'Powder?' I ask. The man nods.

'Tenner?'

'Yeah.'

I take my hands out of my pockets as we walk. The tension mounts as the back of his left hand brushes against the back of my right. All the hairs on the nape of my neck are standing on end and I'm fighting to maintain my 'street' persona. To be caught at this moment would, depending on the size of the stash, put a dealer behind bars for anything between one and four years. All of which means, in the best journalistic tradition, that it's time to make my excuses and leave.

There are limits to how far I am willing to go for a story and, having only narrowly escaped prosecution for having a cache of illegal firearms, ammunition and a quantity of heroin in my house (more on that later) I know the Crown Prosecution Service will absolutely throw the book at me if I'm caught dealing Class A substances to the public, no matter how much I insist I'm only doing it in the name of research.

I did contemplate giving out fake drugs – tinfoil folds of building plaster, cling-film wraps of candle wax, polythene baggies of thistle leaves and so on – but though such actions might not lead to conviction, they are still an arrestable offence. More to the point there are countless examples of dealers being attacked or even murdered for attempting to pull just such a stunt.

Instead I've chosen to work as a virtual dealer, talking the talk and walking the walk right up until the moment when I have to produce the goods, at which point I launch my exit strategy.

The man and I are now walking in time. His hand brushes against mine repeatedly, urgently, waiting for me to turn my palm, take his money and hand over the cocaine. I stare forward and quickly pull my hand back up into my pocket. 'Feds everywhere,' I hiss softly. 'I ain't giving you shit round here, mate.'

He squints ahead, trying to work out who among the crowd might be the police officer I'm referring to.

I nod up the road. 'Try the next guy,' I say.

His face falls a little, his own hand returns to his pocket and he gives me an angry 'what-the-fuck-am-I-gonna-tell-my-girlfriend' glance before slinking off.

Even though I'm not carrying anything, the encounter leaves me almost dizzy with excitement. It is, by all accounts, a common reaction. 'That first deal of the day is sweet,' Lee, the former user–dealer had told me. 'But it's the last deal of the day is the best one. It's like you've got away with it. There's nothing the police can do to you now. All you have is the money and if they pull you over, they're going to have to let you go. I usually get a big stupid grin on my face that won't go away, crank up the tunes on the iPod and head home.'

I manage to suppress my own desire to smile as I make my way back to my spot on the railings, eager to catch my breath before

STREET DEALERS

I go through it all over again. A few moments later I'm brought back down to earth with a bump when I realise that the two dealers from my right have reappeared and are staring in my direction once more. With his taller chum watching on, the pit bull slowly starts advancing towards me.

Studies suggest that around a third of street dealers routinely carry weapons to defend themselves. That means that, statistically speaking, if I don't have anything on me, at least one of the other two does. Rather than waiting to see their next move, I decide to play it safe and check out the dealing scene closer to the canal.

At the first junction, the corner of Buck Street, I pass a man in a bright red top staring wistfully out at the main road. He is so distracted he completely fails to see the large van pulling up behind him or the two police officers clambering out. As their boots hit the pavement he snaps out of his trance and turns to see them. His body tenses as, for a split second, he contemplates making a run for it. But as more officers decamp from the van he realises the hopelessness of the situation and his shoulders slump as he resigns himself to his fate.

With the subject under control two officers from the van begin patrolling the street just ahead of me. The man and woman dealer I saw earlier melt away instantly as the policemen appear, as do dozens of others. It's as if the officers are pushing some giant invisible bow wave ahead of them.

The officer on my left suddenly surges forward towards a group of men leaning between two parked cars, asking one to produce whatever it was he just slipped into his pocket. The man starts to protest just as I walk by and I realise with a jolt that it is the same guy who tried to buy cocaine from me a few moments earlier. His girlfriend is nowhere to be seen.

He catches my eye and for a split second I wonder if he is going to somehow blame me for his predicament. I don't hang around to find out. I look down at the ground and put a spurt on until the sound of his increasingly vocal protests has faded away into the night.

This impromptu police action I stumbled across is the perfect illustration of just why street dealing in an open market is such a high-risk endeavour. There will always be those – especially among the ranks of the user–dealers like Lee – for whom it is the only possible option. But for others wishing to distance themselves from the long arm of the law, the key is to take things to the next level.

Trevor Gentles was the kind of man who excelled at blending into the background. He had the sort of world-weary hang-dog expression that told those around him that he was one of life's also-rans, the type hardly worth bothering with. It was the perfect cover because Gentles, better known by his street name of Sparrow, was a leading 'runner' for one of the most successful drug-distribution syndicates ever to target the streets of Camden.

Only a small proportion of the drugs traded in cities across the country are sold via open markets. Successive police and community crackdowns mean that most of the action now takes place in so-called 'closed' markets. In these dealers will only do business with buyers that they know, or with newcomers who have been recommended by an existing customer. Winning the trust of such a dealer is easy – all you have to do is get hold of their mobile phone number.

In the smallest of operations it is the actual dealers themselves who, having answered the call, make the journey out to the pre-arranged meeting spot and make the exchange. In larger, busier operations, dealers prefer to further distance themselves from possible prosecution by using runners to transport the drugs on their behalf.

Runners are half a step up the career ladder from street sellers. Their job is to meet with the buyers, collect the cash and hand over the gear. Some keep a small quantity of whatever they are selling on them at all times, others walk around with nothing and collect the necessary number of wraps from well-hidden stashes only when they receive a call from their dealer telling them where their next customer will be waiting. Either way, because they have no need to actively draw attention to themselves, they are far more difficult for the police to detect.

Some runners work for a fixed weekly wage and various perks that might include use of a car and mobile phone. Others take delivery of a quantity of drugs for a set price and negotiate with the customers on an individual basis, keeping whatever profits they are able to make for themselves. While that might sound generous, the reality is that it means the dealer is always in control of just how much money a runner is able to make. What keeps the runners towing the line is the dream that they might one day move up to the position of dealer themselves, though in practice such promotions are rare and unlikely.

The Joseph Rowntree study mentioned earlier gives an example of two runners, employed by a relative, who were required to sell 200 bags of heroin and 200 rocks of crack between them in order to earn their wages of just £150 each per week. The runners worked long hours – a minimum of five but up to seven days a week – for this money. Those same sales would net their employer up to £4,000 per week.

(Interestingly, considering how often teenagers protest they have no choice but to work the streets because 'it's better than flipping burgers in McDonald's', a sixteen-year-old working a forty-hour week at the fast-food chain would actually take home £163 after deduction of tax and national insurance. Shelf stackers at the major supermarkets earn a little more.)

With a good network of runners at their beck and call, a dealer need never touch a drug or meet a buyer face to face ever again. And that was just the way that Sparrow's boss, Artley 'Frostie' Henry liked to work.

Just twenty-four years old, Frostie had seven runners on his books. While most dealers prefer to work with people of roughly the same age or younger than themselves, Frostie's approach was the complete opposite. Instead of twelve- to seventeen-year-olds, he believed that non-descript men and women approaching middle age were a far better cover. Trevor Gentles was forty-five. Of the remaining runners Frostie employed the youngest was thirty-eight, the eldest forty-seven.

The gang's operations had been refined into a finely tuned machine. Each morning at his home in Stockwell, south London, Frostie would tightly pack several condoms with the day's supply of crack cocaine and heroin before he'd even had his breakfast. By the time he had finished eating, several young ladies would have come to call for him. Making their way to the bathroom, the women would each take one or two of the drug-filled condoms and insert them deep into their vaginas before climbing into Frostie's car for the start of the journey north.

In Islington, the borough adjacent to Camden, Frostie would park in a quiet side street then hail two black cabs – one for himself, another for his female friends – to take them on the remainder of their journey. Frostie insisted on this long-winded route because he knew he was being watched by local police and felt certain that his car would be recognised and stopped if he drove it all the way into the heart of his drug territory.

Once in Camden, the girls would quickly deposit the drugs at one of the two safe houses that the gang operated and Frostie would be free to strut around the streets as if he owned them. He was stopped and searched on an almost daily basis over the course of two years but was never once found to be in possession of any drugs. He boasted to anyone who would listen that he was untouchable and that the police were too stupid to catch him.

Whenever a customer called the 'drugs hotline' to make a buy, Frostie himself would answer the phone, find out what was required and agree a price. Minutes later Gentles or one of the other runners would be out on the street at the agreed location in order to make the deal. Five times out of ten Frostie would be there too, but he would stand back or wait on the other side of the road. He simply wanted to ensure that everything went smoothly.

Sales took place at various spots all across Camden but one of the gang's favourites was the bus stop outside the Sainsbury's supermarket a few hundred yards down from the tube station. Here both buyer and seller could loiter to their heart's content without drawing suspicion.

Typically Gentles would approach the buyer, his mouth filled with tiny wraps of crack or heroin that could be swallowed at a moment's notice. With Henry watching from a safe distance, Gentles would spit the required number of packages into his hand and swiftly make the drugs–cash exchange. Trusted customers who were unable to come up with money were allowed to pay with stolen goods instead.

Gentles and the other runners would remain out on the streets awaiting details of their next delivery and would return to the safe houses only to replenish their supply of drugs, using the properties as a makeshift warehouse and distribution centre.

Quality control was key to Frostie's success. If you bought a fifteen-pound wrap of heroin that was exactly what you ended up with. There were never any short measures and the quality of the drugs themselves was always consistent. Taking a tip from supermarket strategies, the gang also held regular 'buy two get one free' sales. The business grew so popular that there would often be queues of users lined up waiting for Frostie to arrive in the morning so that he could supply his runners who in turn could start selling the drugs.

One regular customer, John, described a typical scene that took place outside Kentish Town West railway station one morning. 'There were three, maybe four, people, also drug users, waiting for Frostie. Even while we were waiting there were other people joining us. Then I finally saw "Sparrow". Some of the people went over to him but when they came back they said he didn't have anything with him, he was waiting for his boss to turn up.

'A little while later Frostie got out of a taxi and started speaking to Sparrow. He led us off, he and Sparrow at the front. We all trailed behind in a long line until we came to Talacre Road. There were probably about eight of us now waiting. We stood about and carried on waiting while the two of them went out of sight. Then

Sparrow came back on his own and started to sell drugs from his mouth to all of us that were waiting. It was almost a competition to get the drugs first from Sparrow before they ran out. I asked for two wraps of crack and gave him twenty pounds. He spat them out from his mouth and gave them to me.'

What both Frostie and Sparrow failed to realise is that 'John' was an undercover police officer, one of several who had been buying drugs from the gang and keeping them under surveillance for more than three months.

'John' belonged to the Test Purchase Unit – a specialist anti-drugs team and the closest thing British policing has to the squad depicted in the cult American TV drama, *The Wire*. Led by Detective Sergeant Sean Tuckey, a twenty-seven-year veteran of the Met, the elite unit consists of six detective constables (five men, one woman) and one uniformed officer and spends all its time monitoring, investigating and ultimately targeting Camden's various drug-dealing networks.

Inside the TPU's secret base, somewhere in the south of the borough, surrounded by walls covered in pictures of present and future targets, DS Tuckey confirmed the findings of the Joseph Rowntree study that suggested runners like Sparrow often get the rawest possible end of the deal. 'We estimated that Frostie's operation was doing 300 deals a day, seven days a week. That generated a turnover of between £2,500 and £3,000 a day – up to a million pounds a year. Yet as far as we could make out, none of the runners he employed were actually being paid any money at all. They simply got drugs for their own use.'

This meant that no matter what the runners did, no matter how hard they worked and no matter how much money they made for Frostie, they had no chance whatsoever of escaping the position at the very bottom of the organised-crime pyramid. Some have it even worse. 'A runner might be given a bag of fifty wraps and told that he has to bring back a certain amount of money,' says DS Tuckey. 'But in reality the bag only contains forty-six wraps so by the time they are all sold, they are already short. They always end up in debt. It's one of the many techniques dealers use to control people.'

By the time 'John' encountered Sparrow, the TPU team had identified all of Frostie's main runners and rated them among the most active drug pushers in the borough. Little wonder – during a single seven-week period, Frostie took more than 4,600 calls on his hotline. The only thing they couldn't work out was how the runners managed to replenish their supplies during the day. Eventually another one of Frostie's team was followed after he completed a deal and led the police back to one of the two safe houses.

The property was raided early one morning in March 2007. As officers burst in through the front entrance the runners inside sprang into action, launching into an emergency plan they had established for just such an occurrence. While one group began to barricade the living-room door to delay the arrival of the police, others threw drugs out of the rear window of the property or frantically tried to swallow wraps to get rid of the evidence.

When the police did finally make it into the room one man, Conroy Wilson, was seen to have something concealed in his mouth. Making a quick assessment of the situation, the first officer through the door carried out what would later be described as a 'dynamic intervention' – punching Wilson in the jaw. He was promptly grabbed around the throat and made to spit out forty wraps of cocaine and heroin. A further fifty-two wraps of Class A drugs were found hidden under a speaker. A large lump of crack lay on the windowsill, scored with cut marks from the Stanley knife that was being used to cut it up into deal-sized rocks. Dozens more packets of drugs were recovered from the rear of the property where officers, anticipating the occupants might try to dispose of the evidence, had been stationed and watched bemused as it literally began to rain cocaine.

Gentles, who was still out dealing on the street at the time of the raid, was arrested a short time later. He pleaded guilty to conspiracy to supply Class A drugs and was jailed for four years and nine months. Frostie himself was found sitting on a sofa, desperately trying to destroy paperwork that showed the running tally of drug sales and profits. Henry not only denied the drugs charges, he also denied that he was known by the nickname 'Frostie' insisting instead that was his wife's cousin's name, and he was entirely innocent.

Although the TPU had huge amounts of video and surveillance evidence to show that the runners had been selling drugs, pinning any of the trade to Frostie with his hands-off approach proved to be something of a challenge. 'Artley Henry flat out denied that he was known as Frostie,' says DS Tuckey. 'He claimed Frostie was a cousin of his and had fled the country. He tried to say that we had the wrong man.' It was only by showing the pattern of behaviour that followed phone calls requesting drugs, that they were able to convince the jury of his guilt. He was sentenced to nine years.

If you head north through Camden, past Frostie's old haunts, up past the tube station and then continue along the road lined with open-fronted shops filled with tourist tat, you eventually come to the Regent's Canal, the artificial waterway that runs all the way from Paddington in the west of London to the Docklands in the east.

Take a left before you reach the market, cross the canal on Oval Road and you will find yourself in Gilbey's Yard, a quiet, cobbled terrace that runs parallel to the canal and still retains a pair of rusted tramlines from days gone by. It was here, on the first of the two wooden benches that look out over the water, that seventeen-year-old Sharma'arke Hassan received the bullet in the head that ultimately cost him his life.

At around 10.50 p.m. on Saturday 24 May 2008 the Somali-born teenager and a group of friends had just sat down when they were ambushed by a group of youths who had been lying in wait. In the chaos that followed, at least four rounds were fired from a small handgun but only the last one found its target. Sharma'arke collapsed to the ground where, according to eyewitnesses, his attackers kicked him repeatedly before running off.

The bullet was lodged somewhere between his parietal lobe and occipital lobe. Surgeons determined that an operation would either kill him or at best leave him severely disabled. After four days in which dozens of tearful friends and relatives kept a near-constant vigil around his bed at the Royal Free Hospital, Hampstead, Sharma'arke was taken off life support and slowly drifted away into oblivion.

The gunmen did not appear to have any specific target in mind – they had fired at all those sitting with Sharma'arke and any one of them could have been hit. It seemed to be just another teenage tragedy linked to the relentless rise of gun crime in the capital and beyond. But over the course of the four days that he took to die, a very different picture of Sharma'arke began to emerge.

As a runner for local Somali gang The Money Squad (TMS), Sharma'arke had been a key, albeit extremely junior, player in Camden's thriving drug market. The bench he had been sitting on was a regular dealer hangout. A month before he died he had been found guilty at Thames Youth Court of possessing cannabis and offering to supply the drug. Well-known to the police, this was merely the latest in a long line of his clashes with the law.

In September 2007 Sharma'arke had been involved in a pitch battle with members of a rival gang over drug turf. The Money Squad had been vying for control of the lucrative cannabis trade with other gangs including the North London Somalis, the African Nations Crew and the Centric Boyz. In this particular incident both sides armed themselves with metal poles and a variety of missiles as they attacked one another in the midst of Camden High Street. Sharma'arke was arrested in connection with the fight and charged with affray, but this was later dropped.

In November that same year he had been issued with an Anti-Social Behaviour Order (ASBO) which banned him from Buck Street, less than half a mile away from Gilbey's Yard. He broke the order the following day and returned to court the next month. In addition to the ASBO breach Sharma'arke was also convicted of stealing a Cartier watch worth £2,000. His punishment for both crimes was to be referred to a Youth Offending Panel.

In March 2008 he was convicted of threatening unlawful violence and breaching his ASBO for a second time. A week before the shooting he and thirteen other members of TMS appeared at Highbury Magistrates Court when Camden Council attempted to take out a mass ASBO against the gang in a fresh bid to completely curb all their activities. The court heard that as well as aggressively dealing cannabis, members of TMS were involved in assaults, fighting, underage drinking and on one occasion a mass public-urination incident.

With fourteen cocky teens in the dock and dozens of their friends in the gallery, the proceedings soon became chaotic. One youth insisted on referring to the judge as 'bruv' and refused to take his hands out of his pockets. 'It's my hands, bruv,' he taunted him. 'If you want to give me an ASBO just do it.'

The image of Sharma'arke Hassan as a young thug was entirely at odds with the views of many of those within the tight-knit Somali community who had gotten to know him. Sharma'arke's family had fled the deadly upheaval in the African nation when he was just a year old, first taking refuge in Ethiopia before making their way to the UK in 2001. They quickly settled among the 10,000 other Somalis who have made Camden their home.

His father, Abdirahman, an economist who had worked for the Somali Inland Revenue, tutored Sharma'arke in maths so well that he was far ahead of his classmates when he joined Torriano Junior School and he quickly became a 'good, well-educated student'.

He passed four of his GCSEs and planned to retake some of those that he failed. 'He wanted to study business and administration,' said his father. 'He wanted to travel, to go to America and Thailand. We ran from Somalia because of war, gunshots, to come somewhere safe. But he was shot, here. How can that be right?'

The reality was that Sharma'arke, like so many of today's youths, had joined the gang not out of choice but out of self-preservation. With so many rival, extremely violent groups of youths in the area, the only way to ensure some level of protection was to be aligned with one of them. As perhaps the most junior member of TMS, almost all the money he made while selling drugs would have been handed to those higher up the chain. While some saw the gang as a way of life, Sharma'arke was desperate to get out.

'He wanted to turn his life around and get off the streets,' says community leader Ibrahim Isse who became friends with Sharma'arke at the Somali Youth Development Resource Centre in Kentish Town. 'He was physically active and loved sports – especially football. He took advantage of all that we had to offer. He was interested in starting some training courses and getting back into college. He was the sort of youth that made us proud.'

Sharma'arke's mother in particular struggled with the way he was portrayed in the media. 'He was killed. He was a victim. He might have done bad things in the past but he was not a gangster. Would a gangster be home every night at 7 p.m.? Would a gangster be so quiet, so good to children? He was just normal, his friends came in and out of our house all the time. They were teenagers, just ordinary teenagers.'

Following the shooting, the local authorities redoubled their efforts to eradicate the gangs from Camden. ASBOs require a lower level of proof than a criminal court hearing and can be granted on the basis of 'hearsay' evidence. According to local police officers, the introduction of the ASBOs against an earlier gang, the ANC (composed chiefly of the older brothers of the boys who would go on to form TMS), led to an immediate reduction in violent crime and robbery in the area – until the new gang stepped in.

It took several more hearings before the orders, banning the youths of TMS from most of central Camden or from gathering in groups larger than five at a time, were granted. With most of its younger members unable to enter the area and therefore unable to assist in the drug trade, the older, remaining members of TMS quickly moved into the more lucrative world of Class A drug dealing.

It was therefore only a matter of time before they appeared on the radar of the Test Purchase Unit, the same police squad that had ended the reign of Artley 'Frostie' Henry. Led once again by

DS Tuckey, undercover officers began to gather evidence against them by making repeated purchases of heroin and cocaine, first in ten-pound wraps and then in greater quantities until the officers handed over £200 and received an ounce of cocaine in return.

Believing they were still dealing with relatively small-time operators, the team were stunned when one of their targets, Adil Osman whose street name was Top Man, suddenly offered to supply up to ten kilos of high-quality cocaine. Concerned about this sudden rise of the gang member from foot soldier to middleman status, DS Tuckey arranged to buy a single kilo of the drug with the aim of arresting as many of those involved as quickly as possible.

The deal was set up to take place at room 447 of the Premier Inn hotel in Euston the following week. Two undercover officers, 'John' and 'James', first met Ahmed Sadique Ahmed in the car park and handed over £25,000 in cash. Once the money had been counted the pair were sent up to the room where Adil and his friend Kenadid Osman opened up a rucksack containing dozens of packages of white powder.

But TMS had not moved into the big league. Far from it. The drugs turned out to be mostly soap powder. Only 0.88 grams of genuine cocaine, worth around twenty pounds at most, were included in the package. The police had tried to pull off a sting operation but had ended up being stung themselves.

'In many ways they were lucky they tried to sell the dodgy gear to us rather than anybody else,' says DS Tuckey. 'They could have easily ended up being shot dead for pulling a stunt like that.'

Osman, along with the others, was arrested and eventually pleaded guilty. He too had previously been served with an ASBO, which he had repeatedly breached. His latest court appearance was just the latest tragedy to hit his family. His brother Mahir had been murdered by a forty-strong mob in a gang fight in January 2006. Less than a year later another of his brothers, Faisal, was found dead in the River Lea, possibly murdered after an argument over a girl.

As he was being sentenced to a hefty term of imprisonment for drug dealing, Adil told Judge Deva Pillay to go fuck himself. 'I earn more money than you do, mate,' he sneered.

The wily judge didn't miss a beat: 'Not for the next eight years you don't, young man. Take him down.'

Although the action against TMS in the wake of Sharma'arke's death led to a temporary respite in anti-social behaviour complaints and proactive dealing, drugs remain widely available in Camden.

Hundreds of drug deals are still being caught on the area's CCTV cameras that cover the nine key streets. While these figures show a significant drop from the numbers of recent years, insiders say much of this can simply be attributed to the fact that the regular dealers know where all the cameras are and ensure they do their dealing in places where they cannot be seen. Drugs charities use the rising or falling price of drugs to measure the level of supply, and the price in Camden has stayed at or below the national average. Drug-related deaths in the area continue to occur at the rate of roughly one every week.

Towards the end of 2009 Camden High Street received a radial £1.5 million facelift aimed at making the area less attractive to drug dealers and more pleasant for residents. As well as widening pavements and removing street signs and road markings, the scheme also removed the railings that seemed to encourage loitering outside the tube station. But with addicts, tourists and students still flocking to the area each and every weekend, many dealers feel the opportunity to make good money more than outweighs the risks, especially if those getting caught are young, easily manipulated gang members who are almost instantly replaceable.

Although low-level drug dealing will always be a risky occupation, the risks are substantially reduced when a gang is involved. With sufficient manpower to employ lookouts, runners and a network of stashes, those profiting the most can almost entirely isolate themselves from the sharp end of the business.

Artley 'Frostie' Henry got caught because he didn't trust any of his runners and wanted to be on scene when the deals took place so that he could make sure he was not being ripped off. Although they relied on him for their livelihood, none of Frostie's runners had any real loyalty to him.

What separates his organisation from the likes of TMS is the sense of joint enterprise and camaraderie that most youth gangs enjoy. I have come to realise that for every member who goes along with the activities through duress, there are dozens more who eagerly embrace the life.

Which means if I really want to understand the bottom level of organised crime, as opposed to the bottom level of criminality, I'm going to have to experience life in a street gang first hand.

2
STREET GANGS

Joland Giwa, aka Dexter, the self-styled 'General' of one of south London's most notorious street gangs, is about to declare war.

Illuminated by the glow of a street lamp and surrounded by half a dozen hooded members of his crew who crowd in tight around him, he stares intently into the lens of a small video camera as he calmly lays down a challenge to each and every other crew in the capital.

'Ite. It's Dexter, yeah. Man know me. I'm DSN repping Croydon. Croydon is our town. If we catch you in Croydon then it's over. Nobody can't come Croydon and say they are crew, yeah. Don't even come Croydon and fucking say like, like . . . man I ain't got no beef with OC, but don't come Croydon saying you're OC. Are you stupid? Are you fucking dumb?

'If you come Croydon, you mans can only roll around in cars. You can't come Croydon on foot. Say no more. I am the fucking General. I did play a part in the beginning. Ask about DSN, who started it. Get me? I am the fucking General. Say no more, G. Man get to know me.'

DSN stands for Don't Say Nothing, the name of the gang Dexter helped found a couple of years earlier. Since then it has grown rapidly into a force to be reckoned with: there are around twenty or so hard-core 'elder' members and up to a hundred associates. DSN even has a separate 'youth' division known as D2M – Down To Murder. Many key members of both factions, Dexter included, are known for their propensity for extreme violence.

Dexter may not have a beef with the OC (Organised Criminals, a Brixton-based gang) but he does have a major one with the Gypsy Hill-based Gipset and their leader who goes by the street name of Konan. As the filming continues, Dexter gets increasingly excited and agitated. Jeered on by the others, especially his closest confidant Billy 'Thai Kid' Langridge, he begins to deride those who only stab people in the buttocks or legs in the belief that this will not cause a fatal injury.

Wide-eyed, bursting with energy, Dexter spits out his words and gesticulates forcefully to emphasise his point: if you get into a fight with Dexter, he's going to go for the kill. 'Fuck Gipset and fuck Konan, ya pussy,' he continues. 'Yeah. You only shank man in the bum. Get me? You're a bum shanker. Yeah. Me, I'm a badder boy. I've shanked man 'im in the fucking head. I've shanked man 'im in the neck.'

The excitement continues to build as Dexter relates an incident in which he and his brother caught up with a rival gang member who had been trying to make a run for it. 'Me and Moodz started chasing him. Me and my brother Moodz, yeah. Big up Moodz, yeah. We caught him on the grass; we caught him in the park. And I bottled his head. Shanked him in the fucking head! Took off his fucking ear!'

After this Dexter calms down. He smiles and shakes his head sagely as he announces that anyone trying to challenge him and his gang will come away with nothing but regrets. No one has a chance against DSN, he says, but if anyone wants to have a go they are more than welcome to bring it on. 'Man them can try. That's all you can do is try. But me I don't try. I get you. I will get you, G. Physically. I'll get you physically. Fucking real. DSN all day, everyday.'

The video is filmed sometime towards the end of August 2006 when Dexter is just fifteen years old. It takes only a few days before the clip, edited to include a heavy drum 'n' bass music track and gunshot sound effects, has been posted onto the Internet. The first challenges to the supposed authority of DSN, in the form of insulting comments on gang websites, appear within hours.

In the three years that follow there will be countless stabbings, numerous shootings and at least three murders, all a direct result of Dexter's decision to throw down the gauntlet and declare Croydon a no-go area for other gangs.

What follows is the inside story of those years.

For a brief moment it looks as though Radar, a tough-talking, streetwise teenager, is about to cry, the second time in the space of a few minutes that he has been on the verge of becoming tearful. It first happened when he started to talk about the deep love he feels for the friends he grew up with; a misty, faraway expression swept across his young face as the emotions powered through him.

Now, in a split-second of hesitation, I see that same look on his face again, just before he begins talking about the streets where he was raised.

'I love my ends,' he says, his voice thick with emotion. 'I can't explain it. People say how can you love a street or a block of flats, all that, but it's where I come from. It's my roots. Everything that's ever happened to me happened right here. No one can take that away from me, ever. I won't let anyone take it away.'

We've just made the short walk from the quiet residential streets around Wandle Park where Radar grew up, through the covered walkway and across to the bustling concrete heart of Croydon's central shopping area, served by the pedestrianised North End throughfare.

One of London's largest boroughs, Croydon mixes affluent suburbs to the south with seriously deprived inner-city areas further north, and it is here in particular that the gang mentality has taken root.

'You see, you have to have control. If just anyone can walk through your area, it's not right. You wouldn't let just anyone walk through your house, would you? And if someone came into your house and disrespected you and your family, you'd do something about it. So someone comes to my ends and doesn't show respect, I do something about it. I'm not just going to sit there and, you know what, just take it. Naah. It don't work like that.'

For Radar, a fully fledged DSN 'soulja' who joined the gang after serving a lengthy apprenticeship with D2M, day-to-day life is now dominated by an increasingly violent turf war, all in the name of 'repping the ends' or defending the territory.

As well as Gipset, DSN shares borders with the Mitcham-based Terror Zone and a Thornton Heath gang known as SMN. Originally said to stand for 'Straight Merking Niggas' (merk is street slang for murder) this was later changed to 'Shine My Nine', supposedly in honour of a newly acquired gun collection, though the phrase can also be a reference to oral sex.

The first battle took place less than three weeks after Dexter's provocative clip first aired. Up to thirty members of DSN and SMN were involved in a brawl at the massive Whitgift shopping centre late one Tuesday afternoon. By the time the police and security guards managed to break it up, a seventeen-year-old was in a critical condition with multiple stab wounds to the torso.

'When you're in a fight, you don't really have time to think about what you're doing,' says Radar. 'The adrenalin's pumping. It's crazy. You use whatever you can, you do whatever the fuck you can cos at the end of the day, you want to make sure you're the one who walks away.

'You don't hesitate. You do the worst things you can do. If there's something in your hand, you're gonna use it. Swing it out fast and hard. It's a fight. It's not a game. There's a war going on. If you don't, they're gonna happen to you.'

'Sometimes it just kicks off but sometimes you know its coming so people have time to go and get their weapons if they need to. I didn't. I never go anywhere without this.' Radar taps his waistline with the flat of his hand. For a moment I think he's showing me where he keeps his knife but then I realise he is actually talking about the heavy metal buckle on his belt in the shape of a flying eagle. The belts are a DSN trademark and make reference to their Brixton-based allies, the Bird Gang.

'This is a wicked weapon,' he continues. 'Wherever you hit someone, they bleed.'

The following month there was another clash at the Whitgift, but this time footage of the fighting was captured on a mobile phone and uploaded to YouTube by one of Radar's friends. 'Fuck DSN,' said one comment posted in response, 'U man need to start gettin a [bulletproof] vest.'

Alarmed by the growing violence, the Whitgift centre responded by shoring up its security presence and preventing large groups of youths from gathering inside, but the surrounding streets and in particular the local branch of McDonald's remained a magnet for both gangs making further confrontations inevitable.

A few days later a fifteen-year-old DSN member got into a fight in the town centre with an SMN member. After trading kicks and punches the two boys decided to arm themselves, grabbing whatever they could lay their hands on from an unattended street-sweeper's trolley on the side of the road. One grabbed a broom, the other a shovel and they let rip at one another until they were both arrested.

A week or so later yet another mass confrontation was set to take place when police swooped. As many as sixty black youths aged between thirteen and eighteen, some of them still in school uniform, were lined up and frisked in what police described as a pre-emptive measure. Several youths were arrested for breaking dispersal orders, which banned them from congregating in that area.

Then came a fight that started out at Croydon College and ended up at East Croydon train station where a sixteen-year-old from SMN was stabbed twice in the chest before an elderly passer-by stepped in and stopped the attack. The college, the only further education centre in the local area, has often been a flashpoint for trouble.

'There's all type of man dem at the college – DSN, SMN, Gipset, LMD (Lick Man Down), Heathset – but Croydon belongs to DSN, you get me?' Radar explains. 'It kicked off outside the Fairfield Halls big time and when SMN had enough they headed home. But we got one of them Gipset boys by the station. SMN and Gipset roll together so he got shanked and planked.'

'Planked?'

'The boy got humiliated. Owned.'

Soon other gangs decided to follow Dexter's lead and make similar declarations about their own territory, only to receive similar challenges. In November, fourteen members of the Stuck 'Em Up Kids gang (SUK) from Battersea ventured into Mitcham looking for members of Terror Zone.

The invaders were anything but subtle, chanting 'SUK, SUK, SUK' followed by 'RAP, RAP, RAP' to announce their presence as they headed towards one of the area's most notorious estates. At around 7 p.m. they came across a small group of TZ members and gave chase.

'About six of us ran after them until we reached the end of an alleyway,' one SUK member said later. 'We didn't go down because we thought it might be some kind of a trap. Instead we retraced our steps back to Lavender Road where the other SUK members were. On the way we passed a house with some broken bits of furniture outside so we picked up some pieces of wood and planks to use as weapons.'

But the members of Terror Zone, aware of the incursion, called in reinforcements and by the time the two gangs met again, SUK were outnumbered three to one.

Horrified residents looked on as up to sixty youths armed with planks of wood and baseball bats ran at each other near Mortimer Road. Realising their situation was hopeless the SUK decided to retreat but one member, sixteen-year-old Eugene 'Fruge' Attram, fell behind and was soon surrounded.

A fourteen-year-old friend of Attram and fellow SUK member who went to his aid saw what happened next: 'There was about seven people around him and they were punching him in his body, all close like boxing. He was trying to defend himself, trying to throw punches back. He went to the floor but I didn't see how it happened.

'I ran towards Eugene but there was people behind me and I just got a few steps when somebody jumped me. I was only about ten

metres away from Eugene. Someone grabbed me and I was struggling. I think there was more than one person. They grabbed me
round the neck and pushed my head to the floor, all I could see
was the pavement.

'I felt something on my neck and I heard people shouting "Wet
him up, wet him up" [stab him, stab him]. They bent me forward,
it was quite hard. They used quite a lot of force. I was thinking
"I've just got to get out of this" and I was struggling hard.

'I was trying to shake them off, moving my body trying to get
him to let go. Then I felt something on my neck and I was sliced
or something. It felt like a slice. But I didn't see any blood at first.

'Then they just started punching me to my face. Then I went to
the floor and a guy hit me on the head.'

By the time other SUK members arrived to help, Eugene Attram
was unconscious with blood pouring from wounds in his chest,
head and back. He died before he reached hospital.

Two days later, Terror Zone's MySpace page carried the following message: 'You can't move to [attack] the TZ. If you move to
the TZ you will get shanked. Shanking fruge was a warning.'

A short time later the gang uploaded rap tracks to the site. One,
'Got It Good' includes the line: 'My niggas roll with shanks in
their pockets like they're tenners, I roll with a big shank, any nigga
move to me I push the blade through his piss tank.'

Another song boasted: 'We leave niggas yellow-faced like the
murder signs.' And referred to the gang's members as 'certified
murderers' who never snitch to the police.

Eighteen-year-old Terror Zone member Adam Rockwood,
who received a stab wound to the leg during the fracas, would
ultimately be found guilty of Attram's murder at the Old Bailey.
Three other members of Terror Zone were convicted of violent
disorder. As Rockwood was led from the dock by prison guards,
he pointed to Attram's parents and shouted: 'Your kid's a mug,
your kid's a dickhead.'

I ask Radar for his own views on Attram's death. 'He was from
Thornton Heath so as far as I'm concerned he should have been

with SMN,' he says. 'But he's running with people from Battersea. How stupid is that?

'I read somewhere that he wasn't in a gang. But he was there that night. He must have known what was happening. If not then yeah, he was a dickhead. But if he was there to fight, then he got unlucky. Shit happens. You get caught slippin, you get caught out, you die.

'Does it scare me? Nah. Like I said you don't have time to think about it. In that situation it's you or the other guy. The man who killed him, yeah, he'll do a few years in prison but no one is going to mess with him. His rep is secure for life.

'He has shown that he's authentic. He doesn't just talk it, he walks it. You gotta have some kind of bollocks to stab someone right? Well he has those. You do what you have to do to survive, to fit in. And if you live in hell, sometimes you have to turn into the devil. You get me?'

Candid interviews with members of street gangs are nothing new but when it came to researching this book, I wanted to do something a little different.

Most of the time, such interviews only take place in the aftermath of the latest teen tragedy. Everyone is hyped up and reporters and camera crews descend like a plague of locusts in a feeding frenzy.

In the case of tabloid newspapers and certain investigative documentary programmes, interviewees are regularly paid 'fees' in return for their assistance, often under the guise of travelling expenses. The more sensational the story, the higher the payment.

With tight deadlines adding to the pressure to get the best possible story in the shortest possible time, it is all too easy to be taken in by those who know how to play the system.

Furthermore, considering how much time all the youth gangs spend establishing a presence on YouTube and various social-networking sites, it is little wonder that they will jump at the chance to appear on television or in a national newspaper, elevating the status of their gang beyond their wildest dreams. Hence the parade of under-age kids, their faces disguised, swearing blind that they stabbed three and shot four gang rivals before breakfast that morning and that they make £500 selling crack in their school lunch break five days a week.

In a bid to uncover a somewhat more realistic view of what life is really like in today's street gangs I decided to adopt a longer-term approach. To this end I began to make tentative contacts with several gangs in different parts of the country, hoping one would emerge as a strong enough candidate to withstand greater scrutiny. The idea was to be able to cover the shootings, stabbings and beefs contemporaneously, rather than as a knee-jerk reaction to a particular incident.

A few weeks after my first meeting with Radar I heard about another gang fight in Croydon in which a fifteen-year-old was stabbed in the head. I called him up to see if he could provide any more details. It turns out that this time, the action revolved around a group of friends from his old gang, D2M.

'This kid, he's been kicked out of school for something he didn't do, someone from D2M did it, so that means he has a beef with D2M. He was going around telling everyone how he was going to fuck up one man, knock out another, he was giving it all that. But if you got a beef with a man from D2M, you got a beef with all of D2M. That's how it works.

'He made some phone calls to arrange the fight. It was supposed to be at Tesco in Purley but then it got changed to Croydon because some of D2M had been banned from there. He had a knife and a knuckleduster and someone said he had a gun, but gave it to someone else while he was on his way.

'His friends thought they were there just to watch him fight this one man but when they got there and saw D2M in numbers, they just ran. And then the boy who wanted to fight started running and running but knew he couldn't get away. One of the boys caught up with him and tripped him up and he went flying into this shop window.

'Then he was on the ground. And everyone jumped on him. Then he was being whipped with belts and kicked and punched and all the people, all these women out shopping with their kids, they all start screaming and shouting.

'Somehow he gets up again but he'd lost one of his shoes and he's still running until he ends up in a shop doorway and everyone piles into him and that's when he takes out the knife and starts waving it around and that's when my mate took a blade to the head.

'It wasn't bad, not even deep. He was just pissed off that he'd got shanked. He had eight stitches.'

Two months later in March 2007 D2M makes the headlines again because of the trial and conviction of member Adam Eastmond for stabbing seventeen-year-old Gavin Brown to death in October 2005 with a 'Rambo'-style hunting knife.

Eastmond, who was just fifteen at the time, told the court: 'I had joined D2M and got into some trouble with a guy from our arch-rivals Gipset. We had a misunderstanding. He took something from me. Other people started talking and I became paranoid and thought I was in serious danger. Gipset had a bad reputation for violence and I was scared. So I got my hands on a knife.

'I went to the [black] market and bought the blade for ten pounds. I stuck it down the back of my pants and it made me feel safe. I never took the knife to school, but I carried it whenever I went out at night and at parties.'

He claimed that on the day of the killing he had taken the weapon to Parkfields Recreation Ground in Shirley, near Croydon, in order to sell it. But when he got to the park he began brandishing the weapon in front of a small crowd of teenagers and asked them to snap his picture on their mobiles and send it to his.

Gavin Brown was passing by, saw what was going on and decided to intervene. 'What are you doing? Put the knife away.' When Eastmond continued to wave it around, Brown stepped forward and snatched it out of his hand. 'You're not responsible,' he told him. Eastmond tried to retrieve the weapon but Brown told him: 'This is my knife now, you're not going to get it back.'

Eastmond continues: 'I assumed he was joking and I just asked for it back. He turned it around and put it against my right-hand side. I realised he wasn't joking. He said to me "Don't think I won't shank you." I became scared.'

Eastmond jumped forward and grabbed the knife out of Brown's hand. He then tried to use it to stab the older boy in the arm. Brown reacted by punching Eastmond in the face at least two times and the pair fell to the floor, Eastmond still holding the blade.

'Just out of reflex, I swung my arm in a round motion,' he told the Old Bailey jury. 'My eyes were closed. He punched me again, two times. Again as a reflex I swung at him and hit the side of the body. I thought I had missed. I thought each time the knife was going behind him and my forearm was hitting him. He let go of the scruff of my neck and I saw him walking away.'

But Brown had been stabbed twice in the chest and once in the neck, severing both his carotid artery and jugular vein and staggered off gasping: 'I've been stabbed, I've been stabbed.'

He was rushed to hospital but died of massive blood loss. Meanwhile, Eastmond stopped to retrieve his hat and scarf before running away. He was cleared of murder after the jury accepted that he did not set out to kill Brown. He was convicted of manslaughter and sentenced to three years.

'I know Adam,' says Radar. 'He was at my school, one year above. He was D2M. The way the papers told the story it was all wrong. They make Gavin sound like some kind of hero. The guy was a mugger. I know other people he tried to rob. The guy was trying to rob my friend. He and his mates took Adam's knife and bottled him. They could have killed him. He was fighting to defend himself.

'I saw him when he was on bail. He said he's sorry for what happened but he doesn't have any regrets – life's too short for regrets and that if he hadn't done what he did it might be him in a box right now. People say he should say sorry to Gavin's mum but he won't because it won't bring him back so there's no point.'

An internal report by the Metropolitan Police identified at least 169 separate youth gangs operating in the capital alone. A quarter of the groups were believed to have been involved in murders while almost half had been linked to serious assaults. The think tank the Centre for Social Justice believes there are up to 50,000 young people caught up in the lifestyle.

Andrew Eastmond first joined a street gang when he was ten but today, many recruits are even younger.

'You have the generals at the top,' says Radar, 'then the lieutenants, the olders, then the youngers and then the tinys. Olders are usually sixteen and up, youngers are between eleven and sixteen and anyone under that is a tiny. It's not just about age though, it depends how long you've been in the gang and what you've done within it. If you're seen as someone who is authentic, that can push you up a notch or two. That's why Dexter is a general.'

In a kind of underworld apprenticeship scheme, each elder is responsible for one or more youngers who report directly to him. They start out running errands, whatever the elder needs doing. In return they get protection and can call on the services of their elder and the rest of the gang whenever they need to.

'I started out as a younger. I spent the whole time being told what to do and where to go: rob this man, slap this boy, smash that window – before I got in the gang proper. It's a bit of a game. You're just trying to show off to the older kids. You want to be like them so you do the things that they do. Then I got caught with a knife, I was holding it for one of the older kids. Nothing really happened to me because I was too young, but suddenly I had respect, so I got drawn in further.

'Now I'm an elder. For a lot of the youngers, we're their role models. I don't feel bad because anything I do, I do it to survive. If anyone follows me, it's because they want to survive too. They see what's going on around them, they make their own choices. They know who they can trust and who they can't. If something happens, you don't go to the police, you go to the elders.

'Anyway, you don't learn anything useful from school, you don't learn from home; everything I need to know to survive I learned from the streets.'

Radar was expelled from school for the second time a year ago and is now finishing off his education in a pupil referral unit. Like a huge number of black youths, particularly in London, Radar sees his real future in the music industry. Many of the gangs spend as much time swapping insults via freestyle rap lyrics and posting mix tapes on the Internet as they do fighting and committing crime.

It is, for many, seen as the only possible other way of making real money other than criminality. Thanks to the likes of Snoop Dog and 50 Cent, having a criminal record is seen as a badge of honour rather than a problem. It means there is no incentive to stop committing crimes while building up one's musical repertoire.

London's youth gangs used to be split along racial lines, but now geographical location, or more specifically the postcode of the inner-city area you live in, is the most important factor. DSN is made up almost exclusively of those of African extraction. The majority, like Radar himself, arrived in the UK at a young age and can remember little of their native lands. 'As far as I'm concerned, this is where I'm from. This is who I am.'

The main exception to this is Billy 'Thai Kid' Langridge who, as his name suggests, is from South East Asia. SMN has an almost identical racial profile, yet the two gangs are deadly enemies simply because they have allied themselves to different postcodes: CR0 in the case of DSN, CR7 in the case of SMN.

Although various alliances have been struck with other gangs across London in order to allow members of both gangs to travel freely to certain areas, there is no sign of any truce between the two. Instead both gangs continue to bring new members on board and those new members continue to vie with one another to stand out from the crowd.

The desire to rise up the ranks is, according to Radar, a key to many of the random acts of violence that take place around London and beyond. They are simply initiation ceremonies where youngers are carrying out the bidding of their elders in order to earn their spurs.

Radar relates one such incident from late the previous year, preferring to remain a little fuzzy on the full extent of his own involvement. 'This random boy was getting some licks. Punched and kicked, flying kicks too in this café. The elders were holding him down and the youngers were doing the attacking because that was what they had been told to do.

'Then all of a sudden this big white guy who's in the café gets up and goes over and tells them to stop. One of these youngers goes crazy, he picks up a chair and throws it at the man. Then everyone's picking up chairs and throwing them all over the place until the café is totally trashed.'

The Good Samaritan, a thirty-six-year-old rugby player who stepped in to help the victim, needed dozens of stitches to reattach a severed ear lobe caused by the flying chair. The younger who did it was immediately recruited into the gang.

Not all victims of such initiations are lucky enough to survive. In April 2007 fourteen-year-old Paul Erhahon and his friend were passed on the street by a group of young kids in hooded tops carrying sports bags. The youths stopped a few paces away and demanded that Erhahon come to them. When he refused he was told by one of the hoodies: 'This could get physical, and you don't want me to have to come over there.'

The boy, himself just fifteen years old, was Paul Benfield, leader of a Leytonstone gang called the Cathall Boys. Benfield went on to say that he would get the 'youngers' of his gang to do the work for him and promptly made a phone call.

The youngers were around the corner in a KFC restaurant and soon came running. Within a matter of seconds Erhahon was surrounded by the likes of thirteen-year-old Kevin Adu-Marcet and fourteen-year-old Jordan Conn as well as half a dozen others.

Benfield shouted: 'Go on, youngers' and the attack began. From under his jacket Adu-Marcet pulled out a seven-inch samurai sword. The others produced baseball bats and a motorcycle chain.

As the blows started to rain down Erhahon was knocked to the ground but his only concern was the knife. A year earlier he had been stabbed in the leg by bullies at his old school. He had since moved in order to make a fresh start but he still had nightmares about the incident.

As his friend stood helplessly by, shouting 'Allow it, man [leave it, man], allow it' Erhahon realised his worst fears were about to come true and began crying out: 'You can't be shanking me, you can't be stabbing me.'

Adu-Marcet, who despite his age was well over six feet tall, plunged the knife directly into Erhahon's heart. The gang then turned on his friend, stabbing him a total of five times in the lung, back, stomach and twice in the leg.

Erhahon somehow managed to scramble up and make a run for it, chased by a youth armed with a baseball bat. He almost made it to his home. His parents rushed to where he lay in a pool of blood, gasping: 'I'm dying, I'm dying.' He was pronounced dead just half an hour later.

'The shankers and bangers are getting younger and younger because the elders realise they don't have to do their own dirty work,' says Radar. 'There are plenty of youngers who want to make a name for themselves and think the best way to do that is to go shank someone. If you do something like that, everyone gets to know about it and suddenly, you're the man. People respect you, people are scared of you.

'When you grow up in a place like this, that becomes important. These kids grow up seeing this all around them and they want to be part of it as quickly as possible.'

Younger children are increasingly in demand by the gangs for use as couriers, to hide weapons and to run a range of other errands. Although violence undoubtedly exists, few kids of primary-school age feel the same sense of fear as those in secondary school, so different tactics are used to bring in new recruits.

For many boys, the availability of sex is one of the major attractions of joining a gang. Girls within the gangs will often become sexually active at an early age and go on to have several gang members as sexual partners within a short space of time. The higher the rank of the gang member, the wider his choice of possible partners.

There are also reports of children being offered pairs of top-end trainers, brand new and still boxed, in return for joining a gang. If that fails the children are offered a tracksuit to match the trainers.

The money for such activities comes from a range of crimes but most often from involvement in the drug trade. With payments available for working as a simple money courier or allowing items to be hidden in your home, even the youngest members of gangs can find themselves with the ability to earn good money.

Radar told me: 'You get twelve-year-olds who are making more money than their single parent mums make all week and when they go home they get told to stay in school and work hard because that's the way to get on. And all they can think is: "but that's what you did and look how you ended up".'

While members of most street gangs have some dealings with the drug trade, much of DSN's illicit income comes from robbery, either in the form of muggings or raids on shops and other premises. SMN on the other hand is more reliant on the drug business.

According to Radar, there are constant feelers out to try to find SMN's drug suppliers so that they too can be robbed. In some areas children who try to avoid the gangs are forced to take part in robberies and those who refuse risk being beaten up or, in the case of girls, raped. With so much money at stake, gangs have become more tight-knit than ever and eager to ensure there are no loose cannons. Talking to anyone outside the gang about DSN's activities is strictly forbidden, hence Radar's need to remain anonymous.

In May 2007 the leader of SMN, who uses the street name Method, gave an exclusive interview to the *Croydon Advertiser*. Reporter Joshua Layton had spent several weeks tracking down the gangs and would go on to receive a prestigious award for his extensive coverage of their activities.

'There are over a hundred in DSN,' Method told Layton. 'They go round robbing people for no reason. SMN are going the right way. We make our money and protect each other. We don't go around terrorising and robbing innocent people. We try to stop them [DSN] from doing it in our area.'

Among the images used to illustrate the article was a picture showing an SMN youth, his face blacked out, holding a large automatic pistol. 'We don't carry weapons when we're together,' Method explained. 'We don't need them because we've got our fists. But if other people from other areas come into our territory and they have weapons, we can get them too.'

Method had spent time in a young offenders' institution for robbery but told the journalist that he was simply trying to survive on the streets.

'When I came out of jail I wanted to get on with my life but I'm not allowed to. It's a waste of time. I get out of bed in the morning and I have to go probation and do nothing. I'm trying to get out of this – but the system's made for us to fail.'

Radar laughs hard when he reads the article and laughs harder still when I ask if he thinks Dexter might be willing to do something similar.

'OK, for one thing, DSN doesn't work that way. We don't have a leader. I doubt SMN do either.'

Confused, I remind Radar about the video in which Dexter proclaims himself to be the 'General' of the gang.

'You think there's just one general? It don't work like that. Listen, there's more than a hundred men in DSN. If someone comes to Croydon looking for trouble, every one of those men will be there to fight. But the rest of the time, we don't roll together.

'Can you imagine a hundred men going round Croydon together? What kind of stupidness would that be? Half of them have beefs with each other anyway. They don't get on. No way. The other half don't even know each other.'

When it's clear that I'm still confused, Radar slowly shakes his head and says I simply don't understand the difference between a gang and a group of friends.

'All my friends are in DSN,' he tells me. 'These are the people I grew up with. Every man there has a heart for me and I have one for him. There are fifteen of us and everything we do, we do it together. When we roll, we roll as a unit. We are a family, and family look out for each other. When shit happens, you need to know what kinda man you got by your side. There are groups of friends like mine all over Croydon, and all together, they make up DSN. That's how it works.

'Dexter and Thai Kid, they're the originals, they started the whole thing. They're generals, but they're not the only generals.'

I ask again if Radar thinks I could speak to Dexter. He chuckles quietly. 'Dexter's wild, you know. You see this article, the way that Method is putting DSN down, you want to know why he's doing that? I'll show you.'

Radar directs me to a video linked to a MySpace page. At first the images are too dark to be distinct but then I begin to make out what I'm supposed to be looking at. A tall, skinny black teenager is being punched and slapped and forced to strip his clothes. When he is naked he stands in the centre of a circle of other teenagers, covering his genitals with his palms.

He looks terrified, a trickle of blood oozes down the side of his mouth. He is told to repeat the names DSN and Bird Gang again and again. After another slap around the face he is told to show off his gold teeth. Finally he is told to say his name. It is Method.

'That was Dexter,' Radar tells me. 'He and some man found out Method was on our patch in the Rooster's Chicken place and went round there. They gave him a few licks, took his phone and then made him take his clothes off. After they planked him, they hit him on the head with a bottle. [Dexter] doesn't believe in talking things through.'

For a while it seemed as though DSN were on the ascendant, but then a local youth was seriously injured after being attacked with an axe by SMN members who had mistaken him for Dexter. A few weeks later Dexter himself was arrested and charged with the attack on Method that I had viewed on the Internet. According to Radar, police had visited the restaurant and pulled CCTV footage from the cameras inside Rooster's Chicken. Dexter was one of three DSN members they were able to identify.

With overwhelming evidence against him, Dexter knew he'd have no choice but to plead guilty to two charges of false imprisonment and robbery. It was inevitable, he was told, that he would be given a custodial sentence.

Almost all gang members expect to serve time and it is within Britain's prisons that gang culture flourishes. A report on inmates at Long Lartin prison in Worcestershire found that gang culture was rife with new inmates choosing allegiances soon after arriving. 'Inmates state that all violence here is gang related,' the report noted. 'Basically we have adopted the American model. In prison, if you don't belong to a gang, you are in big trouble.'

But in the brave new underworld that today's teenage street gangs occupy, prison isn't considered much of a punishment. Truth be told, it isn't even much of an inconvenience.

3
DOING TIME

I wake with a start and grope around blindly for the phone, dragging it to my ear without even bothering to lift my head off the pillow. The best I can manage is a caveman-like grunt.

'That you, Tony?'

'Uh huh.'

'It's Billy. You all right, mate?'

I manage to open one eye and peer at the digital clock on my bedside table. It is just after 2 a.m.

'I was sleeping.'

'Sorry. Well, I guess you're up now,' he says with a chortle.

I first met Billy, the son of a noted villain from the golden age of crime, while investigating a robbery on a Securitas depot. Pleased with the story I wrote and fascinated by my job, Billy kept in touch and insisted we meet every now and then to exchange gangland gossip. Billy was desperate to escape from his father's shadow but at the same time revelled in the reputation that went along with his infamous surname. The unfortunate combination of a short temper, a long-standing coke habit and a rock-solid right hook meant that by the age of thirty he had spent more time in prison than his father had during his entire life. It also meant that regardless of his achievements, he was destined forever to remain at the rank of foot soldier.

As Billy's voice bounces around inside my head the fog of sleep suddenly clears from my mind. My other eye opens and a split second later I'm sitting bolt upright, completely wide awake.

'Billy.'

'Yeah?'

'Aren't you in prison?'

'For the assault, yeah, that's right.'

'So how come you're using the phone? Has something happened?'

'Nah. I'm on the mobile. Smuggled it in, didn't I. Those little ones fit right up your arse no trouble. I tell you; everyone's got one in here. It's well good. Means you can keep doing business. But hey, you think that's a good story, you wait till I tell you what I heard this morning.'

I reach for a notebook and pen. 'Wait up, mate. Tell me more about this phone stuff first . . .'

Mobile phones have been a problem for the prison service the world over ever since they first became popular, but the issue came to a head in May 2007 during an episode of the popular Irish radio interview and phone-in chat show, *Liveline*.

Known and admired for covering controversial topics, *Liveline*'s presenter, Joe Duffy, was hosting a discussion between *Sunday World* crime journalist Paul Williams and Sinn Fein councillor Christy Burke about the links between the political party and IRA organised crime in Dublin.

Half an hour into the show, a caller phoned in to attack Williams telling him: 'Ninety-nine per cent of what you write is rubbish.' Williams recognised the man's voice at once and told listeners: 'This is "Jack Glenny" [name changed for legal reasons] – a major figure in organised crime.' In the heated, expletive-filled discussion that followed, all of it broadcast live over the airwaves, Glenny accused Williams of stirring up trouble between himself and an armed robber named John Daly. Williams had written that the pair had fallen out, that Glenny was in fear of his life and planning to flee the country before Daly was released from prison. 'You're a fucking liar,' Glenny told Williams, explaining that he and Daly were good friends and that he had even sent the robber a postcard while on holiday in Spain.

At the time Daly was still serving a nine-year sentence for armed robbery and was incarcerated at Portlaoise prison. Used to house all those convicted of membership of the IRA and other paramilitary organisations it is considered one of the most secure prisons anywhere in Europe. An entire platoon of soldiers from the Irish Defence Forces guard the prison twenty-four hours a day and the complex is fitted with anti-aircraft guns, pressure sensors and tank traps. Prisoners are subjected to regular, rigorous checks.

But none of that stopped John Daly from sneaking a mobile phone into his cell in block E1. Increasingly angered by what he heard on the radio show, the hot-headed twenty-seven-year-old couldn't resist calling in himself. 'I can't stay long. I'm in a cell,' he explained. 'Paul Williams, you are a liar. Do you know how much lies you tell every week?'

Daly and Glenny exchanged pleasantries and, after acknowledging receipt of the postcard Glenny had referred to earlier an increasingly agitated Daly went back on the offensive against Williams.

'I have a complaint in against you because if I didn't know Jack Glenny and Jack Glenny did not know me, you're kicking off a fucking gangland war. I'm going on holiday with Jack when I get out.'

Noises could be heard in the background as stunned prison officers arrived at Daly's cell in order to get the phone off him. As Daly was dragged away Glenny brought matters to a conclusion. 'You're a lying cunt,' he told Williams before hanging up.

The political fallout and embarrassment caused by the expletive-ridden phone call from one of the country's most notorious prisoners was enormous and by the end of the month, new legislation had been drafted making it an offence for inmates to possess or use mobile phones.

Officials from the Irish Prison Service were equally outraged and called for an immediate blitz on phones at jails across the country. The results showed the problem was far greater than anyone could have imagined. An astonishing 2,124 illegal mobiles were found and confiscated over the course of the next year. During that time the average Irish prison population was 3,191 meaning that there were around two mobiles for every three inmates.

The blitz uncovered numerous other examples of contraband that had been smuggled into cells including copious amounts of drugs, alcohol, plasma screen televisions, DVD players and even three budgies.

By the time of the crackdown phones had become by far the single most important commodity behind bars. By allowing prisoners to stay in touch with other members of their criminal organisations whenever they wanted and without fear of anyone listening in, they were able to continue to run their criminal empires and jail was far less of an inconvenience than it might otherwise have been.

As the wheels of the Irish underworld temporarily ground to a halt, all the blame was being squarely placed on the shoulders of one man. The death threats began to arrive within hours and Daly was twice moved to other prisons over concerns about his safety in the run-up to his eventual release in August 2007.

With Daly back outside, the situation quickly went from bad to worse. The Gardai, the police force of the Republic of Ireland, became increasingly concerned and offered to provide Daly with safety advice and tips on how to beef up his personal security. He declined.

On the night of 21 October 2007 Daly and friends went out socialising in Dublin city centre. As they headed home in a taxi, stopping at various houses in search of a party, they failed to realise they were being followed by a dark-coloured Toyota Land Cruiser. When the taxi stopped off close to Daly's home at 1.45 a.m., a man jumped out of the Toyota, quickly established that Daly was in the vehicle and then, producing a handgun, fired at least five shots at point blank range before running off.

Daly's dying body slumped sideways onto the lap of the terrified taxi driver who was then unable to unbuckle his seatbelt and remained trapped in the vehicle until the authorities arrived. Having made so many enemies, Daly's death seemed only a matter of time. One detective quipped that the investigation was going well and that they had already: 'narrowed it down to one of two thousand suspects'.

It didn't take long for the shockwaves generated by revelations about the true prevalence of mobile phones in the Irish penal system to be felt, first across the border and then throughout the UK. The number of illicit handsets found in British prisons had been steadily increasing for years and their use by prisoners was becoming a factor in a rising number of trials.

Commenting on the situation, one senior detective told me: 'As long as a prisoner has access to money, a phone and a couple of trusted friends on the outside, they are able to continue running their business almost as well as before. If anything, it's easier because people always know where to find them. They can't suddenly drop off the radar.'

Billy concurs. Crouched down in a corner of his cell, his voice kept low to avoid alerting the screws on night patrol, he agrees that the use of mobile phones on the inside has completely changed what it means to be in prison. 'It used to be that when someone was banged up, everyone on the outside felt safe. But now, people are still proper scared of you cos they know that even though you're away, you're still running the show. And if anyone steps out of line, you're only a phone call away.'

That was certainly the case for south London career criminal Delphon Nicholas who in October 2008 was jailed for a minimum of thirty years after being found guilty of organising the execution of his former friend Andrew Wanoghu, despite being incarcerated at Belmarsh maximum-security prison.

Wanoghu, known as Sparks, was a talented amateur boxer who had fought successfully in the United States. Although he would push his wheelchair-bound brother to church every week, the rest of his life was filled with acts of extreme violence. He once kidnapped and tortured a bus driver whose brother was a rival drug dealer. The man was driven to a flat and chained to a radiator before Wanoghu held a hot iron against his face.

Wanoghu had previously been suspected of shooting dead Damien Cope, whose mother Lucy went on to form the charity 'Mothers Against Guns', but walked free from court when the case collapsed. Two key witnesses withdrew their evidence claiming they were in fear for their lives.

In August 2005, Wanoghu survived an assassination attempt as he left a courtroom where he had watched a girlfriend plead guilty to possession of one of his guns in order to save him from jail. Eight months later he was not so lucky.

Nicholas, who compared himself to the 'Teflon Don' John Gotti, had a history of conflict with Wanoghu, who had shown him great 'disrespect' by robbing Nicholas's father. In the hour before Wanoghu was murdered, Nicholas used a smuggled mobile phone to speak repeatedly to Trevor Dennie, the foot soldier he had asked to act as gunman, and to a female friend whom he had persuaded to lure Wanoghu to the house where the shooting would take place. Dennie, a rapist and drug trafficker, had also fallen out with Wanoghu over drugs and women. He told one friend: 'I've had enough of Andy, he's gone too far. He's barred from the ends.'

In the early hours of 8 April 2006 Wanoghu stepped out of a car outside the home of Nicholas's former girlfriend who had told Wanoghu to come round so they could have sex. He told Sean Albert, the friend that had driven him to Nicholas's ex's place, that he was 'up for a bit of a shagging' and headed towards the woman's front door.

But Dennie was lying in wait. As Albert moved the car to a more discreet spot he heard a series of rapid gunshots. He looked in his rear-view mirror and saw a terrified Wanoghu running towards him. Just as he reached the car he crumpled to the ground, hit in the back by a bullet that pierced his heart. Once the deed was done, Nicholas used his smuggled phone to ring Wanoghu's mobile, just to check he was really dead.

The phone, along with a charger, was discovered in Nicholas's cell two weeks later during a routine search. Forensic examination showed it had been smuggled into Wandsworth prison sometime during the summer of 2005 and used by another inmate who was then transferred to Belmarsh in September that same year. Early in 2006, Nicholas either bought or stole the phone from the original owner and began using it to make calls – mostly to his father or his girlfriend and occasionally to underworld cohorts. In all he made more than 16,000 calls, including dozens on the night of the murder.

During 2009 around 8,400 phones and SIM cards were found in British prisons, equivalent to one for every twenty prisoners. This was a fourfold increase on the number found three years earlier. 'They have become an epidemic,' said one senior prison officer. 'With the exception of a gun, a mobile phone is the most dangerous item a prisoner can have. It's easy for them to set up drug deals, intimidate witnesses and even arrange attacks on prison convoys.'

One seized phone contained, in the words of observers from an independent welfare organisation: 'the most graphic and violent images including forced sex and stabbings'. It is claimed that there have been cases of camera phones being used to take photographs of prison officers so that those on the outside can target and intimidate them. Similarly, video phones are said to have been utilised to call relatives and show live footage of inmates being tortured in order to extort money or drugs.

Although there can be little doubt that smuggled phones are indeed used for such purposes, anecdotal evidence suggests that the vast majority of prisoners use them solely to call their families. Although public payphones are available, their use is heavily restricted and the cost can be ruinous. For convicted inmates unwilling to wait for (or unable to write) conventional letters and allowed only two hour-long visits a month, the ability to call home every night can be a lifesaver. For others, however, a prison mobile is simply seen as a licence to print money.

When low-level drug-dealer Jordan Moore found himself behind bars in Lewes prison he soon realised he had a captive market of addicts and quickly worked out a way to take control and cash in. Until August 2008 he had been part of a small but lucrative heroin and cocaine distribution ring based around the seaside town of Worthing. Once inside he continued to run the business, issuing instructions to his foot soldiers by mobile phone, but expanded his operations to include the prison itself.

Packages of drugs were hidden in socks and thrown over the prison walls to be collected by the inmates at prearranged times. With prices up to ten times higher behind bars than on the streets, Moore found his profits soaring and lavished gifts on his girlfriend who was helping to look after his cash while he served his sentence.

Estimates from the National Offender Management Service, suggest drugs worth at least £100 million are being traded inside British prisons every year. In June 2008 the *Daily Express* reported that the opportunities for making money while doing time were so attractive that some dealers were deliberately getting themselves sent to prison for minor offences. They did this because, once locked up, they could make more in a couple of months than they would during the rest of the year.

Inmates call relatives or friends and get them to deposit the necessary cash in the dealer's bank account. The dealer can then check these deposits via telephone banking and it is only once they have been received that the drugs will be handed over.

Such operations, along with those of the likes of Jordan Moore, may seem ambitious but they are a mere drop in the ocean when compared to the scale of a scheme that was being set up by a man who found himself in court just a few weeks after Moore's appearance.

In July 2009, long-time villain George Moon was found guilty of running an international cocaine ring from his cell at HMP Lindholme in Doncaster. What made Moon's case particularly remarkable was that his chief accomplice, Lee Morgan, was locked up in prison in Panama at the time.

Morgan, originally from Frankley, Birmingham, fell in with what one former undercover police officer has described as 'the number one armed robbery gang in England' during the 1980s.

Former detective Ronnie Howard was part of a covert surveillance team that observed Morgan and the rest of his gang 'casing' a bank in 1986. 'Make no mistake,' says Howard. 'This lot were as savage as they came, and they would not have thought twice about shooting anyone who got in their way. They were in the premier league of their criminal world and lived a champagne lifestyle of fast cars and glamorous women.'

According to sources in Panama, Morgan fled the UK in 1992 to escape charges of importing cannabis and set himself up on a farm in the countryside but soon fell back into his old ways.

Panamanian police swooped on his farm and found 110 kilos of cocaine with a street value of half a million pounds. He was sentenced to ten years in the country's tough El Rencaser prison, considered a 'country club for hardened criminals'.

Sixty-two-year-old Moon, who had already been jailed three times for drugs offences throughout his life and was in Lindholme serving a fourteen-year sentence imposed in 2003, used two Virgin SIM cards and a contraband mobile phone to contact Morgan who had also managed to smuggle a phone into his cell.

Together the pair arranged the importation of twelve half-kilo packages of 77 per cent pure cocaine from Panama and Venezuela to the UK and Republic of Ireland. The drugs were delivered by various postal couriers including Royal Mail Parcel Force, DHL and TNT, none of whom had any idea of the true contents. Moon made hundreds of calls to his connections abroad as well as members of his gang closer to home with the phone he powered using an adapted electric razor while in his cell at the category C prison.

He also used a notebook to store all the telephone numbers he needed, kept a spare SIM card to hand and carefully recorded the tracking numbers of the drug-filled packages being sent out to his trusted colleagues on the outside.

The Serious Organised Crime Agency (SOCA) began their investigation after officials from the National Offender Management Service intercepted a parcel sent to Moon marked 'Legal Privilege Material'. Suspicious that the package was being sent rather than delivered by a solicitor, it was opened and found to contain two SIM cards and a quantity of heroin, which Moon had planned to sell inside the prison, all hidden between fake legal documents.

DOING TIME

When officers burst into his cell to arrest him in November 2008, Moon was on his phone setting up his next deal. He and Morgan had so far earned about £300,000 from their enterprise but detectives admitted they had smashed the operation in its infancy and that, had it continued, Moon would have stood to make millions. Originally due for release in 2010, George Moon will now remain in prison until at least 2019.

The risks are high but with smuggled mobile phones offering so many potential benefits, it is little wonder that some inmates will go to quite extraordinary lengths to maintain lines of communication with the outside world. When officers at Swaleside prison began a routine cell search of one inmate, they couldn't help but notice how incredibly uncomfortable he seemed during the procedure. It turned out that the wonderfully aptly named Tony Pile, serving life for beating a man to death in a race-hate attack, had not only hidden a mobile phone up his rectum but also the entire charger unit.

Pile was lucky. A week earlier Martin Mahoney had tried a similar stunt at Highpoint prison in Suffolk. Having successfully hidden the phone during the cell search, Mahoney discovered to his absolute horror that it had become stuck. He spent several days trying to remove it only to feel the device break apart inside him. Close to passing out with agony, he had no choice but to confess what he had done to prison staff. Rushed to hospital, he required more than 200 internal stitches and surgeons had to remove part of his bladder.

In the spring of 2009, Body Orifice Security Scanner (BOSS) chairs, which can detect small metallic objects such as phones, knives and gun components without the need for intrusive strip searches, began to be rolled out through the prison system and plans were announced to make possession of mobiles a criminal offence. At the same time Norwich prison brought into service Murphy, a fifteen-year-old spaniel, specially trained to detect the scent of mobile phones.

But even if prisoners are denied mobiles, they may still have other lines of communication open to them. According to Bill Hughes, director general of SOCA, some inmates have been able to use gaming consoles to connect to the Internet and then communicate with the outside world using chat rooms or avatars from online games like Second Life. 'One of the issues if you are locked up is how you communicate. What we've been highlighting is that it isn't always a mobile phone. We've seen examples of people using PlayStations, the games you play interactively, to pass messages.' These claims were met with immediate denials from the prison service who insisted that inmates were not allowed consoles that gave them access to the World Wide Web but SOCA said their sources had repeatedly confirmed their claims.

During the autumn of 2009 tests of several systems designed to jam mobile phone and other wireless signals within prison walls were being tried out in various locations. The tests were going ahead despite fears that such jammers might prevent crucial signals from being received by members of the public living or working nearby. There were also concerns about just how effective such technology could be.

In America, where jammers are set to be introduced following an incident in which a man on death row used a smuggled mobile to call a state senator and recite the names and addresses of the man's daughters, inmates have already devised ways to success-fully shield their phones from jamming signals using a few sheets of tinfoil. Satellite phones, which are unaffected by traditional jammers and are now almost as small as regular mobiles, are being adopted as another potential solution.

Mobiles may have made life easier for the criminals but even before they became popular, the fact that inmates were allowed to use phones at all meant many were still able to maintain a grip on their outside interests.

Although all phone calls made from high-security prisons are supposed to be monitored, at least on a random basis, this is often not possible because of staff shortages. And even where calls are being recorded, villains have become adept at dealing with this by using sophisticated verbal codes. New codes are agreed during personal visits and changed regularly. And while prisons attempt to restrict the amount of phone credit a prisoner is allowed to have at any one time, there is a flourishing black market that sees credit minutes changing hands for huge sums.

In open prisons, where regimes are generally softer and convicts are allowed a greater number of luxuries, phone calls are not monitored at all leaving them wide open to abuse.

'I was at [HMP] Hollesley Bay a few years ago,' Billy tells me. 'It was so lax that we used to call it Holiday Bay. If we fancied a change from the usual shitty menu, we'd call up the local taxi firm and get them to pick up an order of Chinese food and a couple of crates of lager from a takeaway and offy down the road in Woodbridge and deliver it all to the perimeter fence. From there we'd sneak it into our cells.

'No one had a mobile back then but everyone was still at it. It was common practice. There was no need for anyone to get their hands dirty – they could just use their money and their contacts to set up deals then wait for the profits to come in. One bloke was in for computer fraud and they let him keep his laptop with him. The whole time he was there, he was taking orders over the phone and arranging deliveries. It was ridiculous.'

Tucked up in a corner of his cell, speaking on his smuggled mobile, it is not surprising that Billy has little confidence that the new measures being introduced to curb phone use will have any great effect. 'We've got one of those BOSS (Body Orifice Security Scanner) chairs here now, but none of the staff know how to use it properly so they just fake it, try and psych you out instead. You have to understand; half the time it's the staff who bring this stuff in anyway.

'If they come across someone in here who wants something badly enough, they can name their price. I'm telling you, a screw can double his salary by bringing in a couple of phones and a few wraps. At the end of the day people are people and nobody's perfect. The chair's a prime example. It's only as good as the people operating it. If someone's being paid good money to turn a blind eye or switch the jammer off for ten minutes every afternoon, then nothing the authorities do is going to stop it.

'People are always going to bring phones and SIMs in here, even if they don't work.'

'Why would they do that?' I ask.

Billy chortles again. 'Listen, mate. If you're a dealer, your mobile phone is the single most important thing you own. We're talking about a phone that rings constantly. Not so much during the week perhaps but night and day at the weekend. Friday, Saturday night the thing's going fucking mental. Ring, ring, ring all the time with people wanting gear. Every call you get, you're earning money. That's your job, that's what you do. That phone's your whole life.

'Without that phone your only way of making money is to go out on the street and sell your wraps, a tenner at a time, to whoever comes by. But you know that sooner or later you're gonna get nicked or robbed or worse. It's a mug's game. Dealing over the phone, that's sweet.

'So if you're sitting at home and you hear the police breaking through the front door, the first thing you do is grab your SIM and stick it down your sock or in your shoe. Either way, the last thing you want is for the police to get hold of it.

'I know people who've been nicked with a couple of wraps and claimed it was only for personal. Then, while they're sitting there lying their arses off, the phone starts going beep, beep, fucking beep and when the police take a gander they've had twenty text messages from twenty different numbers asking: "you got any sniff?" Dropped 'em right in it.

'Now if you're working for a big dealer and you get nicked, the first thing he's going to do is make sure someone else takes over all of your customers so that he can keep selling. If you're working for yourself, you've got to find someone you can trust to take over for you so you've still got something when you come out.'

This, explains Billy, has created an entirely new prison black market in phones. What's being traded in this situation however is not the ability to make calls but rather the information contained on the SIM and within the handset itself.

New arrivals at prisons across the country sell their SIM cards to those nearing release. Depending on the size of the customer network on offer, the cost of such an exchange can easily run to more than £10,000. SIMs have become so important that many dealers keep several of them, all cloned to contain the same information, in case of emergency. 'Think of it like buying a business franchise,' says Billy. 'You put that SIM in your phone and within a couple of days you've got people begging you to sell them gear. At that level none of them are too fussed who answers the phone, just so long as they can deliver. Most of the time it's the runners who hand the stuff over anyway so most of the people who call wouldn't have a clue who they're talking to anyway.

'You can step right into someone else's shoes and start raking in the profits straight away. At the same time, if you're unlucky enough to get nicked and not have a back-up SIM or your phone ends up in the wrong hands, well then, you're for ever fucked.'

When small-time dealer Andrew Law found himself being chased by the police in Gloucester he was smart enough to get rid of any incriminating evidence. Zigging and zagging his way from the park where he had been spotted acting suspiciously, he made his way into Cromwell Street where he dumped his jacket containing £1,400 worth of Class A drugs and his mobile phone into the front garden of a house before making good his escape into the night.

The next morning when he returned to retrieve the jacket, it was nowhere to be seen. Assuming the homeowner had taken it, Law sent a text message to the phone he had left in the pocket. 'Who's got my jacket? I want the stuff back.'

When this failed to elicit a reply he followed it up with: 'If you have got this phone, ring me.' Increasingly concerned about his stash, Law sent more messages. 'I want my stuff', 'Listen, we want the stuff from the jacket.'

Angered by the silence, Law then abandoned any attempt at subtlety: 'Listen, I want those fucking drugs,' he texted. 'I know which fucking garden it was in so fucking answer the phone.' Another message said: 'I will burn your house down. Do you know who I am? Just answer the phone and we will do the deal.' A further message moments later said: 'Why won't you answer the phone? The chances are you don't know what you've got. You can make some money if you get in touch. Otherwise you'll get fuck-all apart from a gun in your mouth.'

Unfortunately for Law, his jacket had been found earlier that morning by a maintenance man and handed into the police who watched with wry bemusement as the increasingly angry messages arrived. Law, a known dealer, was soon identified as the person sending the texts and promptly arrested. He was later jailed for six years.

A soft beep on the phone line tells Billy and me that his battery is starting to run low. I look across at the clock again and see that we've been talking for more than half an hour, almost exclusively on the subject of mobile phones and their pitfalls and benefits to the modern criminal. He is about to hang up when it occurs to me that this wasn't the reason for his call.

'Sorry, mate,' I say. 'What was it you were calling about anyway?'

'Oh yeah. I need a favour. A big favour. I need you to buy me a gun.'

4

GUNS

The disclaimer is as clear as crystal: 'We can deliver all the goods on our website anywhere in the world – it's our speciality! However, some of the items may be slightly or very illegal to import or own in your country or state. So please check with your authorities before ordering (if you are bothered, that is!)'

It's the morning after my late night call from Billy and I've fired up my computer and logged on to the guns2u.com website which he had called to tell me about. Run by a group of Brits based in France, it sells riot pistols, stun guns, CS gas sprays, flare guns and several high-quality replica pistols and revolvers known to be readily converted to fire live ammunition. The company also sells several brands of 'self-defence' guns, identical to the real thing in every way except for the fact that they fire cartridges loaded with CS gas or pepper spray rather than bullets.

While perfectly legal in France and several other European countries, all these items – the CS gas included – are classified as Section 5 firearms in the UK. Possession here is punishable with a mandatory minimum five-year prison sentence.

It's obvious that a story about the site will go down well at the *Observer*, but it will only work if I can show that the company's outlandish claim – delivering to countries where its products are illegal – is genuine. And the only way to do that is to order up a few items and see if they actually get to me.

I spend the next hour browsing through the massive selection of goods on offer, feeling like a kid let loose in a candy store. By the time I've finished I've spent more than £500 and have ordered enough gear to create havoc, at least on a small scale. A few minutes later I receive an email of confirmation from the company along with a note telling me that my items are all in stock and will be despatched within the next forty-eight hours. So far, so good.

That night Billy calls to find out how I got on. He isn't being entirely altruistic – his real motivation behind the tip off is his ongoing quest for the Holy Grail of the modern-day underworld – a source of readily available, reliable and 'clean' – i.e., unused – firearms.

'Don't get me wrong,' he says, 'there's guns out there, but a lot of them are a pile of crap. There are some seriously dodgy conversions that will take your hand off the minute you fire them and then there are loads of war relics with mismatched parts and ammunition that jam up every time you take a second shot. Everything's so unreliable that the minute you get your hands on something that actually works you start thinking to yourself: "what else has this been used for?"'Billy has a point. The gun used to shoot Andrew Wanoghu, the drug dealer whose execution was ordered from prison by Delphon Nicholas, was found eight months later in the bedroom of a fourteen-year-old boy who was keeping it for an older member of a local street gang.

A forensic treasure trove, it was found to have been used in at least seven shootings in the space of just two years.

The gun was first used on New Year's Eve in 2004. A police officer was responding to a 999 call from a victim of a robbery in Brockley Cross and arrived to find three men loitering nearby. As he walked over to speak to them they ran. He gave chase and one of the men produced a handgun and fired a shot, narrowly missing the constable.

Ten months later the gun was used at the Cube nightclub in Camberwell Green, south London, in a petty dispute. The victim happened to bump into a man as he went to the toilet and was shot in the thigh for 'showing disrespect'.

In April 2006 the handgun was used to murder Wanoghu. Three weeks later it was one of several used by members of a north London gang who burst into the M-Blax nightclub in Peckham just before the club was closing and fired a volley of shots at members

of a rival south London crew. In total twenty-one rounds were
fired and three men taken to hospital.

In June 2006 the gun was fired into the air as a 'salute' during a
hip-hop show at Pontins in Camber Sands by a group of teenagers
who had travelled up to the event from London.

A month later it was back in south London again, when shots
were fired at a pool car being driven by rivals of the gun's latest
owner. The pistol was last used in the autumn of 2006 when it was
accidentally fired by a would-be gangster who was attempting to
show off. Soon after that it was given to the teenager and hidden
away until it was uncovered by the police.

The gun was a Ceska Zbrojovka .32 Colt Model 1927, manufactured in Strakonice, Czechoslovakia. It was found ready to fire,
with one round in the chamber and three more in the magazine.
Scratched, battered and not particularly impressive to look at,
the reason for the gun's popularity was simple: while a significant proportion of the black-market guns in circulation today are
converted replicas or re-tooled air weapons, the CZ. 32 was the
genuine article.

Ever since the 1996 Dunblane massacre in which sixteen children
and one adult were shot dead with four legally owned weapons by
Thomas Hamilton before he committed suicide, there has been a
total ban on virtually all UK handguns.

Up until that time two significant, though relatively minor,
sources of guns for the black market were thefts from legitimate
certificate holders and an under-the-counter trade carried out by
bent gun dealers. (Most guns were smuggled in from abroad or
'leaked' from military sources.) The ban would have had little
effect on the underworld had it not coincided with a massive
explosion in illicit gun use.

The rise of the drug trade and the allied need for dealers to
protect themselves meant that suddenly everybody wanted a gun.
'Whatever area of the crime game you're in these days everyone
wants a gun,' an underworld armourer told me soon after the ban
was introduced. 'Right from burglars and muggers to pimps and

fences. Even drug dealers – not the big players but the kids with market stalls selling ten-quid bags of grass – they're all tooled up too.'

Those at the top end of the crime game will always get access to the best weapons. When an associate of the notorious Adams family was arrested with £300,000 of cocaine police were not surprised to find a cache of weapons hidden among the drugs. There were two sub-machine guns, six shotguns and five handguns, all of them brand new. Each weapon was fully loaded and the consignment also contained more than a thousand rounds of ammunition.

With 'real' guns becoming increasingly scarce among the lower ranks, the search was on for alternatives. Deactivated guns, introduced as a sop to the gun lobby after ownership of semi-automatic weapons was outlawed in the aftermath of the 1987 Hungerford massacre, were one solution.

Once genuine weapons, the deactivation process involved removing key components and blocking the barrels to render them inoperable. However, the early deactivation standards were somewhat lacking, particularly when it came to guns working on the 'blowback' principle. Such weapons, which included Uzi sub-machine guns and Mac-10s, both capable of firing up to a thousand rounds in a minute, could be brought back to life in a matter of minutes.

Such 'spray and pray' guns became increasingly popular towards the end of the nineties and by 2000 police estimated that 96 per cent of all machine guns seized in the UK had been reactivated. Although new deactivation standards have since been introduced, the weapons remain the most readily restored to full operation. Every gang of any worth will have a Mac-10 or equivalent at its disposal.

Many such Mac-10s can be traced back to one single source – a man named Grant Wilkinson. In July 2004 Wilkinson, a convicted drug dealer who had also served time for GBH, bought ninety blank-firing Mac-10s using the name Grant Wilson and claiming he needed them as props for a forthcoming James Bond film.

GUNS

Wilkinson paid just over £600 for each gun, £55,200 cash for the entire batch of weapons, and then set about converting them to fire live ammo using an elaborate workshop which he had set up in a shed close to his Berkshire home. Once converted, each weapon was sold through a network of contacts to gang leaders across London and beyond. Each weapon was sold for up to £2,500, meaning Wilkinson's profit on his investment was more than £150,000.

He spent the money on a lavish lifestyle, driving a Porsche and entertaining his girlfriend at five-star hotels across the country.

In the meantime the guns he sold led to a dramatic power struggle within the underworld. In the three years following his purchase of the Mac-10s, weapons from Wilkinson's workshop were used in at least fifty shootings and featured in nine separate murder investigations.

High-profile cases in which the guns were used include the robbery that preceded the murder of PC Sharon Beshenivsky, the murder of fifteen-year-old Michael Dosunmu, shot dead in his bed at his home in Peckham in a case of mistaken identity and the July 2008 murder of Curtis Smith, shot dead outside a nightclub in east London.

Although capable of producing a deadly rate of fire that was ideal for drive-by shootings and the like, Mac-10s are notoriously difficult to fire with any real degree of control. Police report arriving at the scene of shootings where the weapons have been used and finding bullets twenty-five metres to the right and left of the intended target.

Also, although compact when compared to a sawn-off shotgun, Mac-10s and other sub-machine guns are simply too bulky and unwieldy for anyone to keep on their person at all times, at least not without it being obvious that they are packing.

For a while the Brocock ME 38 Magnum air pistol seemed to provide the solution. An air gun traditionally relies on an internal reservoir of air to power its projectile. This can prove highly frustrating for those engaged in target shooting as the reservoir has to be refilled after each shot.

Brocock solved this problem with the introduction of the air-cartridge system. Looking very much like a .38 rifle round, the cartridge contained the pellet and enough compressed air to propel it from the gun. It allowed the introduction of air-powered revolvers that looked and felt like the real thing.

Underworld gunsmiths soon discovered that, with only minor changes, the Brocock could be used to fire genuine .22 rimfire ammunition. Costing only around £120 and with the necessary conversions available for half as much again, the Brocock soon became hugely popular with members of street gangs and low-level associates.

Thanks to this and similar conversions, guns flooded into the underworld. Despite the handgun ban, gun crime more than doubled in the ten years that followed Dunblane. And guns were even edging into popular culture: in 2001 actor and singer Ashley Walters, famous for being part of the So Solid Crew, was caught with a converted Brocock and jailed for eighteen months.

Brococks were banned from sale in 2003 but by then thousands had been sold and remained in circulation. Dozens of shootings, murders and other armed incidents were linked to the guns as well as other converted air weapons.

But those intent on using their guns as business tools rather than fashion accessories were still not happy. 'The Brocock is all right,' says Billy, 'but it's far from ideal. The gun is made out of some kind of alloy. Although it's pretty strong most of the time, I've heard loads of cases where they've exploded when people have pulled the trigger and someone's lost a finger. Fuck that for a game of soldiers.

'Anyway, the chamber is just slightly too big for the .22 cartridge. Some people wrap them in cardboard to get them to fit but it's not perfect. It's all right if you're messing about but if you actually need a gun you can rely on, a gun you actually want to use, the Brocock's not the way to go. Not at all.'

Billy is particularly interested in two weapons that guns2u.com has on offer, both of which now form part of my order. The first is a newly issued replica of the Glock 17L, a hugely popular and highly sophisticated handgun that is used by 65 per cent of law enforcement agencies in the US.

With the exception of the barrel, slide and a few other components, the gun is made entirely from a high-density plastic. Billy believes the new replica may lend itself to being adapted to firing live rounds. The Glock I have ordered comes with a special adaptor allowing it to fire steel ball bearings. In order to do that successfully, it will have to have been constructed out of materials closer in strength to the real thing than those usually used in replicas and blank firing models.

The other item he is interested in is the SAPL pistol, similar to a riot-control device in use by the French police. The GC 27 model fires a special rubber bullet round fitted to a 12-bore shotgun cartridge and is powerful enough to break ribs from ten feet away. Billy believes this too could be adapted to fire lead shot and could be a popular back-up weapon for his fellow gangsters.

Composed entirely of a high-strength polymer, the SAPL will not set off metal detectors in clubs or court houses, a fact which Billy believes could prove highly attractive to many potential buyers. He gives me the name and number of a friend of his who will examine the weapons when I receive them and tell Billy about the potential for conversion.

Like Grant Wilkinson, Billy stands to make huge profits on each weapon if they make the grade. Would I be willing to leave them with his friend? I tell Billy that I'll think about it, but I'm already wondering how I'm going to be able to get myself out of what could become a very awkward situation.

A few days later I get a card from the post office telling me that I have a package waiting for me. I make my way down to the depot, collect my large box and then rush home, eager to delve through the contents.

Everything I ordered has arrived and it has only taken a matter of days. It seems almost too easy. My Glock is contained within what can only be described as a miniature black briefcase and comes complete with a cleaning kit and comprehensive care instructions.

I take it out and hold it. If feels incredibly heavy and, as far as I can remember, very much like the real thing. I pull back on the slide, revealing the barrel hidden within, until it locks, then pull the trigger and watch it slip forward. I slip the magazine in and out a few times and switch the weapon from one hand to the other. It's very clear that this is not a toy, that this is something much more.

If feels incredibly solid and, even though at the moment it is only capable of firing blank ammunition, it delivers a true sense of power. The attraction to young kids across the country is clear. It's all I can do to resist getting up and standing in front of the mirror to see how I look holding it.

Looking down the barrel I see a single spike, the thickness of a nail, about halfway down. That appears to be the only obstruction. This particular pistol is, according to Billy, a new model made to different standards from most others on the market with thicker, stronger steel used in its key components.

Next there is a 200,000-volt stun gun and a 25ml CS gas spray, then a combined device which functions as a stun gun but is also able to spray CS gas out of one of the electrical probes. Each of the stun guns I have received is four times more powerful than the ones in use by the British police.

Towards the bottom of the box I find my GC 27 riot pistol along with the 12-gauge shotgun rounds fitted with rubber balls. The GC feels incredibly light and flimsy, a little like an emergency flare gun, but closer examination reveals just how dense and sturdy the plastic used in its manufacture is.

The device breaks apart like a shotgun and the shells are simply dropped inside. The barrel is closed and then the gun is ready to fire. It's as simple as that.

Underneath the riot pistol are several more boxes of 9mm ammunition for the Glock, some of it blank, some containing CS gas powder.

Finally there is the 'self-gomm' a screw attachment for the Glock, which allows it to fire rubber or steel ball bearings with the force of a bullet. Even without any further adaptation, using this device in combination with the blank ammunition I have received could be a lethal combination.

I take the stun gun out of its box and insert a nine-volt battery. When I press the trigger there's an immensely satisfying crackle as a huge white spark jumps between the prongs.

'It's the perfect weapon for a mugger because it will put anyone down and they won't know what's hit them,' Billy had told me earlier. 'I know of a lot of football hooligans who have them, but they're also common among carjackers. A lot of drug dealers have started using them to torture people who owe them money. They like them because, unlike bullets, knives or clubs, there's no evidence of the attack.'

Possession of stun guns was made illegal in Britain after one was used to rob a postman. Although there have been no fatalities involving their use in this country, they have caused at least thirty deaths worldwide.

The guns2u website explains how they work: 'The stun gun does not rely on pain for results. The energy stored in the gun is transferred into the attacker's muscles, placing a tremendous demand on the muscles. This demand instantly depletes the attacker's blood sugar by converting it to lactic acid. In short, he is unable to produce energy for his muscles, and his body is unable to function properly.'

Conservative estimates suggest there are as many as 10,000 stun guns in circulation in the UK and that the number is growing fast. More and more are being intercepted in the post and recovered during police searches for drugs.

A few days later I make my way over to an estate in west London to meet up with Jay, Billy's gunsmith friend. Once I'm safely inside his second-floor flat and the curtains have been drawn, I open my rucksack and hand over the Glock and the GC 27, standing by nervously while he examines them from every possible angle.

'What you want to know, I guess,' Jay says at last, twisting the Glock in his fingers, 'is whether or not this can be made to fire real ammo. The short answer is no. This isn't a deactivated weapon, this thing was never the real deal, it's a fake. A copy. The barrel isn't real so even if I drilled out the obstruction, it wouldn't take a bullet.

'That said, the barrel is by far the easiest part of the gun to replace, but even if I did that it wouldn't do you much good. What they've done here is really quite clever. They've obviously thought this through. A lot of the internal components are mismatched. The magazine is too narrow to hold anything with a bullet in it, the ejector claw won't handle anything other than 8mm ammo and I'm guessing that the clearance on the slide won't allow live ammo to be used.'

He shakes his head. 'At the end of the day everyone thinks that a gun that can fire blanks can fire real bullets too but that's just not the case. A blank has only a fraction of the explosive power in a full cartridge. Also, in a blank, there's nothing in the way of the gas that comes out of the barrel. With a real gun the bullet effectively seals off the barrel until it reaches the end. The pressures are enormous.

'Even a real gun has its limits. You ever heard of a squib load? It's when a bullet fails in the chamber or gets stuck in the barrel. If that happens and you fire another shot behind it, even a real gun will explode, fall to pieces. People just don't understand how powerful these things are.'

'Now this thing on the other hand,' he picks up the SAPL, 'this is a beauty. You put the right load in this, you could take someone out, no problem.'

'The right load?'

'You can get shotgun cartridges with less powder than usual. They use them for kids and women who want to go clay pigeon shooting but are worried about recoil. They still pack enough lead shot to reduce a target to dust at thirty feet. Imagine what they'd do to someone's face close up.

'You'd only get the one shot, but the truth is, if you're using something like a Brocock, you've probably only got one shot anyway before it takes your hand off.'

Jay also wants to have a look at the stun gun that I brought along. After he has finished he asks, on behalf of Billy, if he can hang on to the GC 27 and the stun gun with gas attachment. Billy does, he explains, expect to run into a little trouble when he gets out of the prison and is eager to have something to defend himself with that won't see him go down for murder.

I lie and tell Jay that I can't leave the items with him at that moment as I need to keep everything together so that I can be photographed for my *Observer* story. In fact, the story is already completed and will be running that weekend but there is no way in the world I can leave any of the items for Billy to get his hands on, even if he was responsible for giving me the story in the first place.

Billy is disappointed but seems to understand. In any case, his real concern is to find a gun that can be converted. That, he tells me, will be literally worth its weight in gold.

The story I write ultimately focuses on the stun gun, following a huge robbery in which they were used that same week. I plan to write follow-up pieces in the weeks to come about blank firing guns that can be converted to fire live ammo, but then both Billy and I are beaten to the punch.

Manchester gangster Bobby Tyrer seemed to have found the Holy Grail.

During a visit to Cologne in 2004 he wandered into a gunshop and was stunned at the models that were available over the counter without the need to even produce so much as a driving licence.

German gun law was tightened up in 2003 – following a massacre at a school in Erfurt – but it is still much easier to buy weapons than in the UK.

The Brocock ME 38 with its air cartridge system was on sale but so was a nearly identical model made by noted German sporting arms manufacture Cuno Melcher which was made to fire 9mm blanks containing CS gas. These and other guns by the company were as sturdy, if not more sturdy, than the Brocock. Surely it wouldn't take much to adapt them into reliable weapons for the underworld.

Keen to put this theory to the test, Tyrer bought sixteen of the guns and smuggled them back to England on the cross channel ferry. Back in his home town of Gorton, he contacted his friend David McCulloch, owner of DMC Engineering which operated from a mill in Ancoats.

McCulloch, a qualified engineer by trade, examined the weapons and announced that, using his computerised lathes and general expertise, he could convert each gun to fire live ammunition. Some parts would have to be drilled out, others completely replaced at a cost of £100 a time, but it could be done. To ensure the guns were completely safe, McCulloch suggested making their own ammunition so as not to overstress the components.

Tyrer already knew that he could sell the finished guns for at least £700 a time on the streets of Manchester and so was born a lucrative business.

Tyrer made repeated trips back to the shop in Cologne and then contacted Cuno Melcher's factory direct and, claiming he was a dealer with a company in France, got them to sell him their guns at the wholesale price.

In the space of little more than a year, working with his brother Jamie and some other trusted friends, Tyrer smuggled and converted 274 guns making profits of tens of thousands of pounds. The guns were initially brought back on the ferry by Tyrer personally before he switched to using the postal system.

This would prove to be his downfall. In July 2005 a consignment of guns was accidentally delivered to a shop in Levenshulme. Staff opened the package and, realising what was inside, immediately called the police.

Tyrer and his gang were ultimately convicted and sentenced to long prison terms but the guns they had bought and converted were already out in the community. In October 2005 one was used to rob shopkeeper Jagdish Patel. When he resisted he was shot in the head and survived only because the bullet bounced off the side of his skull and hit the ceiling. 'It smelled of firecrackers and I fell back thinking I was hurt. It's only because the gun was not 100 per cent accurate that I'm here today,' he said later.

One turned up in the summer of 2006 when Brian Walsh used it to shoot dead his estranged wife Pauline before heading to a graveyard and shooting himself in the chest. Pauline survived after emergency surgery to remove the bullet but Walsh was dead on arrival at hospital.

Another cropped up in April 2007 when sixteen-year-old Gorton teenager Kasha Peniston could not resist disobeying his mother. She had brought one of the guns to the family home to hide for a boyfriend and, after burying it in the garden, told her son not to touch it.

Kasha, who was left in charge of his twelve-year-old sister Kamilah and two younger children, dug up the gun and was playing with it in his pocket in the living room when it suddenly went off, the bullet hitting Kamilah in the centre of the forehead as she sat on the sofa.

In a panic, Kasha carried his sister out into the street and called neighbours for help. The little girl was rushed to hospital but doctors were unable to do anything for her. The next day, her mother's birthday, they switched off her life-support machine.

Hundreds of guns converted by Tyrer's gang remain on the streets but by the time the police had closed their operation down, the converted Cuno Melchers had already been superseded by a weapon which, in the space of just three years, became the most popular in all of gang land and would ultimately be responsible for more murders than any other converted gun.

One Sunday night in October 2007, eighteen-year-old student Philip Poru was sitting in a car with friends in Plumstead, south London, when the vehicle was approached by two men who demanded to know what they were doing and where they were from.

When one of Poru's friends explained that they were from Peckham, one of the men pulled a handgun out of his jacket. It was tiny and looked like a toy, a cap gun. A silencer attachment had been fitted to the end of the barrel. It was only when the gunman pulled the trigger and fired several shots into the silver Ford Fiesta that the passengers knew that this was no Halloween stunt. Witnesses said they found the teenagers slumped out of the car, two of them bleeding heavily. They were screaming that they had been shot by a Somalian gang.

Poru died later that night, his friend spent weeks in hospital recovering from his wounds. Both had been unwittingly caught up in an ongoing turf war between gangs from different African nations.

The gun that killed Poru was another conversion, but one that reached new standards of quality and deadliness. 'They are extremely well engineered,' says Tony Miller, a senior forensic scientist. 'They use a steel tube which is properly rifled so that the bullet spins when it's fired. They don't jam and there are no problems with accuracy. There is no difference in performance to a real handgun.'

The Makarov pistol was the standard sidearm for the Soviet military and police force between 1951 and 1991. Based on a relatively simple design, the gun was cheap to make and proved sturdy and reliable.

In the late nineties Russian company Baikal, the largest manufacturer of hunting and sporting guns in the world, decided to produce a copy aimed at the growing market for 'self-defence guns' for women concerned about rapists or muggers. An alternative to carrying a can of mace or pepper spray, the guns had an 8mm barrel and fired pellets that released clouds of tear gas but would have added 'scare' value when produced, which would hopefully drive an attacker away before it became necessary to pull the trigger.

The copy, named the Baikal IZH-79 was introduced in the late nineties and immediately proved popular. Like my Glock, most guns manufactured specifically to fire blanks or CS gas cartridges are made of cheap components and aren't robust enough to fire real ammunition; the Baikal, however, was different. It was made of solid steel.

Sometime in 2001, several Lithuanian criminal gangs, impressed by just how well-constructed the Baikal was, set out to discover its full potential. Engineers spent hours in backstreet garages and farm workshops experimenting with barrels of different materials and calibres to see which would work best.

Early conversions were unsophisticated, could fire only 5.45mm ammunition and sold mostly to the Russian market where genuine handguns were scarce. But the most lucrative market lay in the West.

Lithuanian gangs had been active in Britain since the start of the new millennium, mostly in the sex industry where they trafficked in large numbers of East European women to work as prostitutes. From there the gangs developed sidelines into the highly lucrative cigarette smuggling business and soon found themselves in contact with gangsters – most of whom assumed they were Russian mafia – desperate to get their hands on guns.

The first Baikals to arrive went down a storm. One consignment of ten actually led to a bidding war when it arrived at a Hackney club in 2006. But those early models were far from perfect and British buyers demanded modifications.

They wanted guns that fired 9mm bullets, supplies of factory-made ammunition, and they insisted on silencers. British gangs already had their Mac-10s and similar weapons for distance work. What was needed was an effective, reliable gun for self-preservation but most of all for close-up assassination, hence the need for a silencer.

Next time round, the criminal gangs got it just right. Compact and reassuringly solid, the latest generation 9mm Baikal IZH-79 fits comfortably in the palm of a teenager's hand and weighs, unloaded, a modest two pounds. A brand-new Baikal can be bought for as little as £1,200 from gangs in the UK's larger cities, though the usual price is closer to £2,000. With the silencer, it can be used discreetly at close quarters, meaning targets rarely escape with their lives; it is now so widely available, so reliable and so accurate that it has completely changed British gang culture and street crime.

In its 2008 report on the threat of organised crime to the UK, SOCA noted that since 2006 the seizures of guns in the country have increased both in number and in volume of weapons, and 'of the seizures, there has been an increased trend of Baikal gas pistols converted to fire 9mm ammunition entering from Lithuania'.

One of the first gangs to get involved in the trade was part of Lithuania's most feared criminal syndicate, the Baubliai gang. The pistols could not be bought legally in Lithuania but the Baubliai gang obtained vast numbers over the counter from Russia and neighbouring Latvia where they could cost as little as eight pounds each. Using a series of secret workshops at their base in Alytus, a small town in southern Lithuania, the gang began the process of converting the weapons.

After conversion the guns can be purchased in Lithuania for 590 litas – about £140 – but in Britain they change hands for around £2,500. For that sum a Baikal will be delivered shrink-wrapped in heavy-duty plastic complete with twenty rounds of ammunition and a silencer.

The Alytus production line converted countless weapons before a major joint operation in 2008 by the Lithuanian police and secret services, SOCA and the Metropolitan Police smashed the ring in a dramatic armed raid. It led to the arrest of six men, including Remigijus Laniauskas, a former soldier in the Soviet army.

In an earlier British court case of three other Lithuanian gun-runners, Laniauskas was named as the head of an organised crime group that had been supplying guns to the UK. His chief accomplice in the UK was softly spoken Romas Dumbliauskas who, despite having lost his sight during a gang shoot-out in Amsterdam, was a senior member of the Alytus syndicate.

The guns had been smuggled into the UK hidden inside vehicles. Dumbliauskas's cover as a car dealer allowed him to import

GUNS

vehicles in which he hid weapons. Some of the guns were smuggled inside car batteries that had been lined with lead. This ensured they did not show up on X-rays. The transporters were driven across Europe by 'mules' with clean driving licences and no criminal records. The gang masters also paid private individuals already travelling to the UK to act as couriers.

But the guns still had to go through one further person. In order to distance themselves from the hardware, the gang ensured they were sold on to a 'fence' in the UK, who would then sell them on the streets.

Forty-two-year-old divorcee Jeanette Hodges, is a fence for the Lithuanian syndicate. She also has an impressive wealth of underworld contacts in the UK, many through her son Trevor Hodges, who was then in jail for his part in a string of extremely violent car-jackings.

Trevor Hodges exploited his time inside to build up a lengthy client list for his mother, including members of some of London's most notorious gangs, the Muslim Boys and the Peckham Boys; members of the latter were jailed for the murder of schoolboy Damilola Taylor.

Jeanette Hodges built up a friendship with Dumbliauskas and his gang when she began selling their cigarettes, so when her son's contacts asked her to source guns she immediately turned to the Lithuanians. She could get guns within four to six weeks.

Unaware she was dealing with undercover police officers, Hodges explained that the price was between £1,200 and £1,400 per gun if they were bought in bulk. A one-off order would cost £2,250. She and the rest of the gang are now behind bars.

Smashing the syndicate had an instant effect on the market. According to SOCA, 9mm ammunition was going for fifty pence a round on the street; after breaking the Baubliai supply chain, prices went up to three pounds a round.

But any lull in activity was only temporary. According to SOCA, many other gun-running syndicates exist and Baikals continue to arrive in the UK in batches of up to thirty at a time. Another group importing Baikals to the UK was run by former veterinarian Andrius Rauba. He was able to obtain the original weapons for around ten pounds each but sold them for £1,500 to British gangsters.

Scotland Yard detectives keeping London criminal Gerry Smith under surveillance, watched him negotiate the purchase of eighteen of Rauba's weapons from a Lithuanian arms dealer at Café Rouge in St John's Wood, north London.

A month earlier, three Lithuanian men were jailed for a total of thirty-two years at Southwark crown court in London after smuggling what the judge called an 'assassin's armoury' of weapons into Britain. Andrius Gurskas, twenty-six, Orestas Bublilauskas, thirty-four, and Darius Stankunas, thirty-four, had hidden Baikal handguns along with hundreds of bullets in the modified fuel tank of a Vauxhall Astra. Officials from Lithuania's Office of Organised Crime and Corruption say the weapons came from Rauba.

Baikals are now so ubiquitous that it seems they are being used almost exclusively.

In Sheffield, the gang warfare that led to the murder of Tarek Chaiboub, seventeen, has been waged largely with Baikals. Chaiboub's friend and fellow gang member, Jonathan 'Venomous' Matondo, sixteen, was shot dead with a Baikal in October 2007.

Less than a year later police found a Baikal at the home of a thirteen-year-old boy in New Cross, South London as part of a wider investigation into gang crime in south London. The boy, who said he was looking after the weapons for a nineteen-year-old gang elder, was the youngest child ever arrested in possession of a firearm.

The gun and two silencers were wrapped in a pillowcase inside a rucksack.

Labelled a persistent offender, the boy had received two reprimands – one for robbery, the other for threatening behaviour – in the weeks before the discovery. He was then made the subject of a six-month referral order after being found with a meat cleaver at school.

One evening in October my then girlfriend and I go out to see a show in the centre of London and, at the end, make a last-minute decision to spend the night at her place rather than mine. The following morning I wake and switch on my mobile, which immediately starts to ring. I hit the answer button.

'Hello, this is Detective Sergeant Ashton. Could I speak to Mr Tony Thompson.'

'Speaking.'

In my line of work there's nothing that unusual about receiving calls from police officers, though what happens next is somewhat disturbing. The officer recites my full address and asks if I currently live there. My heart sinks.

'Oh shit. Has someone broken in?'

'Yes, sir.'

'Oh no.'

'I broke in. About two hours ago. Myself and thirty officers from SO19.'

For a moment I am rendered utterly speechless. 'Why? Why would you do that?'

'I think you already know, Mr Thompson. And I would like you to come here as soon as possible. Then we can discuss it.'

I jump into my car and head towards home, arriving some twenty minutes later. As I pull into my road I can see dozens of officers both in plain clothes and in uniform, milling around the entrance to and in and out of the hallway of my flat. Neighbours are peering through their curtains, wondering what on earth is happening. They are not the only ones.

As I get out of the car and make my way towards the entrance I feel as though I'm being watched by a thousand unblinking eyes. The heavy front door has been smashed off its frame, the distinctive circular imprint of an 'enforcer' entry tool is on one side of the letter box. The officers part and the detective sergeant I spoke to on the phone steps forward.

He shows me a search warrant and explains that they have gone to my flat because they believe I am in possession of illegally obtained firearms.

'I'll show you where they are,' I say.

The detective sergeant repeats my admission of guilt back to me and I confirm it once more so that others can hear. There is no way I can possibly take it back. With officers either side of me, just in case I should make a break for it or try to destroy some potential evidence, I am asked to lead the way through my flat.

The living room is a sea of chaos. There are papers and clothes and books and boxes everywhere. It is as though a tornado has torn through the place, destroying everything in its path. It is exactly as I left it the night before.

We reach the bedroom and I pull open the drawer to reveal the guns. The officer then tells me that I am under arrest and reads me my rights.

'Is there anything else here you shouldn't have?'

I shake my head.

'We're not worried about the cannabis,' he says.

I snap to attention. 'I don't have any cannabis,' I protest.

'Really, we're not bothered about it.'

'What cannabis? I honestly don't have any.'

The DS points to a bookshelf in the corner of the room. 'That cannabis.'

I look over and see two small polythene bags filled with a green leaf-like material and suddenly all is clear. A couple of months earlier I'd written a story about legal alternatives to marijuana and come away from the supplier with several bags of products with names like Kratom and Damiana, none of which I'd tried but had simply stuck on the shelf and forgotten about.

'That stuff's not real,' I said.

'Really, Mr Thompson, we're not bothered about it, not under the circumstances.'

My protest was more about the fact that I didn't want the officers thinking I was a regular drug user than anything else. But then it occurred to me that, over the years, in the course of my work as a crime reporter I had done all sorts of things and collected all sorts of bits and pieces that might not reflect well on me. One thing in particular stood out above all the others.

While researching an earlier book, *Gangs*, I had smoked both crack cocaine and heroin, purely for journalistic purposes you understand. In the case of the latter, I purchased two wraps from a dealer in Southall. I smoked one that afternoon in the flat of a man named Jas, the other I had brought home and . . . oh shit . . .

'There is one thing,' I say sheepishly.

'And what would that be, sir?'

'Um. In the drawer with the guns. There might be some heroin in there.'

The detective sergeant's eyebrows rise slowly. 'How much heroin are we talking about?'

'Just a wrap. You know, ten quid's worth.'

'I see.'

'I don't use drugs.'

The officer's eyes flick over towards the bags of 'cannabis' sitting on the shelf.

'I really don't. I know how this looks but oh, never mind.'

'Mr Thompson, you do not have to say anything . . .'

This time I decide to take his advice.

Over the next hour very little is said at all. The police officers are going through my flat with a fine tooth comb, bagging up anything at all that seems to be evidence. Perhaps it's because of the heroin but they all seem utterly convinced that there must be something I'm holding back.

And then they find the hole in my kitchen wall. Ever since I moved into the flat I've been planning to renovate the kitchen but have never got round to it. One of the things I planned to do was fill a hole in the side of the wall where the bricks show through which was there when I bought the place. Until then, I had simply covered it up with the countertop.

The DS takes me into the kitchen and asks me what I use the hole for. The hole is about a foot wide and two inches deep. I try to explain that it's just a hole but I'm starting to feel as if the whole world is conspiring against me.

A short time later the DS comes to me with another question. They have found a large, narrow black bag under my bed. It's a carry case for an electronic keyboard that I occasionally play very badly. 'It looks like a carry case for a hunting rifle,' the detective sergeant says.

'Oh good grief.'

'Do you have a rifle?'

'No, just the guns, just the heroin.'

We both stare at the floor for a moment before the officer speaks again. 'I have to ask you. Why on earth do you have so many guns here?'

'Well, because I was doing a story on them.'

'A story?'

'Yeah, I'm a journalist.'

The officer stares at me for what seems like a very long time. A very, very long time. Then he turns on his heels and walks away. I hear whispers in the corridor and suddenly everyone seems to be on edge. Up until that point I'd just assumed that everyone knew I was a journalist, that I'd written the story and not bothered to hand the weapons in afterwards. Now for the first time I realise that the team involved in the raid had absolutely no idea.

It is only later that I will learn that I have been caught up in Operation Bembridge, a massive nationwide operation aimed at people buying illegal guns over the Internet. More than 5,000 officers have been involved in simultaneous raids on seventy-eight addresses across the country.

Things rapidly become increasingly farcical. The arrest team had been given my date of birth but it had somehow been mixed up. When they find my actual passport, they therefore assume they have found a cunning forgery.

They also get extremely excited when they find a Barclaycard receipt showing a cash transfer of £34,000, clear evidence that I have been involved in some kind of criminality. That is, until I point out the small symbols on the side of the box showing the figure.

'This is from when I was in Africa. Those are Kenyan Schillings. It's about two hundred quid, not thirty-four thousand pounds.'

The attitude completely changes. It's not that anyone was being particularly nasty before – at all times the officers were incredibly professional and courteous – it's just that they thought they were dealing with a scumbag gun-toting gangster and were keeping their distance.

When the DS returns, he seems much more relaxed. 'There are a couple of concerns. The main one is that, if we walk away now and you're hiding something from us, we might be all over the papers tomorrow. I can see the headlines now: police came to my house to look for guns and here are the six rocket launchers they missed.'

'I don't have anything else.'

'So you say. But they want to be sure. They're thinking of calling a Phoenix team.'

This specialist search unit will tear my entire house apart. They'll lift up floorboards, probe into cavity walls, they will quite literally leave no stone unturned. Furthermore, I will have to pay for any damage they cause. The Met's rules are simple. If they break down your door and don't find anything, they foot the bill of putting everything back exactly the way if was. If they find anything, then you're on your own. I've already admitted having illegal firearms on the premises. And heroin. Cannabis or no cannabis, I'm fucked.

'Surely that won't be necessary? How about if I prove that I only ordered the items that I have here?' Having received permission to use my computer – the officer warned me in no uncertain terms that if at any point it looked as though I was trying to erase evidence I would be forcefully restrained – I log on to my webmail account and print out a copy of the delivery note guns2u had sent me.

The officer scans the list. 'Is everything on this list in that drawer?' he asks.

I think back to my last phone call with Billy and his request to borrow the CS gas and the stun gun. He'd even offered to pay me for them and pointed out that, had it not been for his help, I would never have known about the website in the first place.

'I understand, Billy, really I do,' I had explained, doing my best not to antagonise him. 'But supposing you use them to do someone and then it comes back to me. I just can't take the risk. I'm sorry.'

As I look at the DS I'm sure the relief at having made the right decision back then shows on my face. 'Yes, everything's there. Nothing is missing. Nothing's been fired. I haven't even opened the packets on some of them.'

I print off a copy of the story from the *Observer* which I wrote about buying the guns and dig out a copy of my last book. 'Oh that Tony Thompson,' says one officer. 'I've read that. It's good.'

I'm escorted down to the police station and booked in by the custody sergeant. By now I'm being treated as something of a minor celebrity. It's my first time seeing this process from the inside and the DS helpfully talks me through everything and even offers to show me around.

The custody sergeant, a stern-faced brunette, begins making her way through the list of standard questions that need to be asked when booking in a suspect. 'Do you have any difficulties understanding English? Do you require any medication?' and she records my answers directly into the computer terminal in front of her.

'What is your profession?'

'Journalist.'

She taps a few keys, hesitates, backspaces, taps a few more, then sighs and leans forward: 'How do you spell that?'

I impress myself by not only managing to stifle my giggles but also stopping myself from hitting back with the obvious question: 'Do you have any difficulties understanding English?' When I look over at the DS he is smiling and shaking his head slowly.

After I am photographed, fingerprinted and have my DNA taken I am led to a cell to await the arrival of my solicitor. It's soon clear that I am not cut out to be a villain. After an hour in my

cell the complete lack of any form of stimulation is utterly intoler-
able. After two hours I'm ready to call my girlfriend and get her to
smuggle in a rock hammer and a Rita Hayworth poster so that I
can start working on a *Shawshank Redemption*-style escape.

After three hours I am taken to the interview room. The brief
session consists of my explaining how I came to be in possession
of the guns followed by the DS reading extracts of my article and
book to prove that I never intended to hide the fact that I had
purchased them. Just simply forgot to hand them in.

The next morning I have the slightly surreal experience of reading all about myself in the tabloids courtesy of a story in the *Sun*.

THIRTY-seven suspects were arrested yesterday after police
seized a huge haul of weapons bought and sold on the Internet.
Among the men held were a police officer, a doctor and the
Observer's crime journalist Tony Thompson.

Met Commander Steve James said: 'Some of those arrested are
criminals who were exploiting the Internet to get weaponry into
this country. We believe two of them are underworld armourers
who were supplying firearms to criminals.

'Others arrested were just fools and naively bought weaponry over the Internet. They now have to face the consequences
of their actions which they knew were illegal and can expect a
minimum sentence of five years imprisonment for possession of
firearms.'

The overall haul from all of Operation Bembridge is quite breath-
taking: 108 handguns, thirteen rifles, four sub-machine guns and
seven shotguns. A World War Two Sten gun, assorted .22 rifles,
Berettas, Glocks, Walther PPKs and hand cannons. Six flare guns,
ten CS sprays and thirteen Taser stun guns capable of delivering
electric shocks. Five thousand rounds of ammunition and tools for
converting imitation guns.

I spend six months trying not to think too much about my
case before the CPS most graciously announces that, on the

recommendation of the arresting officer, they will not be taking any further action.

My own brief foray into the world of gun crime may be over but for the rest of the underworld it continues to gather momentum.

In the months that follow I read about one raid in Lithuania where police uncovered a stash of Agrams – lightweight, rapid-fire machine pistols made in Croatia – alongside dozens of converted Baikals that were destined to be shipped to Britain. The same Lithuanian gangsters who have managed to gain a foothold in the UK gun market – which by all accounts they are attempting to exploit in order to propel themselves into the highest levels of the drug trade – are, it seems, eager to bring newer, more sophisticated weapons into the country.

But for the foot soldiers occupying the lowest levels of organised crime, the search continues for a holy grail of affordable, reliable weaponry closer to home. The latest contender is the Olympic BBM 9mm revolver, legally sold on British high streets for use as a starting pistol.

Painted bright orange to comply with new legislation which states that imitation firearms must be made to look unrealistic, the gun can be legally purchased at dozens of stores for around eighty pounds. Underworld armourers have found that the weapon is sturdy enough to have its barrel drilled out and that the chamber is capable of holding and firing 9mm ammunition.

To assist with concealment and help with street credibility, the bright orange finish is removed and the gun is sprayed matt black. In this new form the gun changes hands for up to £600. According to the Metropolitan Police, during the year that followed the first appearance of the new weapons, four out of every ten guns seized that were capable of firing live ammunition turned out to be Olympic BBM revolvers.

Such weapons are, not surprisingly, most popular among the new breed of street gangs cropping up in inner cities all across the country. During several of my interviews with Radar, the member of Croydon's DSN gang who I had been talking to on a regular basis, told me that he could get his hands on virtually any kind of gun at short notice. His comments echoed those of Jean 'Method' Tomety, leader of rival gang SMN. In an interview with the *Croydon Advertiser* in 2007 he had boasted that his gang liked to use their fists but that they could 'get weapons if they needed them'.

Both gangs had posed with guns on the Internet (many were probably replicas or BB guns) and bragged about the arsenals at their disposal, yet despite numerous violent clashes between the two factions, guns had never been used. Both sides would undoubtedly have preferred to keep it that way but by the time Method gave his newspaper interview, forces beyond the control of either gang seemed to indicate that an escalation of the violence was inevitable.

It was around this time that the Metropolitan Police released the results of its most recent study into gangs. A Home Office report, published in 1997, had identified seventy-two street gangs in England and Wales. Most of the members were white and their average age was between twenty-five and twenty-nine.

The Met's report identified 257 gangs in London alone. The vast majority of gang members were black and the average age of those involved had fallen dramatically. With all the gangs in the capital feeling increased pressure from rivals, it was becoming increasingly clear that the best way forward was to build up a proper arsenal with which to wage war. It was also clear that, unlike the battles that had taken place between the two gangs in the past, people were about to start dying.

All across London, and particularly south of the river, gun crime was rising and the foot soldiers of the street gangs were almost always the victims. When DSN's Dexter had declared war on other gangs who dared to enter Croydon, the talk had been of 'shanking' and 'bottling' rivals. Less than a year later a sharp spike in the number of gun deaths involving teenagers was making headlines in the national press.

In February, three south London youths had been shot dead in three separate incidents in the space of eleven days, all the result of disputes and 'beefs' between rival gangs. One of the shootings took place on the borders of the territory that SMN and DSN claim as their own.

More murders followed in quick succession and while not all of them involved guns, it was clear that the landscape of London's gangland was changing dramatically, that guns were the way forward and that if the members of DSN wanted to survive, they would not only have to arm themselves but also be prepared to use their weapons with deadly effect.

'It's not a question of if,' Radar told me at the start of that summer. 'It's just a question of when. It's going to happen sooner or later. The only thing I can't tell you is which side is going to pull the trigger first.'

5

STREET GANGS II

Matthew Dunn was taking stock in the basement of the south Croydon jewellery shop where he worked with his father when the front door buzzer sounded, prompting him to stop what he was doing and make his way upstairs to answer it.

Seeing a hazy figure through the partly glazed doorway Dunn instinctively pressed the button on the counter to release the lock. He regretted it immediately. 'A man stepped halfway through the door and was holding something under his jacket,' Dunn said later. 'I could see he had used a box to wedge open the door and I instantly knew what was going to happen. He produced a gun and pointed it at me. Two others came in with scarves covering most of their faces. The man with the gun came around the counter and said: "Stick 'em up." I was terrified. I just did not know how far they were going to go.'

Pointing to a cabinet, the man with the gun demanded to know what was inside while one of the others brought out a large hammer and started smashing display units and grabbing valuables. At that moment Dunn's father, Terry, came into the store from an ante-room holding a wooden tray full of rings and bracelets. Unsure of how many other staff might be lurking out of sight, the raiders panicked, shoving Terry Dunn hard in the chest before running off. In their haste the raiders had missed out on a decent payday: most of their haul was cosmetic jewellery. The most valuable item was an £800 gold watch.

The gunman was Ronaldo Robb, at the time just seventeen years old, a leading member of DSN. The man with the hammer was Louis Wynter, a year older than Robb, and also a well-established DSN 'soulja'. The raid took place in July 2007, midway through the year that would for ever change the face of street gangs.

According to Radar, the robbery was part of a wider play by DSN to maximise its earnings in order to buy more weapons so that members could defend themselves against attacks from outsiders and, if necessary, launch full-scale assaults on rivals. SMN had generally made most of its money from the drug trade, DSN had long preferred a more active approach to criminality

The raid on the jewellery store was the start of a spate of robberies across Croydon carried out by DSN members. It was also a sign of a worrying and seemingly unstoppable evolutionary process as the gang moved from being a group of young boys who sought safety in numbers to proactive criminal collectives seeking monetary gain through the use of violence. 'It was a crazy time,' says Radar. 'Crazy twenty-four seven. The elders were expecting all sorts of shit. Everyone had to do their bit, everyone had to do work. There's no arguing. That was just the way it had to be. It was about money but it was also about knowing who you could count on.'

On several occasions, elders within DSN had been pressing Wynter to join in with the robberies in order to prove his loyalty to the gang, but he had repeatedly turned them down. In the end he was picked up by one of the gang's 'pool cars' as he waited at a bus stop on his way to college. It was only when he was given a bandana to wear and saw the gun that he realised what was really going on. When he refused once more he was threatened with being shot in the leg – an increasingly common 'punishment' meted out by gang members for acts of disrespect.

Robb, on the other hand, was a seasoned veteran by comparison. He had carried out at least four previous robberies and had a history of being involved in serious violence. 'Robber by name, robber by nature,' says Radar. 'That boy was never happy until he was taking something that didn't belong to him.'

A month later Robb was one of another group of DSN members who took part in a vicious robbery on a Crawley to Croydon train. The gang had chosen their target with care, launching the raid at a time when the carriages were packed with hundreds of youngsters returning from a major under-eighteens' event. Robb and the others made their way through the carriages, cornering victims and taking anything they could get their hands on. Necklaces and bracelets were ripped away, mobile phones, cash and jewellery were all collected. Anyone who tried to resist was punched or head butted in the face. Many of those who were attacked were just fifteen years old.

Radar says nothing about his own involvement in these activities but in our next meeting he is showing clear signs of increasing affluence. He wears an enormous padded black coat over a pastel-coloured collarless shirt that seems to glow against his smooth black skin. The gold chain around his neck looks thick enough to secure a small yacht and dangles like a glittery noose.

In the weeks that follow, as the body count of young teenagers stabbed or shot to death on the streets of London reaches an all-time high, the robberies by DSN members continue. Dexter, who has been released from prison after serving time for the assault on Method, steers DSN towards further criminal activity and soon there are armed raids on taxi drivers, assaults on the homes of suspected drug dealers, robberies at fast-food stores, corner shops and dozens of violent muggings. Dexter is soon back behind bars though, having been caught taking part in a violent car jacking. The situation soon becomes so serious that Croydon Police announce the formation of a special unit aimed at tackling the borough's gang problem. The unit plans to eradicate all street gangs operating in Croydon within a year.

Among the first to be targeted by the unit are two members of SMN – Tyrell 'Drastik' Ellis and self-proclaimed leader Jean Louis 'Method' Tomety, the one who had given the interview to the local newspaper and also the one who had been attacked by Dexter.

According to the police both Method and Drastick had been responsible for numerous acts of street robbery, assault and threatening behaviour. The pair had also breached previous agreements aimed at regulating their behaviour. New ASBOs are issued and both youths are banned from Croydon and Thornton Heath town centres for two years, banned from seeing members of their gangs and from seeing each other.

A week later SMN hits back with a new media offensive. A man called 'Sarge', a high-ranking general within the gang, gives an interview with the Sunday tabloid, the *People*, about his life in the gang. He claims to earn up to £500 per day selling crack and cocaine and states that senior members of the gang have twenty-four-hour access to weapons.

'It's important youngers prove themselves if they want to join,' Sarge tells the reporter. 'They have to show they can handle anything, and that they are prepared to fight to the death if necessary.' According to the article a major attraction of gang life for many young boys is the opportunity to have lots of underage sex. Some girls are attracted by the money and the danger while others simply wish to be associated with the gang because of the protection it affords. One twelve-year-old is quoted as saying: 'You can have sex with much older girls because they're up for going with a bad boy.'

A few weeks later the same paper runs another feature on SMN, this time interviewing Sarge's girlfriend, Aliyah. She talks about being part of a 'harem' of women that competes for the attention of the leading members of the gang, the lucky ones becoming serious girlfriends rather than just casual flings. She also claims that new recruits have to have sex with all the male members of the gang in one night before they are accepted.

The next time I see Radar I ask him if that depiction of women within modern street gangs is at all accurate. He smiles. 'There are no girls in DSN, but there are plenty of girls who want to be seen with us,' he says. 'The badder you are, the more girls you get. You can do anything you want. That's just the way it is. You get me? The more men a girl is with, the more protection she's going to get.

'The girls like the money too. If you're in a gang, you're making money, though nobody makes anything like the paper they say they do. It's all an act. They call it balling. If you're balling, you're spending everything you have to look as good as possible, to live as big as possible. You get a taxi five minutes down the road, you buy a new ring instead of keeping the money to feed your family for the next six months, you buy brand-new £150 trainers every week that you don't even need. It's all about showing off as much as you can. I know some fourteen-year-olds who've been out shotting [selling drugs] and have bought themselves cars. You look at them and you think: "where you going with that?"

'When you're balling, the girls come calling. The girls are the ones who carry the drugs and the guns. If you have something you need to hide somewhere, you take it to a girl's house. Some gangs have girls in them and those girls are rough! They want the same rep as the guys do. They do all the same things. They want to be the best, they can be dangerous. Like Pitbull. She was a soldier.'

'Pitbull?'

'That was the girl who got killed round here last month. Sian Simpson. She wasn't in DSN but she was one of us, in spirit.'

The name rings a vague bell and I shut my eyes in concentration, trying to recall the details of the case. I finally remember that I read about the murder but dismissed it as there seemed to be little connection to gangs like DSN and SMN. I do a quick search on my phone for related news stories and soon find a story from the local paper that talks about how seventeen-year-old Simpson, a promising student, was stabbed to death after trying to break up a fight. 'She was a good girl doing a good deed,' one friend said. 'She tried to stop the violence. She was there to protect.'

Radar shakes his head slowly. 'That's not the way it happened at all. Not even close. You're fucking kidding me right? I knew her. We all did. We called her Pitbull. That was her street name. She wasn't breaking nothing up. She was there to fight. She got stabbed with her own fucking knife.'

Radar patiently explains that the trouble started because a boy, Nathan Davidson, had decided to visit the four-month-old son he had fathered with his ex-girlfriend, Chantelle Campbell. Unfortunately for Davidson Daniele Cooke, his new girlfriend who was pregnant with his child, found out about the visit – which was taking place at Davidson's mum's house – and decided to go and confront him. 'You hear what I am saying, yeah?' she said in a message left on his mobile phone voicemail. 'I am coming to your mum's house so if she's there she's going to get fucked up and so are you.'

When Chantelle Campbell found out what was happening, she panicked and phoned round several friends to get them to come to the scene thinking that there would be greater safety in numbers. One of those friends was Sian Simpson.

Cooke arrived at the house with her best friend Chelsea Bennett and three other girls. With a heavy storm raging, Campbell and Simpson, both armed with ten-inch steak knives, went down to the grassy area outside the block of flats they had been inside to confront them.

Cooke and Campbell began arguing. 'I know who the father of my baby is, how about you?' was one exchange. Then Bennett approached Simpson and began arguing with her. The row got more and more heated until Bennett exploded with rage and punched Simpson several times. Then Bennett tripped and fell into a kerbside puddle, causing a few of the girls watching the fight to burst out laughing.

At this point, Simpson pulled out the knife and the crowd of up to thirty girls that were looking on began shouting out 'stab her, stab her' as Simpson advanced. 'She had the knife and she kept coming,' Bennett said later. 'She jumped on my back and started punching my head. I saw the knife on the pavement. I picked it up. I thought she would be scared. I thought she would stop running towards me. I wanted to get back into the car and her to stop running at me. I got up very quickly. I was trying to block her and push her away.'

The next thing Bennett knew was that Simpson had kicked her, hard, sending her reeling back into a puddle once more. Simpson was looming over Bennett but suddenly she stepped back. She backed into a car then slumped to the ground and rolled over on to her front. Bennett did not realise she had stabbed Simpson but the blade had pierced the girl's heart and she was as good as dead before she hit the ground.

The screaming stopped and a terrible silence descended on the scene. Bennett ran off, locking herself in a friend's car. But before she could get away the vehicle was surrounded. Simpson's friends began kicking the vehicle and throwing bricks. They were still trying to get to Bennett when the police finally arrived. Bennett was arrested at the scene when she pulled the brown-handled steak knife, used to stab Simpson, from under the car seat.

Radar shakes his head slowly and whistles through his teeth as he recounts the death of his friend. 'Sian was there because Chantelle begged her to be there. That's the truth. No one made her do it. Those girls were stupid. They should have been fighting that boy, not fighting over him.'

By the end of 2007 Sian Simpson's name is just one among the twenty-six teenagers shot or stabbed to death in London that year. She is the only girl on the list and her killer, Chelsea Bennett, is eventually cleared of murder after a trial at the Old Bailey.

This is also the year that eleven-year-old Rhys Jones is shot dead in Liverpool, an event that prompts many gangs across the country to keep their heads down because of intense police and public scrutiny. Tensions between DSN and SMN continue to rise but there are no major confrontations.

One judge is so angered by the steady tide of cases involving the gangs – one day three of the five local courts are hearing separate cases involving DSN members – that he publicly condones the gang, naming and shaming several members and hitting them with maximum sentences to discourage others from following in their footsteps.

In the meantime the issue of girl gangs rises to the top of the agenda as figures are released showing that teenage girls are responsible for 15,000 violent crimes per year. Two teenagers from the East London Girls Over Men gang are jailed after kidnapping and assaulting a sixteen-year-old girl who 'dissed' the mum of the gang leader. At least one member of the gang filmed the assault on her mobile phone.

Stories also emerge of girls allowing themselves to be brutalised simply in order to be accepted by the gangs. Some tell of being raped by several members, others talk of having to carry out attacks on members of the public. One girl claimed to have been raped at the age of thirteen. Others told of being used as decoys to enable male members of the gang to carry out robberies.

In March 2008 Jean Louis 'Method' Tomety, leader of SMN, is deported back to the Ivory Coast after being involved in yet more criminal activity including drug offences and robbery. Despite having arrived in the UK at a young age, he had never applied for British citizenship.

A few days later a group of DSN members take some of their newly acquired guns – supposedly paid for with the proceeds of the numerous robberies and raids – and force their way into a council flat in Woodville Road in Thornton Heath. They were looking for Older Troubz, the street name of Sudanese-born Hamid Baballa. At twenty-six he was a veteran gang member and the main dope dealer of DSN rivals SMN.

'They got a tip off about where he was dealing from and headed over there to rob him,' Radar tells me. 'They got inside and put a gun to the man's head and told him to tell them where the drugs were or he'd die. He said, "I ain't got no drugs. Don't know what you're talking about." And they look around and see that there's nothing, not so much as a joint. The address they've been given is obviously wrong so they leave it.'

In fact the gang were far closer than any of them knew. Older Troubz lived right next door to the flat they raided. When the occupants of the home that had been raided complained to the police, local detectives realised the gang's mistake and raided the flat next door.

It was empty but the police came away with three carrier bags of 'skunk', a gold Rolex and £4,500 in cash. After the raid the flat was secured and when Troubz failed to appear to collect any of his personal items, police decided to search the property again. This time they found a revolver hidden in a bandana. Guns, it seems, are everywhere.

For the next few months the situation seems to calm down, but in the summer of 2008 Croydon plays host to a case that will make headlines around the country. It is also a case which demonstrates just how deadly the women involved in the gang world can truly be.

He was never short of female attention. Tall, slim with intense eyes, a wicked smile and the confidence to match, he had always had some or other girlfriend on the go since the tender age of thirteen. But this time round, something was different. This time he was completely and utterly smitten.

'She's so beautiful,' he told his mother, a wistful, faraway expression spreading across his face. 'I'm in love. I really am. One day she's gonna be my wife and we're gonna have kids and everything.'

There were several pictures of the girl, Samantha, on his mobile phone and he couldn't wait for his mum to see them. 'I remember thinking she was really pretty and nice to look at,' she said later. 'He really cared about her.'

Shakilus Townsend, had started seeing fifteen-year-old Samantha Joseph around six weeks earlier when their eyes met across the top deck of a bus. They exchanged text messages and then began meeting up regularly. Before long he was totally obsessed and Samantha was all that he could talk about.

It wasn't entirely mutual. After a couple of weeks Samantha had told Shakilus that she already had a boyfriend and wanted to keep things low key. She told him that if they were seen out together, he should tell people that he was her cousin. He reluctantly agreed.

Samantha had come to England as a child with her mother, Sheila, who worked as head chef at a pub in Brockley, south-east London, while her father and elder brother had remained behind in their native Trinidad. Despite this unconventional arrangement and the strains of being brought up in a tiny flat above a high-street bookmakers, the young Samantha did well at school and showed a particular flair for art.

She and her mother were said to be incredibly close – one was rarely seen without the other – but that changed when Samantha blossomed into a strikingly pretty teenager and found herself preferring the attention of boys to that of family.

One such boy was eighteen-year-old Danny 'Tamper' McLean, a leading member of Shine My Nine. Having lost her virginity at fourteen, Samantha was soon in an intense sexual relationship with McLean and fast becoming embroiled in gang life.

Within a year of meeting McLean she had been excluded from Norbury Manor Girls High School for fighting and referred to a specialist education centre. She didn't care – she was totally besotted with McLean, though the relationship was far from perfect.

While Shakilus continually showered Samantha with gifts and attention – he was planning to buy her a puppy for her birthday – McLean never ever took her out, never spent any money on her and basically just used her for sex. McLean also had a furious temper and had slapped, punched and kicked Samantha on numerous occasions leaving her covered in bruises.

Shakilus was prepared to play the waiting game, convinced it was only a matter of time before she left McLean behind completely. At one point the pair had even met and McLean, believing the story about Shakilus being a member of his girlfriend's family, declared him to be a 'cool guy'.

But then one of Samantha's friends told McLean what had really gone on behind his back for the past month, which instantly ended the relationship. McLean was furious – not only had his girlfriend of eighteen months betrayed him but, once he learned who Shakilus really was, he realised she had done it with one of his gang's sworn enemies.

A few months earlier Shakilus had wandered into SMN territory and been challenged with the usual 'what endz you from?' by McLean's friend and fellow gang member, Andre 'Tiny Bouncer' Thompson. When Shakilus refused to answer, Thompson pushed him. Shakilus responded by punching Thompson in the mouth so hard that he knocked out his two front teeth, then calmly walked on.

Within hours of being dumped, Samantha decided that she had made a terrible mistake and could not live without her McLean, or the status that having a leading member of SMN as a boyfriend afforded her. She promised to do anything to keep him sweet and win him back.

That 'anything' turned out to be leading Shakilus into a trap so that McLean and his friends could teach him a lesson he would never forget. 'It was something along the lines of "if you still love me, you will set up Shak",' Samantha said later. 'I just went along with it.'

Shakilus soon heard rumours and later received threats from McLean and others but wasn't particularly worried. He had grown up in a tough neighbourhood and, as his encounter with Andre Thompson had shown, was more than capable of looking after himself.

At thirteen he had been convicted of common assault and a year later had been found carrying an axe in the street. He also had convictions for robbery and carrying offensive weapons that culminated in five months spent at a young offenders' institution. He went by the street name of Bugz but was not affiliated to any particular gang. He had a reputation as something of a tearaway and had often been in trouble with other boys around his home area. At one point his home was attacked by a gang of stone-throwing youths.

By the time he met Samantha his mother insisted that he had turned over a new leaf, but his profile on social networking website Bebo showed him wearing a stabproof vest and holding a knife. The picture was captioned: 'I'm a sweet boy, slash your face up if you fuck around with me.' Another picture on the same site showed him posing with his finger on the trigger of a large semi-automatic pistol.

It was for this reason that McLean, who initially had considered exacting his revenge on his love rival in a traditional mano-a-mano fashion, rapidly changed his mind and decided to take some backup along for the ride.

He chose Andre Thompson, of course, but also Tyrell 'Drastik' Ellis and his brother Don-Carlos, aka Rugrat, who had become leader of SMN following the deportion of Jean Louis 'Method' Tomety earlier in the year. Drastik was still the subject to a two-year ASBO for gang-related crimes at the time while his brother was on bail for a previous incident.

The pair had once been promising street dancers, taking lessons at Streatham Park in Wandsworth, south-west London, from a local teacher, but had to give up after postcode rivalries between gangs in the capital meant it was no longer safe for them to travel outside their home turf. 'You have to stay in your zone,' Radar had once told me. 'If you stay in your zone then you're safe, if you step out of your zone there's not going to be anyone to protect you. You could end up dead.'

McLean's assault team also included a public schoolboy who left a promising future behind because of his association with McLean. Andrew 'Fenza' Johnson-Haynes, eighteen, was educated privately at Emmanuel School in Wandsworth from 2001 and then Portland Place School, central London, between 2005 and 2007.

He studied at Richmond College for four months and in September 2008 registered at Croydon College for a diploma in sport. Johnson-Haynes regularly played for the London Irish Amateur Rugby Club as a wing and full back and worked at McDonald's.

On the morning that the trap was due to be sprung, Samantha spoke to a friend and explained what she was about to do. Told that it was wrong for her to allow the two boys to fight in that way she claimed she had no other choice. 'Tamper wants to get Shak set. Either I get the beats or he gets the beats.'

'You shouldn't do it,' the friend said. 'Shak's innocent. He didn't know you had a boyfriend.'

'It's not just because of that,' Samantha replied. 'It's because he punched up another bloke's teeth already.'

An hour or so later, on a sunny July afternoon in 2008, Samantha met up with Shakilus on the pretext of introducing him to one of her cousins. Seeing this as a sign of real progress in the relationship, the smitten teenager eagerly agreed.

As they travelled on bus number 450 together through south London heading towards Thornton Heath, Samantha chatted on her mobile phone to her cousin. Bugz could only hear half the conversation.

At one point her cousin asked her: 'Are you getting Shak set?'

'Yes,' said Samantha.

At this point Shakilus started to become suspicious. 'I hope you and your cousin aren't getting me set.'

Samantha smiled sweetly. 'Do you really think I'd do that?'

A few moments later Shakilus' mother called. It would be the last time she would ever speak to him. During their chat, Samantha continued to send text messages. Shakilus assumed that they too were to her cousin but in fact she was contacting McLean to say they were nearly at their destination.

A few minutes later she and Shakilus got off the bus and headed towards a quiet cul-de-sac where Samantha claimed her cousin lived. They had gone only a few paces when they heard shouts of 'Get him, he's over there.' Witnesses reported seeing five or six black males, dressed in hooded tops with bandanas covering their faces, rushing towards the pair. Shakilus made a run for it but McLean and his friends were on bicycles and caught up with him easily.

First Andre Thompson hit Shakilus around the side of the head with a baseball bat knocking him down to the ground. The others then pounced and began to rain down a flurry of punches and kicks as Samantha looked on, laughing.

In the seconds that followed Shakilus was stabbed five times with at least two different knives. When it was McLean's turn to wield the blade, he pushed it in deeply and twisted it before pulling it out, leaving a gaping hole that pierced his victim's liver. More kicks and punches followed. Thompson swung his bat again but this time caught McLean with a glancing blow to the side of the head, splitting the skin with a deep gash.

By now residents of Belauh Crescent had been alerted to the sounds of shouting and screaming and had come out of their homes to see what was going on. One of the first on the scene was warned off by the attackers who told her: 'We know who you are.' More residents soon appeared and, deciding that their victim had learned his lesson, the members of SMN turned and fled.

They left a mortally wounded Shakilus on the ground crying out: 'Mummy, Mummy, Mummy ... I don't want to die'. One eyewitness said later: 'He was tiny and looked terrified. There was loads of blood. He was crying for his mum over and over again. Even when the ambulance came he was trying to take off the oxygen mask and speak to the ambulance crew to tell them to call his mum.'

Shakilus died in hospital a few hours later. He was already the thirty-third teenager to be murdered that year, the eighteenth in London.

Footage from a CCTV camera taken a short while later showed Samantha walking beside McLean, carrying his hooded top and a cream-coloured handbag stained with blood. They stopped off at a newsagent to buy plasters for McLean's cut head and concocted a story to explain his injuries. If anyone asked, both he and Samantha would confirm that he had been attacked by members of DSN.

Later than day McLean and Samantha logged on to Shakilus' Bebo account and deleted it in an attempt to destroy any evidence that the two had known each other. She called her friends and told them to delete Shak's phone number from their mobiles.

'I could hear Tamper in the background saying "my head's hurting, it's bleeding",' one friend recalled. 'She said he'd been hit on the head with a baseball bat and sounded like she was in a panic.'

When the friend found out that Shakilus had been murdered, she rang Samantha again. 'I was asking her if she did that thing I told her not to do. She said "what thing, I don't know what you're talking about."'

'Did you stand there and watch him get beaten up?'

'No, I just walked away.'

When questioned by police Samantha Joseph claimed she had left Shakilus at the bus stop but an eyewitness reported seeing her, wearing a distinctive orange floral dress, with the gang shortly after the attack. Detectives who interviewed her for several hours over three days recalled her 'cold and calculating' demeanour. She told the arresting officer that she could not be involved in the crime because Shakilus had been her boyfriend.

The same friend later received a call from McLean who told her that Samantha had been arrested in connection with Shakilus' death. 'I said good, I hope she gets the maximum sentence possible. Tamper then said "It wasn't meant to happen like that." He sounded like he was telling the truth – like he was upset about what happened, like he didn't mean for him to die.'

But if McLean had any regrets about what had happened, they were not shared by the other members of SMN. The Ellis brothers both posted videos of themselves 'spitting' – freestyle rapping to music – on YouTube and the website of music magazine *NME* and boasting about the exploits of SMN. In one clip the pair pose with a pitbull on a chain while rapping about being 'down for the killing' and making gun signs to the camera.

Rugrat and Drastik go on to discuss attacking people with bottles, carrying guns, shootings and hitting women. At one point Rugrat compares his weapons with those of insurgents: 'You don't wanna see me on the backstreet, when I've got the black heat, cos I'm strapped like Iraqi. When I've got the .22 trust I'll leave your brains on the backseat.' Meanwhile his brother brags about carrying an Uzi gun saying: 'I'm licking off shots like Arsenal.'

Once the Ellis brothers were arrested, the videos quickly sparked an online war between supporters of SMN and friends of Shakilus, both of whom traded comments. One friend of the victim known as Madreps123 said: 'fuck all u heath prickz if i catch any of u ur fucked try kill ma boy r.i.p shak. An dat yoot who sed we shuld get over it fuck him and his brothers dnt care if ur a big man fuck u.'

Another message by a user called vwoke read: 'U lot killed a little boy, ova a little girl. And wasted ur lives. U boys r guilty, and u know it, ur gonna get locked up, all da mandems u fink u have now, r gonna 4get u sooner or l8tr.'

But other SMN members were happy to boast about the murder. 'It Was Rugrat And Drastik My Cuzzinz Who Shankd Dat Shaki Ute' said djmvp99. In another southlondonslumz wrote: 'big up drastik shanked up dat shakilus yute nicely. Soon come home.' Joseph's online accounts were also flooded with comments. One warned: 'remember you set shak up you bitch. And he loved yooooh. YOU IZ FUCKED!'

Some time over the summer I lose touch with Radar. The mobile phone number I have for him rings without being answered for a couple of weeks before becoming completely unobtainable. He also no longer responds to emails sent to the special address we set up to enable us to contact one another. It will be several months before I find out that he, like so many of his DSN colleagues, has been arrested and sent to prison, in his case after being convicted of a brutal assault. In all up to twenty-five members of DSN are behind bars while most of SMN have been arrested or deported. Croydon police proudly proclaim that its gang unit has been a huge success and that the problems of the past are finally at an end.

For a short time it does indeed seem that Dexter's declaration of war on other gangs was the beginning of the end for DSN, the first nail in the coffin so to speak, but it soon becomes apparent that reports of the death of the organisation turn out to be wildly exaggerated. In the days of the Kray twins back in the sixties, gangs were nothing without their leaders. If you took out the top man, the rest of the organisation collapsed like a house of cards. But today's gangs have what can best be described as a rolling hierarchy which makes them far more resilient: if the man at the top gets taken out, there's an endless supply of replacements waiting in the wings. Not all will be criminal masterminds and some will be only barely competent, but when it comes to foot soldiers, such considerations are unimportant. Far from being dead and buried, the reality was that a whole new generation of young gangsters, many operating under the DSN banner, were about to take things to a whole new level.

A few weeks later a local reporter who I had got to know tipped me off about a new wave of Internet activity involving youths claiming to be part of DSN. I followed the links that had been sent and found several pictures from someone calling themselves 'croydontown' of gang members posing with guns and other weapons. Close ups of the ammunition and magazines of the various firearms had left experts to conclude that the weapons were genuine. The profile included the comment: 'If you get shanked, don't say nothing' and was seen as an act of blatant defiance by the gang in the face of police claims that they had been destroyed.

The move was also aimed at sending a message to a newly emerging gang threatening to move in on DSN's patch. The GMG (Get Money Gangsters) had sprung up in the Thornton Heath area around six months earlier and were getting a reputation for being heavily involved in violence and street robbery.

Aged between twelve and sixteen, the gang was believed to have up to twenty-five members and to have grown out of a music group that had been meeting up on a regular basis. During a series of pre-emptive raids on GMG members in October, police recovered several items of stolen property including a number of credit cards and offensive weapons. But still the violence continued.

With no way to get in touch with Radar and no other close contacts within the gang, I find myself without an insider's view of the goings on at DSN at a time when the level of violence in Croydon seems to be escalating dramatically.

A few days after the murder of Shakilus, two police officers are hospitalised after being attacked by a thirty-strong mob of boys and girls – said to be members of DSN – who react with fury when the officers attempt to make a girl pick up a piece of litter.

The officers suffer multiple bruises and are bitten several times during the assault that takes place in broad daylight in the middle of Croydon High Street. The incident prompts headlines in the national press: 'Town where even the police get beaten up' and leads to calls for a new clampdown on gang activity in the area.

Later that same month Barnet FC footballer, Oliver Kingonzila, nineteen, is stabbed to death in a fight outside Croydon's E Bar. Although not a fully fledged member of DSN, Kingonzila whose street name was 'Dropz', was well known to dozens of members and considered to be an honoured associate. In the wake of his death scores of gang members sign up to online tributes to pay their respects to the latest fallen soldier.

In November a senior police officer tells the *Croydon Advertiser* that for the first time in months, there has been no gang-related violence in the town centre. But it soon emerges that a brand-new threat is just around the corner. The guns that DSN had so carefully acquired are about to be put to the test as the remaining members quickly find themselves involved in a major beef with a new rival gang known as LMD – Lick Man Down.

A week after the police claim, an eighteen-year-old DSN member is attacked at a tram stop by two members of LMD, suffering appalling injuries when his head is repeatedly stamped on during the brawl. A few days later in what appears to be an act of revenge, a member of LMD is shot in the arm in Thornton Heath.

At around 9 p.m. the following evening at the top of Derby Road, twenty-year-old student Ricardo Cox is walking home from the local KFC with his older brother Oniel when a Honda Civic pulls up alongside them.

'They stopped and asked us: "Do you know anyone in the Bird Gang?"' Oniel recalled later. 'We said "no we don't."'

The car drove off but turned around at the top of the road and passed the brothers once more. As it did so, shots rang out. The brothers began to run but Ricardo managed only a few yards before he collapsed, having been hit twice in the chest. 'He told me to call an ambulance,' said Oniel. 'We were just yards from home.' Ricardo never made it. He died within the space of an hour.

Initially thought to be another gang revenge attack, it quickly emerged that Ricardo Cox was a hard-working student and had no known connections to any particular faction and had never been in trouble with the police. It seemed to be a case of mistaken identity. 'It is my belief that the victim was totally innocent,' said the officer in charge of the investigation. 'He was in the wrong place at the wrong time.'

The car the gunmen had been driving was found a week later on Mitcham Common. It had been set alight in a bid to destroy all the forensic evidence relating to the murder. The car, which had been stolen from Tulse Hill a couple of weeks earlier, had also been fitted with false number plates. Although such measures are not exactly rocket science, they showed a degree of pre-planning and thoughtfulness that had until then been mostly absent from street gangs. While the membership seemed to be getting younger, the gangs at the bottom of the criminal career ladder appeared to be getting far more sophisticated.

I made my way back down to Croydon in the days following the shooting of Ricardo Cox, eager to gather some inside information about what was happening. I soon found myself surrounded by a wall of silence. Part of the problem was the ambiguous nature of what had been said before the shooting: it simply wasn't clear whether the gunmen were members of DSN and looking for rivals or members of a rival gang looking for members of DSN.

The remaining members of DSN were clearly keeping an extremely low profile but once more it was not clear whether they were doing this because they were concerned that they might be the next target or because they believed they had overstepped the mark and wanted to disassociate themselves from a completely unforgiveable act of violence.

But the violence doesn't stop there. After a brief respite for Christmas and New Year shots continue to be exchanged between DSN and their rivals, though seemingly without anyone being hit.

In April 2009 alone Croydon Police deal with twenty firearms incidents with the weapons being discharged on at least six occasions. In one a fifteen-year-old from Thornton Heath was left seriously injured after being shot in the head by a man who escaped on a bicycle, a few days later a twenty-year-old received a serious gunshot wound to the arm while on 15 April a twenty-one-year-old was left blinded after being blasted in the face outside his home.

In May 2009, DSN's general, Dexter, the man who in many ways started all the trouble, finds himself back in the headlines. From inside his cell at Rochester Prison, using a smuggled camera phone, Dexter uploads several pictures of himself onto his Facebook page. Close to the end of his sentence, Dexter also adds the message: 'Dexter will be touching road real soon.'

The pictures showed him posing topless – his muscles bulging as a result of extended time in the prison gym – and also showed a few of the creature comforts he was allowed in his cell including his own television, stereo and kettle. The images caused a storm of protest and prison authorities promised a thorough investigation. In the meantime the remaining members of DSN were getting ready to celebrate: 'We are getting our general back,' one told the *Croydon Advertiser*.

A few days later Wesley Blake becomes the latest victim of the violence in Croydon, shot twice in the chest while sitting in a car. The twenty-seven-year-old father of three was believed to have been involved in a feud between DSN and Gipset. He managed to escape from the vehicle and tried to get help by knocking on doors down the street before collapsing. He was pronounced dead on arrival at hospital.

Soon afterwards yet another senior DSN figure, Ashley 'Caste' Sheridan, appears back on the streets having been released from prison after serving a term for burglary. Stopped by local police while walking through Croydon town centre, part of a policy of putting 'pressure' on known gang associates, Caste was found to be wearing a bulletproof vest. He told the officers that he had received word while in prison that he would be shot as soon as he returned to Croydon.

Within a week he had been sent back to prison for breaching his release conditions but was back in Croydon in plenty of time for the start of the summer. At around 11.30 p.m. on 15 July, Caste stopped off at Kebabs Delight Burger in Woodside for a bite to eat. He had only been inside for a few seconds when a masked gunman burst in and fired a shot at him, narrowly missing his head. A second shot hit Caste square in the chest, just above the heart.

The attacker then fired at a CCTV camera, attempting to destroy the telltale evidence it contained, then ran out of the shop and jumped into a dark green Mazda MX5 which sped off towards South Norwood, hitting a road sign and a transit van on the way. The car, which had been stolen from Penge a few hours before, was found abandoned in South Norwood the following day. Shotgun cartridges were found on the front seat. Caste, who is believed to have been wearing his bulletproof vest at the time, survived the attack but has been a keeping a low profile ever since. The gunman was said to have been tipped off about his whereabouts by a group of girls connected to a rival gang who had spotted Caste earlier in the evening.

Later that month the authorities claim another scalp when Dexter's right-hand man, Billy 'Thai Kid' Langridge, is convicted of robbery and sent to prison for nine years. Croydon Crown Court hears that he was part of a trio who held up two young brothers at knifepoint during a raid on their home. They rushed inside the house and held a knife to the throat of one brother and then put a knife to the other's chest and demanded money and jewellery. The trio then chanted 'DSN, DSN', before running off.

It's around this time, with DSN dominating the headlines once more, that I unexpectedly hear from Radar. He has served his time, earned his freedom and is eager to see me again. We arrange to meet up in a north London fast-food restaurant. I arrive late and when I walk inside I'm shocked to discover that I hardly recognise him. Just under a year in a young offenders' institution has changed this once slight teenager beyond all recognition. Physically he has grown much larger and has a weathered, weary expression on his face that was completely absent during our previous meetings. It takes only a few minutes of conversation for me to see that the changes are not just cosmetic – Radar is a different person inside too.

The reason we are meeting so far from what he would normally consider to be his home turf is that Radar is taking a break from DSN. He finds himself caught between two opposing worlds and is unsure which one he wants to make his home. His time behind bars was a far from pleasant experience, but not so bad as to make him want to completely give up a life of crime. The decision he now has to make is whether to put the gang behind him and try to move on with his life or whether to become even more involved in the hope of moving on up the career ladder.

He has reached this point because, having spent extended time with those in positions slightly higher than his own, he has a newfound understanding of the way everything fits together. In between huge mouthfuls of chicken and chips – pretty much the only food he has eaten since getting out of prison – he tells me how the latest round of tit-for-tat shootings taking place all across London are directly related to the jailing of two key figures in the drugs underworld.

According to Radar the two men occupied senior positions in the distribution chain that provides crack to many of the capital's most notorious estates and the shootings are the result of the battle to fill the void they have left behind. 'For the first few months, there were enough drugs in circulation to satisfy demand. Also one of the men, because he was on remand, was able to have visits every day, so he was able to keep his business going. That all changed a few weeks ago, when he went into prison proper. Now everyone is fighting to try to take over his business. What will eventually happen is that a couple of the rival gangs will get together, make an alliance and move into place. Once that happens, things should calm down again.'

In the meantime, anyone who willingly gets involved in the ongoing battles has to be prepared either to lose his own life or take that of another. The fights and shootings are not just about territory, they are also about respect and reputation. 'No one will admit it to you, but the truth is that there are a lot of scared people out there. They are scared for their lives so they get a gun. When they have a gun they feel safe, which is stupid cos a gun ain't got no other purpose than to kill someone.

'Guns are respect. On the street, respect and reputation is everything. If you have a gun, you make sure everyone knows about it. People say: "Don't fuck about with that one, because you'll end up dead." But that means people overreact. You get a situation where someone doesn't even have a reason to shoot, but he does it anyway because he wants the rep that comes with pulling the trigger and doesn't want to risk the other guy getting his shot in first.

'But now the people with the guns are getting younger because the olders are getting smarter. They realise they don't have to go out and do their dirty work any more because there are so many youngers willing to do it for them. You get some kid to do the shooting, the older gets what he wants and the younger gets a gold chain or something.

'You imagine, if you're fourteen and you're at school with a big gold chain around your neck, you're the man. There ain't gonna be nobody with nothing better. That's why they do it. These kids grow up seeing this all around them and they want to be part of it as quickly as possible.

'None of them takes time to think. There are two kinds of road people out there. The first are the ones who plan ahead and think about what they are doing. They will only kill someone if they think it is going to further their career and be good for their business. The other kind are the people who don't think about the consequences, the hotheads who shoot first and ask questions later. They're the ones who shoot you if you step on their trainers or just look at them funny. They want respect and they think the quickest way to get it is to go out and shoot someone with a bigger rep than they have.

'Now I've done time, I'll be the one they all look up to. If I go back down Croydon I'll get kids wanting to be my younger. They want my protection, my rep. But all they want to do is go out and fight. You can't make a living like that. This postcode stuff – it's all such foolishness. You live on one side of the road, I live on the other so I'm going to kill you? Nah man. I saw a boy the other day wearing a T-shirt with "NW9 till I die" printed on it. I thought to myself no mate, when you die, NW9's still gonna be there. All these guys repping the ends, they all live in council flats. They don't own any part of the place yet they're ready to go out and kill over it. And when they get rehoused, what ends are they gonna be repping then? You heard about Dexter? They're talking about deporting him back to Sierra Leone. Go rep that, motherfucker.'

Radar bursts out laughing at his own joke. 'Dunno. Maybe I'll go back down there, take over, make DSN into my own gang, a real gang. My mum's like, why do you have to go back there, why can't you just move on? But even if I stay up here, it ain't gonna make no difference.

'People always say, just walk away from it – but you can't do that. It's not that easy. The drugs, the guns, they're everywhere. Ninety per cent of the people I know are involved in this thing. I've been to prison, I've got friends who are still there. I've got friends who are dead, but that's just the way things are. I can't walk away from my entire life. It's the only thing I have. If I walk away now, it's all been a waste. Nah. The only thing I can do is keep going down the same path and hope it leads somewhere. Not to the graveyard, not right back to the same fucking estate you started from, but somewhere else. Somewhere better.'

PART TWO
MIDDLEMEN

6

THE FUGITIVE

Not every junior member of a gang is destined to remain on the bottom rung of the career ladder. Organised crime is a true meritocracy and opportunities for promotion, whether as a result of death, imprisonment or expansion of business activities, present themselves on a regular basis. The key is being sharp enough to spot the openings as they appear and ruthless enough to eliminate anyone or anything that gets in the way.

William and Gary Carruthers were not twins – Billy was the elder by two years – nor were they from the East End of London. They did, however, hate authority, share a predilection for extreme violence and yearn for money and power, so it seemed perfectly natural that they should model themselves on their idols: Ronnie and Reggie Kray.

The pair started out small, bullying fellow pupils at Brinkburn Comprehensive School in south Tyneside into handing over their lunch money and valuables. On those rare occasions when the brothers encountered someone who refused to be intimidated or looked as though they might put up too much of a fight, they simply brought them into the gang for a cut of the profits.

Most of these new recruits were classmates of Billy or Gary and around the same age. Allan Foster was a couple of years younger but the thick-necked bulldog of a boy was stocky and cocky enough to stand up for himself. Impressed as much by his tenacity as his solid right hook, the brothers eagerly welcomed Foster into the fold.

Within the space of a few months the Boys of South Shields (BOSS), as the gang was now known, had become a force to be reckoned with and had a reputation that stretched far beyond the school gates. During vicious pitched battles with rival gangs from other schools, most of which took place at local fairgrounds, BOSS always came out on top, enhancing their reputation further still.

By the time Billy and Gary left Brinkburn Comprehensive, they had upwards of twenty dedicated followers and were more than ready to become something more than just a simple street gang.

It was the early 1990s and the era of acid house was just beginning. Along with the music, the huge outdoor parties and, of course, the drugs, came new opportunities to make money. Having nearly two dozen burly lads at their disposal, all of them handy with their fists, the Carruthers decided to move BOSS into the security business.

The principle was a simple one: if you control who and what goes in and out of every rave, club and pub, you control who deals the drugs, which in turn means that you can ensure that you get a cut of every pill, tab, or snort that is sold.

Soon BOSS were either working every door or had reached an agreement with bouncers to allow their dealers, and only their dealers, free access to the premises. A few clubs tried to resist, but they were soon intimidated into towing the line after repeated acts of vandalism and endless fights breaking out threatened to drive away all their clientele.

'Basically everyone was shit scared of them,' one former Tyneside club owner told me on condition of anonymity. 'You really just lived in fear. They would come in and deal drugs openly and you just had to let them get on with it. That's how dangerous they were. No one was ever going to be stupid enough to say anything against them and they knew it. As far as we were concerned, they were untouchable.'

Over the course of the next few years the gang's earnings increased to the point that several members were taking home as much as £1,000 per week selling ecstasy, cannabis and amphetamines to eager clubbers. Foster, still the youngest member of the gang, took to the good life like a duck to water, splashing out on clothes, cars and jewellery. He would think nothing of gambling thousands of pounds at a time on horse racing or football matches, safe in the knowledge that if he lost, another pay day was just around the corner.

Occasionally rival firms would attempt to muscle in on the lucrative world of nightclub security in the area. BOSS saw them off with a shocking level of brutality that saw kidnappings, punishment beatings and threats of kneecapping.

Working on the principle that any sign of weakness could be exploited by enemies, no debt was considered too small to collect. When a female ecstasy user fell behind with her payments she was visited by members of the BOSS gang and beaten about the head with a knuckleduster. She was told that unless the debt was repaid immediately, she would be wearing 'concrete boots'.

One venue that remained stubbornly outside the influence of BOSS was the massively popular Oz nightclub. Housed in a massive and virtually windowless warehouse close to the town hall, Oz featured an indoor waterfall and dance floors on two levels. Clubbers flocked to the place in their droves and the BOSS gang were determined that only their dealers should profit from them.

In July 1994 a group from the gang tried to storm Oz. The management and security staff, led by head bouncer Kevin Nightingale, managed to repel the attack but knew only too well that they had not seen the last of them.

On 28 August the same year in an apparent show of strength, BOSS attacked a group of men at a stag party in Hartlepool. Police who attended the scene described it as 'a massacre'. The next day two members of a rival gang were shot, not fatally, outside the Simonside Arms in South Shields.

The following month, around twenty members of BOSS, including Allan Foster and the Carruthers brothers, were arrested in connection with the attack on the stag party. When police raided their homes they uncovered a huge cache of weapons including sawn-off shotguns, machetes, hunting knives and axes. They also found £150,000 worth of cannabis and ecstasy.

It seemed like the beginning of the end for BOSS but astonishingly, due to a legal loophole, they were all released on bail and allowed to return to their homes. Picking up right where they left off the gang launched a campaign of terror against the security staff at Oz, still hoping to force the management to allow their dealers to operate there.

All the bouncers were targeted – usually singled out and beaten to a pulp by men wearing balaclavas – but the worst attacks were reserved for Kevin Nightingale. In the space of a few weeks the thirty-three-year-old father of two was shot at with a crossbow, had his home petrol-bombed and was peppered with shotgun pellets. Yet he still refused to allow the dealers into the club.

At around 2.20 a.m. on 17 February 1996, Nightingale had finished a shift at Oz and was walking up his cul-de-sac having been dropped off at the top of the road by friends. Inside the family home his wife of seventeen years – they had been childhood sweethearts and married at sixteen – was woken by a series of loud bangs followed by the sound of squealing car tyres. Rushing downstairs, she found her husband collapsed outside the front gate of their home, bleeding heavily from gunshot wounds to his head and chest. He died soon afterwards.

One member of the BOSS gang was among those originally charged with Nightingale's murder but the case was dropped due to lack of evidence. To this day it remains unsolved.

In the aftermath of the killing of Nightingale, the gang continued with its usual business, now more cocksure than ever that its reputation for violence would protect its members. Although the trial was fast approaching Foster, the Carruthers brothers and the others were convinced it would fall apart due to lack of witnesses.

In the meantime BOSS began to diversify. Anthony Marshall, a local businessman, was coerced into carrying out a series of mortgage frauds that netted the gang tens of thousands of pounds. Marshall himself received only a few hundred for his efforts. Having not initially realised exactly who he was dealing with, Marshall soon became terrified about the prospect of the gang approaching him again.

When he was arrested, it didn't take long for him to start to sing about his involvement with the BOSS. Signed up to the witness protection scheme, Marshall became the first of a series of those who had fallen foul of the gang to give evidence against them.

The next was a mother-to-be whose boyfriend had been forced to sell ecstasy after running up debts with the gang. She too was taken into the witness protection scheme, given a new identity and rehoused in a different part of the country. 'He had known some of the gang when he was younger,' she said later. 'We got into debt and I didn't know what was happening. They used to come to our flat to sort out drugs with my boyfriend. He was supposed to owe them £1,500. When some of them threatened him with baseball bats over the money I knew I had to tell the police. I am not afraid for my life. I did what I thought was right.'

The Crown soon had sufficient evidence to proceed against seventeen members of the gang. Two trials followed with the defendants in one changing their not guilty pleas to guilty on the second day in the light of an overwhelming prosecution case. Judge Helen Paling told the gang that they had held the seaside town to ransom for far too long. Passing sentence at Newcastle Crown Court, she told them: 'This was a lucrative and dirty business backed up with violence and threats of violence. Sometimes there was violence for its own sake in the clubs where drugs were sold and there was violence to dealers who were behind with payments. As one witness said, "You did not need to be threatened. Their presence was enough."'

Billy Carruthers was given fourteen years for conspiracy to cause grievous bodily harm and conspiracy to supply drugs. Foster, still only twenty, was sentenced to eleven years for the same offence. Gary Carruthers received eleven years for conspiracy to supply drugs. In total, members of the gang were sentenced to 153 years of imprisonment. It was, at the time, the largest sentence handed down on a single gang in British legal history.

Foster became a model prisoner, thereby ensuring he was released as quickly as possible. But it was all an act. Foster had been out of prison only a few months before he went back to his criminal ways.

Using contacts he had made while inside, Foster joined a gang of drug smugglers bringing shipments of cannabis from Amsterdam into the country along the Norfolk coastline. Foster's role as a 'fixer' was to arrange transportation of the drugs from a lock up in Bury St Edmunds to Tyneside.

The drugs were due to arrive in mid-November 2001. Foster arranged a number of vehicles to travel in convoy and chose a trusted friend from prison, one-time armed robber Steven Bevens, to drive the vehicle containing the drugs.

The pick-up went smoothly enough: 250 kilos of cannabis resin with a street value close to £1 million were taken from the lock-up, stuffed into seven holdalls and a rucksack and placed into the back of the Mercedes van Bevens was driving. But when Bevens stopped off at a petrol station on the A63 near Hull, officers from the National Crime Squad swooped.

Foster, at the back of the convoy, could do nothing but keep driving. Bevens was arrested right away and would later be sentenced to six years after pleading guilty to possession of cannabis with intent to supply. Naturally enough Bevens refused to name anyone else involved in the conspiracy. Instead he told the cops that he had been paid anonymously to deliver the van and its load to a location in Hull, thus eliminating any link to anyone from Tyneside.

However, Bevens soon learned that he and Foster had been under surveillance and had been seen together several times during the days leading up to the bust as they planned their operation and made their way to and from the pick-up. He warned his boss that it was only a matter of time before the authorities came calling.

But Foster already had an ace up his sleeve. A few months earlier he had begun to frequent the Marlbro gym in the centre of Seaham. At only five foot eight inches, Foster was a little below average height but more than made up for it by developing a powerful physique through working out regularly.

THE FUGITIVE

The gym was run by Bruce McCall, a successful amateur body builder, who had taken it over from his father a few years earlier. Born and bred in the tough mining town, McCall had worked in the gym since the age of eighteen before making use of his solid physique to get work as a bouncer at bars across Sunderland and in South Shields.

When McCall took over the gym quickly became popular with doormen, bouncers and 'hard nuts' from across the region. To inspire them to work harder, he ensured that the trophies he had won at bodybuilding contests were on display in every corner. For those who wanted their results to come more quickly, McCall was there to supply them with illegal steroids that he imported from China.

The fact that McCall was willing to openly break the law at his place of work made those members of the gym who earned their living in less than legitimate ways feel a little more easy about the fact that his closest friend and main training partner was a member of the Old Bill.

John Jones and Bruce McCall had known each other since their Seaham schooldays. While McCall started work at the gym, Jones trained to be a plumber, completing a City and Guilds course in the trade before joining the local water company as an inspector.

It wasn't until 1992 when, eager for a change, Jones joined Northumbria Police, working his way through various departments until he ended up in CID. By then the pair had been training together regularly and McCall knew they were close enough for Jones to turn a blind eye to the occasional indiscretion.

Jones had his own reasons to keep his profile as low as possible. In the late nineties he had joined the intelligence division of Northumbria Police's Crime Operations Department and become responsible for cultivating, recruiting and managing 'Covert Human Intelligence Sources' otherwise known as informants, most often known as grasses.

Jones first spotted Foster at the gym in early 2001 soon after his release, and it wasn't long before he became aware of the man's pedigree as a former member of the BOSS gang. But the gym was considered neutral ground and ever since Jones had broken the ice by showing Foster the proper way to use a piece of training equipment he had been struggling with the pair had reached the point of having the odd friendly chat.

Foster was facing up to nine years in jail for the cannabis importation and was keen to find a way to reduce it. He knew from experience that there was only one way to get his sentence cut – he would have to become a grass. He confided in McCall who suggested his 'copper friend' might be able to help him out.

Foster told Jones that he could lead police to a cache of guns in London. Jones explained that the information would not be of much use unless he was able to provide a name linked to the guns. Foster eventually admitted the guns belonged to James Freeman, a member of a notorious east London crime family. Freeman, it just so happened, was terminally ill at the time.

Because the intelligence went outside the Northumbria Police area, Jones passed it on to a contact in the National Crime Squad (now part of SOCA). Officers from the squad got in touch with Foster and signed him up as an official informant. The guns were found exactly where Foster said they would be – in the boot of a car parked in Plaistow, east London. Freeman, languishing in hospital and close to death, was not arrested or interviewed in connection with the find.

In March 2003 Foster was arrested for his part in the cannabis seizure. He remained on bail until April the following year when, despite acknowledging his role as the head of transportation in the smuggling gang, he received just three years.

Steven Bevens, the man who had been arrested with the drugs in his van, was just halfway through his own six-and-a-half-year sentence. Confused about why Foster had gotten off so lightly, he confronted him about it. According to Bevens, Foster explained that it was all an elaborate scam and that McCall and Jones were both in on it.

'He told me he had met a person at the gym called John, a police officer,' Bevens said later. 'He told me he came up with the idea of getting the weapons himself, stashing them in the car and then striking a deal with the police as if he was an informer, which he wasn't, because he put them there, he bought them himself. He told me the police officer John was the person who advised him on how to put together the deal, and that's how it originated.

'Foster said John advised him on how to talk to his handler so that he came across as a real informant. It was all part and parcel of him getting bail [before he pleaded guilty]. He alleged to find out information about these guns, but it was all just fabrication, he did it himself.

'After that, John said that as part of his job with the police, he would occasionally come across information that might be useful to us. Foster told me that if the police were ever planning to do a raid, John would tip us off.'

Bevens also claimed that Foster told him that the night before he had started his prison sentence, during a farewell party at the Tall Trees nightclub in Yarm, he had given Jones an Armani suit with £1,000 stuffed into each pocket. Prior to that he had given him a large-screen plasma television. Once he was out, Foster told Bevens, they would be putting Jones on the payroll.

Once again Foster had played the system and continued to do so once he started his sentence, getting transferred to Moorland Open prison in Doncaster within a matter of months on account of his good behaviour.

Foster was soon allowed out on day release in order to work and quickly came to a mutually satisfactory arrangement with his employer: he wouldn't bother to turn up and the employer wouldn't bother to report his absence to the prison authorities.

Despite the fact that he was technically still serving his sentence, Foster took full advantage of his newfound freedom, regularly travelling back to South Shields but also going as far afield as Manchester and Liverpool in order to continue brokering drugs deals. Foster even found time to socialise, spending time with his girlfriend and even going to a bodybuilding contest in Merseyside with McCall and Jones.

By now Foster had moved up a notch or two in the drugs world and was bringing significant amounts of cocaine and cannabis into the North-East. In one typical deal he paid fisherman Craig Cole, owner of the trawler *The Wayfarer*, to bring two holdalls of drugs into the country along with his haul of shellfish, knowing that Cole would easily be able to avoid the usual customs checks.

Steven Bevens, finally released from his own prison sentence, became Foster's main bagman, collecting cash from his network of dealers and occasionally transporting money or drugs on his behalf. Foster's team also included Derek Blackburn, whom he and Bevens had met at Moorland prison, and David 'Noddy' Rice, another veteran of the ecstasy scene who had a big enough customer base to shift all the cannabis and cocaine Foster could put his way. A fitness fanatic, Noddy was yet another regular at McCall's Seaham gym.

With sellers and distributors spread around the country, Foster emerged from prison to find himself at the head of a fast-growing and incredibly lucrative drugs empire, producing more money than he knew what to do with.

Bevens would pocket up to £5,000 a week working as Foster's henchman, and would collect up to £100,000 per week in cash from Foster's drug deals.

Foster moved his long-time girlfriend, Shareena McAuley, into a plush detached property and spared no expense on the furnishings. Eager to maintain a degree of freedom within the relationship, he also rented a riverfront apartment in Sunderland and a mews house in the upmarket Kensington area of London.

Although McAuley was less than happy with the arrangement, she knew better than to complain about it. She had fallen under Foster's spell at the tender age of thirteen and had stuck with him through thick and thin ever since. Nothing, it seemed, could break the hold he had over her. Whatever happened, she stayed as besotted as ever. She remained devoted to him through his stints in prison, fought back the tears when she found out about his numerous affairs with other women and was always willing to give him just one more chance after he'd subjected her to yet another beating but promised it would never happen again.

In return Foster took care of all the bills and expenses and gave McAuley a monthly allowance of around £1,600, most of which she spent on designer clothes. Despite being top to toe in Gucci and Prada and the fact that she had a choice of three brand-new cars to drive – an £80,000 Porsche Carrera, a £60,000 Range Rover and a £44,000 Mercedes – McAuley claimed jobseekers' allowance.

Extra money was available if ever Shareena wanted it. On one shopping trip to London the pair spent £15,000 on clothes in the space of a few hours. They were living what would later be described as a 'Posh and Becks lifestyle'. Foster always made it crystal clear to her that the money, and the luxury that went with it, was his, and if she left him, she would walk away with nothing.

But though Foster had come a long way since his days with the BOSS gang, he hadn't quite made it to kingpin status. Kingpins tend to keep their distance and rarely get caught with anything illegal in their possession. They do their best to avoid coming up on the radar of the local law enforcement authorities. If someone steps out of line, they have people working for them who will be despatched to deal with it. If Foster had been a true kingpin, he would have never have gotten his hands dirty.

With the money rolling in and DC Jones as an ally, Foster became ever bolder as Sam Hamadi, managing director of an exclusive jewellery store in the Gateshead MetroCentre, was about to discover to his cost.

Hamadi had first met Foster when he came into his shop to purchase a £7,000 diamond-encrusted Rolex watch. Hamadi believed he was dealing with a successful businessman who had an eye for the finer things in life and ensured he gave the customer his full attention. After that both Foster and his girlfriend Shareena, became regulars at the store.

Foster purchased a ring for £8,000, and in November 2005 he took away a £9,000 Cartier watch on approval, returning a few days later to pay for it in cash. A week after that he took away a £33,000 ring on approval, but returned it to the store.

Having built up a high degree of trust, Foster went back to the shop and told Hamadi that he was now acting on behalf of a Newcastle United footballer who was looking to buy a 10-carat diamond piece as a gift for his pregnant wife.

'I didn't inquire who the footballer was, as I trusted Allan and did not feel it necessary,' said Hamadi. 'If he didn't want to tell me it was up to him. He gave me the impression he moved in these circles, so probably kept deals confidential. I told him to give me a few days to get hold of something.'

The following week Hamadi called Foster and told him he had four pieces to show him. There was a diamond baguette worth just under £100,000, diamond earrings worth £20,000, a solitaire ring worth £40,000 and a smaller baguette worth £35,000.

'Foster showed interest in the £100,000 ring, and said he would go and show it to the person and come back the following Friday either with payment or to return it.'

Friday came and went and Foster didn't show up. Because of his long history with the customer, Hamadi was not initially concerned. He let a few more days pass before trying to call Foster, only to be told by McAuley that Foster was out of the country on business.

Again, Hamadi bided his time but as the days turned to weeks and the weeks turned to months there was still no sign of Foster or the ring. Once or twice he managed to get through to the man on the phone but as soon as he gave his name the line would go dead.

By the spring of 2006 Hamadi had finally had enough. Having no idea of who Foster really was and no knowledge of the man's fearsome reputation, Hamadi did the one thing Foster had failed to anticipate: he called the police.

Since their friendship had begun Jones had checked Foster's police file 168 times. Of all the informants who were in Jones's care, the most checks he had made on any individual was 139, on someone who had passed on information eighteen times. Jones had only once entered intelligence provided by Foster.

On one occasion, according to Bevens, Foster took £2,000 in cash into a room at the gym where Jones was waiting for him. 'When he came out, he didn't have the cash any more.' Bevens claimed that Foster told him that he was paying the officer that amount on a weekly basis.

The gangster certainly appeared to be living a charmed life. Whenever the police would get a rock-solid tip about a dealer within Foster's network, they would arrive to find no drugs and no sign of drug use on the premises. Whenever they were told a delivery would be arriving at a certain place and certain time, they would get there to find the supposed meeting spot deserted.

Whenever undercover officers tried to infiltrate supposedly well-established drug networks, they would be told that the participants had retired and were no longer interested in anything criminal. Unaware that Foster was being tipped off about their actions well in advance, the numerous police teams working the drug beat put their lack of progress down to nothing more than poor intelligence and bad luck.

In April 2006, as a thank you for all his assistance, Foster arranged to take Jones to London for an overnight trip. They started out in the Prada shop in Chelsea then made their way down to Foster's mews house. That evening the pair were picked up by chauffeur-cum-minder Niyazi Hassan who had been told to take the men out and ensure they had a good time.

They started out at the Bardos Wine Bar in nearby South Kensington where Foster and married man Jones took a fancy to a couple of girls at the far end of the bar. Eager to fulfil his obligations, Hassan went over to the women and made the introductions.

After a couple of drinks with their new companions, Hassan took all four of them to the exclusive Wellington Club in Knightsbridge, a favourite hangout of A- and B-list celebrities where seats near the dance floor are only given to those willing to spend a minimum of £500.

Hassan waited outside with the limo and a couple of hours later Foster and Jones returned having left the women inside. They then made their way to Stringfellows to see the lap dancers and stayed until the early hours of the morning when they were driven back to the mews house.

Foster then called up a local escort agency and asked them to send three girls over. The trio, Rose, Danielle and Sarah, arrived soon afterwards, just as the men had finished snorting some lines of cocaine.

Rose sat next to Jones who told her he was married and into property. When Foster took Sarah upstairs to the bedroom, Jones and Rose followed. Danielle asked Jones if she wanted her to join him and Rose for a threesome. Jones initially said yes but quickly changed his mind after learning it would cost extra.

As it was, even one girl turned out to be one too many. Naked in the bedroom with Rose, Jones was unable to get an erection. 'I've taken too much coke,' he told her.

All told, Foster spent more than £10,000 entertaining John the copper that night. It seemed like a good investment – Foster knew that a key reason he had managed to be so successful and stay off the radar was because of the information Jones provided to him. But then it all went horribly wrong.

On the morning of 30 April, just weeks after their jolly boys outing to London, Foster's home in Sunderland was raided by a team of officers looking for the ring that had been stolen from Hamadi's jewellery shop. Foster wasn't home at the time and got tipped off about the raid in plenty of time to avoid getting arrested, but he was still furious – he'd heard nothing about it from Jones at all.

But Jones could not have helped even if he had wanted to. Foster's name had not been entered into the police computer in connection with the proposed raid. Jones had been as much in the dark about it as Foster was.

With the villain still on licence from prison, even being arrested on suspicion of the theft would be enough to send him back to jail to complete his full sentence. With a major consignment of drugs arriving in the UK that weekend Foster had no choice but to go to ground.

He stuck around in Sunderland long enough to supervise the delivery of his latest batch of cocaine then fled to Spain using a false passport in the name of Sean Michael Wilkinson that he kept around for just such an emergency. Before heading off he left a message for Jones telling him that he was going on the run.

'Allan went off in such a hurry that he left a lot of loose ends behind,' one of his former associates, Lance, told me. 'Because he wasn't on the scene any more, he couldn't put pressure on people the way he had done before. People starting defaulting on debts, taking the piss like, because they all thought he couldn't come back.' One dealer in particular was causing Foster considerable grief: David 'Noddy' Rice.

Noddy had always been one of Foster's most reliable and trustworthy dealers. Unlike many of those that Foster dealt with, Noddy was allowed to take his drugs on credit, just so long as he ensured that Foster received his money on a mutually agreed date. Rice used to joke to friends that his 'bail' was running out whenever it got close to payday, but he always managed to come up with the goods.

Foster trusted Noddy so much that he even let him transport vast sums of money around the country on his behalf. The pair socialised regularly and Foster even bought presents for Noddy's children on their birthdays.

As part of the gang's 'inner circle', Noddy soon became good friends with Steven Bevens as well. The pair would often go drinking together and Bevens visited Noddy at home on numerous occasions, also getting to know many of his seven children.

Noddy had not always had it easy. In February 1996 he was jailed for five and a half years for possession of ecstasy with intent to supply. Early in 2002 he was left scarred for life after he was slashed across the face at the Eivissa nightspot in Winchester Street, South Shields. He and a female friend were attacked on the dance floor in front of terrified drinkers. He required plastic surgery on a wound stretching from his ear to his chin.

In August of the same year Rice escaped jail after admitting assaulting a police officer and possession of cocaine. Rice struggled so violently when he was arrested police officers were forced to use a CS spray to restrain him. He was sentenced to a 150-hour community service order.

It was only when he began working for Foster's organisation that his life seemed to get back on track and he started to make good money. Noddy idolised Foster and made it clear that he would do anything for him. 'I trust him like a brother,' he told his mother. Noddy also told how Foster had bragged on numerous occasions about having a police officer in his pocket.

As soon as Foster left the country, Noddy started to relax and his debts to the organisation rapidly built up to the point where he owed £36,000. Foster made a few calls but Noddy made excuse after excuse and didn't seem at all in a hurry to pay what he owed.

It wasn't just the money. Foster also had other worries about Noddy. He was convinced that he was responsible for his girlfriend finding out about his most recent indiscretion, something he was now getting constant grief about. If Noddy couldn't be trusted to keep his mouth shut about Foster's personal life, could he really be trusted to be discreet about his business dealings?

But Noddy was hugely popular, especially at the gym, and if too many people found out that he was getting away with taking Foster for a ride, others might try to do the same. Foster needed to send a message. One that would be heard loud and clear throughout the organisation.

On the evening of 23 May 2006, Steven Bevens travelled round to Noddy's home where the friends spent the evening drinking tea, watching football and chatting about nothing in particular. Before he left, Bevens arranged to meet Noddy the following day to discuss his debts. Noddy promised to bring as much cash as he could scrape together in the time.

Early the next morning Bevens drove to Doncaster and picked up Allan Foster who had flown back to Britain that morning, using the same fake passport, from Tenerife where he had been hiding out. From there the pair drove up to South Shields and, after a brief stop at a service station, headed towards a car park close to the popular beauty spot of Marsden Bay where they had arranged to meet Noddy.

The picturesque coastline at that spot attracts dozens of walkers and nature lovers, drawn by the stunning beaches and rock formations. Noddy came here to the main car park every day in order to chill out and read his newspaper. This time, on the seat beside him, was an envelope containing £6,000 in cash, which he planned to hand over as part payment of the debts he had built up.

At around 4 p.m., as Noddy was on the phone to his solicitor, a black Ford Mondeo pulled up alongside him, its passenger door opposite his driver's door. Noddy looked over and realised too late that the two occupants of the Mondeo were both wearing balaclavas. The passenger window rolled down and one of the men raised a semi-automatic handgun that had been fitted with a silencer and fired several times.

Noddy was hit but still managed to scramble across the seats to the passenger side of his car and open the door. Bleeding heavily, he tried to drag himself away from the vehicle to safety. In the meantime the gunman calmly got out of the Mondeo, walked around to where Noddy was crawling across the ground, and shot him repeatedly. With eight bullets now in him, Noddy stopped moving but just to be sure, the gunman leaned forward and fired a final shot into the man's forehead at point blank range.

The brutal execution was carried out in full view of dozens of witnesses.

Peter Oliveros had been at a car park at Marsden Bay in South Tyneside preparing for a stroll with his wife Lorna. He heard 'cracks' from the direction of two parked cars as he reached into his own boot. 'There was a panicky scream and I looked back at the car and that's when someone came out of the passenger door, staggered and collapsed on the ground. He was not moving at all.' Oliveros saw a second man with his arm outstretched walk towards the figure motionless on the ground.

'There were two or three loud shots. I still didn't believe what I was seeing. The man with the gun walked right up next to him so he was standing at his feet and pointed down towards the body. It was extremely deliberate. I didn't believe it was for real on a sunny afternoon by the seaside.'

The gunman then made his way back to the Mondeo where Bevens drove at high speed to nearby Lizard Lane. There the car was set on fire to destroy any forensic evidence and the two men transferred to a waiting orange van.

Foster had known about the money in the car that Noddy had brought with him but had not had any interest in it; Noddy had to be dealt with ruthlessly. And in doing so, Foster would also send a message to other dealers so that they would all think twice about crossing him.

Behind the wheel of the waiting orange van was Derek Blackburn, another member of the gang who Foster and Bevens had met in prison. Blackburn had met the pair at Doncaster services earlier that day and driven them to Lizard Lane. He was then told to wait in the van while the men drove off in the Mondeo.

Blackburn assumed that Foster and Bevan were heading off to do a drugs deal. It was only when they returned half an hour later, torched the getaway car and, still wearing masks, jumped into the back of the van through the rear doors that he realised they had been involved in something far more serious.

'What the hell have you done?' gasped Blackburn.

Foster smashed the flat of his hand against the side of the van again and again. 'Drive, drive, drive!' he screamed.

Blackburn put the van into gear and drove up the A1 before pulling up at a lay-by near Scotch Corner. He then listened with disbelief to the conversation taking place behind him.

'Did you see where the first bullet went?' asked Foster.

'It went through the arm didn't it? In his arm and collarbone and then through his chin,' came the reply.

Blackburn watched at the pair got changed out of their masks and dark clothes.

'Foster put his tracksuit in a plastic bag and when I looked there was a gun on the top. He said: "I'll not shoot you." Bevens was taking his own tracksuit off and Foster said, "Steve's got more to worry about because he set him up." Bevens wasn't looking very happy.' Blackburn asked why the person had been shot. 'Who dares, wins,' said Foster.

Foster and Bevens spent the next week hiding out at a flat in Essex. Foster was then taken to Luton airport where he boarded a flight back to Spain. He has not been seen since.

The investigation into the murder of David 'Noddy' Rice was led by Detective Superintendent Barbara Franklin, one of Northumbria Police's most experienced homicide operatives. From the time she received the call about the incident, Franklin initially worked thirty-six hours without a break followed by a series of gruelling twenty-hour days. Foster's name came up almost immediately, but as soon as the team began pursuing that line of inquiry, they ran into a wall of silence.

'Foster had a history of violence,' says Detective Superintendent Franklin. 'He was feared by many. Throughout the inquiry we had problems with people not wanting to speak to the police because of the fear Allan Foster would get them and kill them.'

But it didn't end there. When officers went to see the Rice family, they found that even they were unwilling to speak to any member of the inquiry team.

'Why won't you talk to us?' asked one flabbergasted detective.

'Because everything and anything we say to you will get back to Allan Foster,' came the reply.

'What makes you think that?'

The family members looked at one another then explained that they believed that Foster had managed to corrupt a local officer who was able to provide him with inside information.

Quite what was going through the mind of Detective Constable John Jones at this point in time is a matter of speculation, but he was clearly a very worried man. While officers attached to the murder squad were running around like headless chickens, chasing a thousand and one false leads, Jones kept his head down, seemingly hoping the whole thing would somehow blow over.

Despite knowing that Foster had fled to Spain earlier in the year, knowing that he had returned to personally carry out the murder, despite having spoken to him less than an hour before the shooting took place, Jones said nothing. When the murder squad came to the intelligence unit to see if anyone there could help them he gave nothing of value. He kept quiet about the address of Foster's London mews house and didn't even hand over any of the mobile phone numbers he had for him.

Despite the lack of assistance from within, Northumbria Police made significant progress with the case, identifying Bevens as having a connection to the murder within days. Foster's right-hand man was duly arrested when he returned to South Shields from the Essex hideaway to take over the day-to-day running of the drug empire.

But although the officers knew Bevens was involved, they had very little evidence against him and were on the verge of dropping their case when they stumbled across Derek Blackburn. Having effectively been tricked by Foster into taking the pair away from the scene of the murder, Blackburn realised the only way to avoid a conspiracy charge himself would be to grass the killers up.

Thanks to Blackburn, the mobile phones that Bevens and Foster used on the day of the murder were recovered from the waters off Roker Pier where they had been thrown in.

Bevens was charged and stood trial for murder in March 2007. Initially pleading not guilty, he changed his mind five days into the proceedings once it became clear that Blackburn would be giving evidence against him. Sentenced to life with a minimum term of twenty-six years, Bevens then decided the time had come to seek mitigation of his own and agreed to give evidence against DC Jones.

Arrested in June 2007, Jones initially refused to answer questions put to him. He made an official statement, part of which read: 'I have never received any sort of benefits as a result of my contact with criminals. I have never knowingly or intentionally given any information obtained as part of my police activities to an unauthorised person.'

Investigators were sceptical to say the least: given the number of times Jones accessed Foster's file, he could never have remained convinced that Foster had turned over a new leaf and become a reformed character, but Jones stuck to his story. The officer insisted Foster told him he was manager of an industrial-cleaning company, had a share in two guest houses, and had renounced his former life of crime.

In a second statement, made the next day, he said: 'I will be honest with you, I did like the lad. I got on really well with him. I deny absolutely receiving any money or material benefit as a result of any corrupt relationship with criminals.'

Jones told officers he had paid for his own drinks during the night out in London, which he said was a 'one off'. 'I certainly didn't know about any cocaine. I never saw any cocaine and I was never offered any. I totally deny taking or having any cocaine, I totally deny attempting to have sex. I totally deny it. I wasn't using escorts, it had nothing to do with me.

'I was foolish to go down, I realise it, but I didn't realise he was going to murder somebody. I thought he was finished with criminality. I thought he was a mate who was a reformed character, and wanted to get on with his life. I liked the lad. I have been a fool, stupid. I never received anything off him. I never warned him about anything. All I want to say is if I've done wrong it has not been done maliciously.

'I certainly never received any money off Allan Foster at the gym whatsoever. That is total and utter fabrication, that didn't happen. I was never on the payroll of anyone at that time apart from Northumbria Police.'

Jones resigned from the police force immediately and went back to plumbing before becoming a lecturer at Newcastle College. Tried in December 2008, Jones denied four counts of misconduct in public office but was convicted by the jury after seventeen hours of deliberation. He was, however, acquitted by the jury of accepting money in return for confidential police information – an allegation for which there was no evidence other than Bevens' testimony. He was jailed for five years.

The fact that Foster has managed to keep such a low profile has led some to speculate that he may in fact be dead. Detective Superintendent Barbara Franklin has certainly received intelligence to that effect but has 'not got a body to match that intelligence'.

There is also the fact that just as much intelligence exists to suggest that Foster continues to be alive and well and make the most of life on the run.

Although Foster has not been seen since, his reputation continues to influence events in the area. In August 2007, nineteen-year-old Ryan Burn, one of Noddy Rice's seven children, was arrested at Newcastle Airport after getting off a flight from Thailand.

Three knuckledusters and six extendable batons were found in his luggage and he was charged with being in possession of offensive weapons. Burn explained that he believed Allan Foster was intent on carrying out retribution on his family and that he was in constant fear of his life. Instead of a prison sentence he was given a community service order.

A little more than a year later Burn was dead, having collapsed after sampling a selection of drugs at a party.

A few months later Foster's girlfriend Shareena McAuley was jailed for eighteen months for money-laundering over £65,815 – the proceeds of Foster's drugs dealing – found stashed at her mother's house in South Shields.

With Foster nowhere to be seen, all her ready cash seized and no way to get hold of any more, Shareena had been declared bankrupt shortly after his disappearance. The relationship had ended and she had lost everything that had gone hand in hand with it. The judge who sentenced her sympathised with the fact that the life she had once lived had 'turned to ashes'.

* * *

Eighteen months after the murder of Noddy Rice I travelled up to Newcastle in an attempt to uncover more about Foster's background, in particular his time with the BOSS and his transition from street gang member to leading criminal middleman.

Lance, a former associate of Foster, had promised to introduce me to several colourful characters from the local underworld who worked with the man at key points in his criminal career. While some of them had once been loyal members of his extended firm, they had since turned against him as a direct result of his actions. 'Foster didn't get to the top on his own,' Lance told me. 'He used people, manipulated them, shat all over them and left a whole load of shite behind when he pissed off.'

Lance and I have never met but we have spoken on the phone several times and I have given him my physical description. He still works within the nightclub security business and arranges to meet me at the end of the night outside the club where he is working the late, late shift.

I arrive at the stylish waterside venue a few minutes before 3 a.m., just in time to see the first few hard-core clubbers emerging out of the exits and heading for the line of taxis that snakes its way along the main road. I can still hear and practically feel the steady thump, thump, thump of bass coming from within the club so when I call Lance to tell him that I am here I expect to have to shout to make myself heard. Instead, when he picks up the phone there is very little background noise. Subconsciously I find myself pondering the fact that the bouncers must have access to a sound-proof restroom or office.

'Lance, it's Tony.'

'Nice one, mate. Where are ya?'

'At the club.'

'Whereabouts?'

'By the entrance. Where are you?'

'Round the back. You need to go round the back.'

'How do I get there?'

'There's an alleyway on the left. Go down it. I'll meet you by the back entrance.'

GANG LAND

We finish the call just as the main doors swing open and two large men, one black, one white, both wearing dark suits, emerge. Directly behind them a group of giggling girls in high heels and sparkly micro-miniskirts emerge and make their way unsteadily down the steps.

I turn and gingerly make my way down the narrow gravel-lined alleyway which is still filled with puddles from the night before. At the end, to the right, is a small courtyard that leads to the back entrance of the club. There is a heavy iron door next to a fire escape leading to the upper level. The door is open just a crack and inside I can see several men milling about, dressed in the same doormen outfits as the pair at the front. I assume one of them is Lance and step back a little, waiting for him to emerge. When nothing happens, I call Lance again. I peer through the crack to see which one of the bouncers I am talking to but none of them seems to be on the phone. After a few rings Lance's voice comes on the line.

'Where are ya, Tone?'

'I'm near the back door.'

'You're there right now are ya?'

'Yes, I'm right there.'

'OK. Just give me another minute. Yeah, one more minute.'

As I put away my phone I hear the faint ringtone of another, coming from the room where the bouncers are milling about. Inside a tall man with dark-blond hair and a misshapen nose is speaking into a handset and nodding vigorously. Within seconds of that call finishing the atmosphere in the anteroom suddenly changes. The men I have been staring at are suddenly spurred into action. One of them picks up what looks like a baseball bat, another appears to slip on a large brass knuckleduster.

It suddenly dawns on me what is going on. I have been lured into a trap. With the benefit of hindsight I see that, from the first moment I got in touch with him, Lance was never particularly happy about the line of questions I was asking. Despite everything he has done, Foster still has many friends in the area – or at least

140

people who feel it is best to keep on his good side, just in case he comes back.

There's no way of knowing whether the men at the club simply want to scare me into dropping this part of the story or whether I'm about to get the shit kicked out of me but I decide not to hang around long enough to find out. I'm only a few feet away from the back door but because they are surrounded by bright lights and I am in virtual darkness, I'm invisible to them. Before the bouncers make their way to the door I quietly slip away and vanish into the shadows.

A few days later, safely back in London, I hear from a contact in Marbella, the coastal town on Spain's Costa del Sol, with details of a possible lead on the whereabouts of Allan Foster. As soon as I finish the call I turn to my computer and open up a budget airline website so I can book a flight and try to track them down.

7
COSTA DEL CRIME

You can't quite see the Mediterranean from the white benches that sit outside the gleaming glass frontage of Sinatra's Bar and Grill, one of the hippest hang-outs on the marina at Puerto Banus in the Costa del Sol. The view is completely blocked by the hundreds of luxury yachts that fan out in all directions. What you *can* see from here is a seemingly endless parade of top-end sports cars as their owners slowly cruise along the Calle de Ribera, past the dozens of sumptuous open-fronted restaurants, in search of the best parking and posing spaces.

Beyond the marina, to my left and right, sandy beaches stretch off into the distance; somewhere behind me looms a massive upmarket shopping complex that is a favourite of the local rich and famous. It's mid-spring and with the sun beaming down from a cloudless, pale blue sky it's easy to see why this place has been so appealing to fugitive British criminals for so many years.

I rushed out to Spain after hearing about the arrest of two men from Newcastle whose extraordinary reaction to a relatively simple misdemeanour had convinced officers from the Guardia Civil that they must be hardened criminals on the run who would go to any lengths to avoid being caught. The pair were approached after police spotted them urinating outside a video shop in Alhaurin el Grande, a hillside development some thirty miles west of Marbella. The officers asked the men to stop urinating and identify themselves. One told them his name was Paul and threw over a passport but when the men from the Guardia Civil opened it up it was immediately obvious that the document belonged to someone else.

As the officers stepped forward, 'Paul' pulled out a semi-automatic handgun that he had concealed in his trousers, pointed it at the head of the nearest policeman and pulled the trigger. The gun jammed. 'Paul' immediately re-cocked the weapon to free the blockage and swung it across until it was pointing at the head of the second policeman, then pulled the trigger again. Incredibly the gun jammed for a second time. As the officers drew their own weapons and began a three-way Mexican standoff, Paul's friend, who had pulled out a knife the moment the confrontation had begun, realised the odds were not in his favour and decided to make a run for it.

With the notoriously reticent PR department of the Spanish police refusing to release anything more than the most basic details about the incident, speculation was rife that either the unidentified trigger happy Geordie or his blade-wielding friend may in fact have been none other than the fugitive Allan Foster. By the time I arrived in Marbella the pair had still not been officially named and were yet to appear in court, so I decided to turn my attention to some of the other characters who have made this part of the world their home.

Spain first developed its reputation as an idyllic gangster bolt-hole in 1978 when a dispute over the ownership of Gibraltar resulted in the collapse of a hundred-year-old extradition treaty with the UK. The loophole was closed in 1985, but by then dozens of gangsters had set up shop there and had no desire to go home. They soon discovered that, even if the authorities caught up with them, there was no need to organise a hasty farewell party – a third of all extraditions collapsed at the first hurdle while a clever lawyer could easily ensure proceedings in the remainder dragged on for months if not years.

A new 'fast-track' extradition introduced in 2001, means that fugitives can find themselves back in the UK within weeks, yet the Costa del Sol along with the Costa Blanca to the north west, continue to be incredibly popular with those trying to evade the long arm of the law. They are also, according to a new generation of villains moving in on the area, the perfect place from which to run a drug-smuggling empire.

Thanks to its extensive coastline and its linguistic and cultural links to Columbia and the rest of South America, not to mention its proximity to Morocco – a key source of cannabis resin – Spain has long been a major gateway for drugs coming into Europe. British and Irish gangsters have always been involved, but in the last decade or so that involvement has become far more extensive.

'Time was, most of the crims who came to Spain were hiding from something,' says Jake, a mid-ranking drug dealer originally from Liverpool who has agreed to be my guide to the local expat underworld, something he has been a part of for more than a decade. 'Nowadays, the people who come here, people like me, they come to work. That's all there is to it.'

In 2006 police from Britain and Spain launched a joint campaign to round up fugitives amid concerns that both Costas were becoming a major hub for British organised crime. A list of wanted fugitives is now published each year and circulated throughout the expat community (Allan Foster's name was added in 2008). The initiative, known as Operación Captura, was set up after SOCA identified the areas around Malaga and Alicante as a key base for those directing international drug-trafficking networks with tentacles leading to the UK.

It takes only a few hours in Jake's company for me to appreciate just how real those links are. We have our first drink at Sinatra's, then move along the marina to a table at a second bar. It is while we are there, sipping at our beers, that the first of several familiar faces passes by. A couple of them are notorious villains from the golden age of British crime who have long since served their time and are here for the climate, but some are younger, more ruthless characters from the London and Essex underworld whose mugshots I can recall seeing in connection with numerous cases over the years.

I start to feel incredibly exposed and uncomfortable and so does Jake – although he is usually based much further along the coast he is concerned that if some of his 'colleagues' see the two of us together they might get the wrong end of the stick and assume he is giving information about them specifically, rather than the scene generally. As we're both getting a little hungry we decide to move to a nearby fish restaurant and take a well-shaded table towards the back where we are hidden from prying eyes. Even before our next drinks have arrived Jake is already feeling far more at ease and begins to open up about his life.

'There are lots of different groups out here. None of them work in the same way and hardly any of them get on. Some came to try something new, others got sent here by the people they're working for. That's the situation I'm in. For this thing to work, you need someone on the ground. Being here means you are where the action is. The closer you get to the source, the bigger your profits and the lower your risk, right. And of course the weather's great most of the time.

'Some lads come here and try to get hold of a kilo or two to take back but that's all small time. You can't operate at my level unless you're somebody. It's not hands-on. I'm not actually going out and collecting the stuff. My job is all about arranging for goods to go into one place and then go out of another. I never actually get my hands dirty. But that means that unless people trust you, they won't let you get involved. My reputation and that of the people I work for is the reason I can do what I do.

'It's mostly coke. That's where you make the best money. We deal with big loads and that's a lot of bread. Some people go for puff but we don't like it. Takes up too much space, stinks like shit. Anyway the demand isn't there like it used to be. But everybody likes coke. They can't get enough of it over there. Honestly, the amount of stuff we send through, I don't know where it all goes. Fucking everybody must be at it over there twenty-four seven.

'Most of the stuff we get comes direct from Columbia via Italy. You've got the main men over there, the main men back home and me right here, in the middle. And that's just how I like it. Most of the time there isn't much to do. I always say it's a bit like being a jumbo jet pilot. You're busy as fuck for take off, busy as fuck for landing but in between you can just sit back on your arse and let the fucker fly itself. Ninety per cent of the time that works fine. You only need to step in when something goes wrong. But of course, if something goes wrong, then you can be well and truly fucked.'

For obvious reasons Jake won't talk about the current methods his organisation uses to get drugs in and out of Spain and then from there to the UK, but he's happy to tell me about what they did when they got started a few years ago.

'My boss was over in the south on holiday and he got to know this Colombian guy who was running a Spanish restaurant in Marbella. One thing led to another and before you knew it, my boss had paid for two of this man's relatives to fly to Spain to meet with him. Getting the tickets for them was an act of good faith, a way to show he was serious. It was a man and a woman that came over, a young couple, only in their mid-twenties I think, but they were working directly for the head of one of the big cartels, a guy called Juan who was based in Medellin.

'He had a pilot who worked for Avianca and was happy to do the odd run as he could always get stuff through. Security wasn't quite so tight back then. The thing is, when you're dealing with new people, nobody trusts anyone. With cocaine, no one ever wants to pay for anything up front. Everybody wants to wait until they've been paid before they hand over any money to the people above them. But when it comes to bringing the stuff into the country, somebody's got to fork out. My boss didn't want to get ripped off and Juan was worried that there were leaks in our organisation.

'I got asked to come over with the money and hang around to keep an eye on things. Back then no one checked money coming out and if they did, you just said you were buying property. That's all changed now. The first load we did, the drugs were supposed to be in a couple of suitcases with false bottoms, ten kilos in each one. But when we got hold of them, they were empty. Just clothes. No drugs. *Nada de nada.*

'Turned out it was a dummy run. Juan didn't tell us because he wanted us to believe it was the real deal so he could check us out.

He said his pilot was just too valuable to lose. I was pissed off and my boss was really pissed off but we could see his point. After that, we started to get stuff through on a regular basis. We've got a few different routes, a few different concealments, we're making good money. It's a great little thing we've got going.'

According to Jake many of the larger shipments of cocaine that are brokered in Spain enter the UK via Ireland. With more than 3,000 miles of rugged coastline, thousands of tiny inlets and rapidly changing, utterly unpredictable patterns of extreme weather, the waters around the Emerald Isle provide perfect cover for the drugs gangs. This 'back-door' route to the UK is not without risks but for every shipment that is lost or compromised due to stormy seas or bad luck, dozens more get through.

The vulnerability of Ireland's coastline was first highlighted more than a decade ago by the US Drug Enforcement Administration. The DEA found that vast swathes are 'nearly impossible to patrol'. It concluded: 'Ireland's isolated coasts are ideal for shielding offload operations. The country's internal role as a transit point will accelerate as drug trafficking organisations continue to favour using the island for continental and British-bound cocaine and hashish shipments.'

With so many drug operations making use of the island, Irish gangsters have in recent years become some of the leading figures in Britain's drugs underworld and are now one of the biggest ethnic groupings in Spain. Many chose to relocate after the launch of the Criminal Assets Bureau which began seizing houses, cars and cash if criminals were unable to prove they were purchased with legitimate funds. In some cases this sudden influx of new blood has threatened to disrupt the carefully balanced equilibrium that Jake and his fellow smugglers have established.

'Some of the lads who come over, especially the young Irish lads, they've seen and heard about what goes on over there and they want to be part of it,' says Jake. 'They might have been the big cheese back home on some fucking rubbish estate and they get here and start acting the same way. That doesn't go down well, doesn't go down well at all. There are a lot of seriously big players here from places like Russia and Turkey. If you deal with them you can't fuck about. They won't hesitate to put a bullet in you.'

Two Irish dealers who learned this to their peril were Shane Coates and Stephen Sugg, leaders of a gang known as the Westies because they hailed from the western part of Dublin.

Friends ever since their teenage years, the pair started out stealing cars and committing robberies, activities which soon led to numerous convictions. In the late 1990s, they saw a vacuum in the hash and heroin trade and decided to move in. They quickly built a lucrative dealing network and formidable reputation based on the use of extreme violence.

Chilling ruthlessness was their trademark – unpaid debts of as little as ten pounds could result in a severe beating. When a drug-addicted mother of nine fell behind with her payments, they used lighted cigarettes to burn her breasts in front of her children in order to 'encourage her' to find the money to pay them. When another woman crossed them, they chopped off her hair and smashed up her home and car. One junkie nicknamed 'Smiley' owed the gang £200. Sugg smashed all his teeth, slashed him across the face and beat him with an iron bar in a public park. At least three other small-time dealers were tortured over bad debts. Dozens more were beaten and tortured with knives, vice grips and iron bars.

When a rival heroin dealer, Pascal Boland, tried to expand his operation into the Westies' territory one of his dealers was severely beaten and told to pass a mobile phone number to his boss. When Boland called the number he had been given he was surprised to find himself speaking directly to Coates and Sugg. The pair told him to stop selling on their patch or he would die. 'Fuck off,' he retorted, 'you're nobodies!' A few days later, as Boland parked his car on the driveway of his Dublin home, a hooded figure emerged from the shadows, produced a handgun and shot him at least eleven times at point blank range. Boland died where he fell. Although police attempted to bring several cases against the pair, the fear they generated among those around them meant that no one was willing to give evidence.

It was, however, inevitable that one day Coates and Sugg would come up against someone equally ruthless. Sugg fled to Spain after a narrow escape during an attempt on his life. A few weeks later his brother, Bernard, was shot dead as he drank in a Dublin pub. Sugg was joined by Coates who fled Ireland after being injured in a shoot out with members of the Garda. Taking advantage of their connections among expat criminals on the Costa Blanca, the pair quickly tried to muscle their way to power using the same tactics they had employed back in Dublin.

After a series of rows with criminals from London, Liverpool and Lancashire to name but a few, the pair suddenly vanished in January 2004. Six months later their bodies were found encased in concrete beneath a warehouse floor in an industrial area close to Alicante. Coates and Sugg are thought to have been lured to the warehouse with the promise of a big drug deal before being over-powered, tied up and shot in the head.

In early 2008 it was a similar story with Paddy Doyle, a leading figure in the local cocaine trade. He had survived a vicious turf war in his native Dublin that claimed the lives of at least ten gangsters but soon bit off more than he could chew when he relocated to Spain. After a night of heavy drinking Doyle got into a fight in a bar and left his victim badly beaten. What he did not know at the time was that the man he had fought with was the close friend of a Russian mafia leader living on the Costa. From that moment on, Doyle's fate was sealed.

A few days later he was travelling in the front passenger seat of a BMW X5 driven by a friend on the way to Estepona when he was ambushed by two men who opened fire from a passing green car, smashing the windscreen of the Beamer and leaving a trail of bullet holes down one side of the vehicle. The driver of the X5 lost control and spun off the road. Doyle, already injured, ran for cover but one of the gunmen pursued him and fired at least two shots into his head at point blank range. The driver, crouching in terror nearby while his friend was murdered in front of his eyes, was allowed to live. Doyle's execution was, according to local detectives, highly professional, bearing all the hallmarks of someone with extensive military training. It was mostly like the work of someone from the Spetsnaz, the Russian special forces, many former members of which now work for the crime bosses on the Costa del Sol.

Soon after Doyle was killed seven British men, including one from Tyneside and another from Liverpool, were arrested following the discovery of 140 kilos of cocaine hidden in secret compartments in furniture in a van in Estepona.

Coates, Sugg and Doyle were not the only ones. In January 2009, just a few months before I arrived on the Costa del Sol, yet another notorious underworld figure from Dublin had been murdered in a gangland-style attack. Thirty-year-old Richard Keogh had been drinking in a casino bar in Benalmadena with a well-known South American drug dealer and was on his way to his car with his wife when a car pulled up alongside him and a man began shooting at him. Keogh was hit twice and tried to escape but fell. His killer then stood over him and fired round after round into his head and body. At least twelve shots were fired in all.

Although he had only one minor traffic conviction, Keogh had previously been a major player in the Irish drugs trade and had fled to Spain following an attempt on his life in November 2007. Then, while putting out his household bin at his home in Duleek, a gunman who was lying in wait fired five shots at him. Keogh picked up his two-year-old son who was standing beside him and ran into the house, bleeding heavily from wounds to the shoulder and arm.

The would-be assassin tried to get into the house but Keogh's wife slammed the door in his face. The gunman then fired into the door, smashing the glass and sending bullets flying into the hallway. The whole incident was captured on an elaborate CCTV system that Keogh had installed in his home following earlier threats. The suspected gunman was later captured and placed on an identification parade, but Keogh refused to pick him out. It is believed he had attempted to resolve the dispute himself. Although it appears to have worked in the short term, it remains uncertain whether his death was connected to his dealings in Dublin or to those in Spain.

Plenty of Brits have also been caught up in the gangland violence of this new frontier. In October 2008 a nightclub security boss from Liverpool miraculously survived being shot five times after leaving a popular diner just yards from the Puerto Banus marina. The thirty-three-year-old was hit in the eye, the groin, pelvis, right leg and right arm after being blasted in broad daylight by a lone gunman in front of dozens of witnesses. The shooting came just months after the murder of Colin 'Smigger' Smith, former right-hand man of the notorious Curtis Warren. Smith, who was also based in Puerto Banus, was shot dead in Liverpool after being followed back to his native city by Colombian drug barons he had fallen out with.

Prior to that the dismembered body of a murder suspect and drug dealer wanted by Scotland Yard was found in two suitcases dumped on wasteland close to the resort town of Torremolinos. Scott Bradfield, who was on the run, was about to be extradited from Spain, leading to speculation that he was murdered by fellow gangsters fearful that he would give evidence against them. His body is thought to have been dumped by his killers as a warning to other dealers.

At least fifteen British and Irish gangsters have been killed in Spain in the past ten years. The figure could be higher, as several other dealers have disappeared, apparently without a trace. Because some of them had fled to Spain as fugitives, the authorities have no effective way of keeping track of them. There have also been scores of other victims of other nationalities including French, Colombian, Algerian and of course Spanish. In one three-month period alone, eight suspected traffickers were killed. Many have been gunned down as they were eating meals in restaurants in a throwback to the Chicago of the 1930s. While some of the deaths can be attributed to battles between rival factions, there are undoubtedly times when they are the result of the gangs simply fighting among themselves.

With so much bloodshed taking place on the Costas, it is no surprise that many British gangsters have chosen to move their operations further afield. In particular, many have now set up shop on the one particular island of the Balearics where they have discovered a whole new, incredibly lucrative drug market. It was only a matter of time before the violence that had plagued them on the mainland followed suit.

From the moment you enter the slip road out of the airport that joins you up with the E20 highway towards Ibiza Town, you are left in no doubt whatsoever just what this island is all about. Every single one of the massive billboards that line the route advertise one thing and one thing only: clubs.

Corporate logos, pictures of world-famous DJs and scenes of frenzied foam-covered dancers 'having it large' stretch out as far as the eye can see. Ibiza's tourist season used to run from March to November in common with the other Balearic islands but, since its reinvention as a partygoer's paradise it is crazy busy between June and the end of September and a virtual ghost town the rest of the year. In the main resort areas not only do many of the bars and restaurants shut down after the club closing parties, they go further and take away all their fixtures and fittings, making it seem as though they never even existed.

A large proportion of the estimated 1.8 million annual visitors to Ibiza hail from the UK and a considerable number of those Brits are aged between eighteen and thirty. It is said that there are more Brits in Ibiza during the summer than in any place on earth outside of London. While not everybody who travels here does so to end up dancing the night away at the likes of Pacha, Space and DC10, the numbers that do have made the clubs a vital part of the island's economy.

Everything here is geared towards making the clubbing experience as trouble-free as possible. The bigger venues refund taxi fares for groups of three or more; 'disco buses' shuttle between clubs twenty-three hours a day for bargain-basement fares and discounted packages that include club tickets, transportation and accommodation are widely available. But there is a flipside to all this: the unique combination of demographics and clubbing opportunities mean that as well as being party central, Ibiza has also become the biggest captive market for cocaine and ecstasy dealers on the planet.

The availability and range of drugs on offer in Ibiza is legendary. A huge proportion of young clubbers seek out dealers almost as soon as they arrive. Ralph from Birmingham first went to Ibiza in 1997 for two weeks of non-stop partying. 'We didn't take any drugs with us – we didn't have to. You could get anything you wanted out there and it was cheaper and superior in quality to anything you could get here. I've been back every year since and it's the same. Last year we hired a minibus to pick us up from the airport and before we'd even got our seatbelts on the driver asked if he could sort us out. It was amazing.'

Every summer hundreds of kilos of cocaine and hundreds of thousands of ecstasy tablets are dispatched to the twelve-mile strip of sand and rock in the Mediterranean. The profits are phenomenal. The dealing gangs buy in ecstasy in bulk for a few cents per pill and sell it on to clubbers for between €4 and €10 a time. Cocaine sells for up to €80 per gram. The prices are significantly higher than back in the UK but thanks to the added frisson of excitement that comes from being on holiday, buyers seem more than happy to pay a substantial premium.

During the peak clubbing months it takes only a brief stroll along the San Antonio seafront to see just how all-pervasive the drug business on the island is. As I browse the souvenir stalls on either side of the promenade a black man approaches selling silver bracelets and sunglasses. In his deep African accent he asks if I would like to buy any of his wares and I say no. Without missing a beat he immediately launches into his alternative sales pitch: 'Anything else? Cocaine? Skunk? Pills?' I walk away, only to find myself repeating the same exchange every few yards as more dealers approach me. Across the island all of the *pastilleros* – pill pushers – operate with a similar degree of utter impunity.

The prohibitively high cost of entry into the clubs and drinks at their bars means that many holidaymakers feel they have no choice but to seek alternative forms of stimulation to keep up with the standard schedule of heavy drinking at beach parties during the afternoon followed by heavy drinking at bars in the evening followed by non-stop clubbing from 2 a.m. until 7 a.m. At the height of the season up to 40,000 ecstasy tablets are consumed each and every night in Ibiza. Ketamine, GHB, cocaine, marijuana and acid are all widely available. In Britain clubbers may go out and take drugs once or twice a week but in Ibiza they attempt to do this night after night after night. Inevitably some users run into problems; the island's main Can Misses Hospital deals with more drug-related cases per head of population than anywhere else in the world.

Long before I travelled to Ibiza I had heard that the drug trade on the island was dominated by gangs from Liverpool. This was confirmed by my Spanish contact Jake. 'The first time I went to Ibiza I never had a chance to ask any one for drugs. Every single bar or club I walked past had some scouser outside who'd point and me and shout: 'Buy one shot, get one free. Coke, E, speed, hash, buy it you cuuunt!' I mean it was just so blatant it was unbelievable. I think it's calmed down a bit now, but the people at the top are still the same.'

Back in July 2006 heavily armed officers from the Spanish National Police swooped on yachts at the marina in San Antonio and recovered more than 800 kilos of cocaine. Among those arrested were two Britons from Merseyside and a known Irish drug dealer who had relocated his operation to Spain in a bid to escape the attention of the Garda National Drug Unit. As part of the same operation, officials from the Serious Organised Crime Agency raided four homes in Liverpool later the same day.

At street level, the dealers are switched regularly to keep one step ahead of the authorities. They are recruited all over Merseyside, often from outside magistrates' courts, and offered a plane ticket and two weeks in the sun, plus wages. Many who accept find the work so lucrative they become regulars. 'I don't bother trying to sell back home any more: too many Old Bill around,' says Darren, a dealer from Bootle. 'The money I earn here is more than enough to keep me going for the whole summer. Sell a few pills, shag a few birds and then drink myself silly. It's magic.

'The Spanish police class ecstasy as a soft drug, on the same level as dope, so long as you don't have too many on you, they'll just take them off you. End of story. But you don't even have to worry about being caught, especially in the high season, there are so many people around, the police are reluctant to do anything. They don't want a riot on their hands.'

For more than a decade the dominance of the Mersey gangs went unchallenged until other firms – in particular those from Newcastle and Manchester – cottoned on to just how lucrative the trade was and decided to try to grab a piece of the action. A series of minor clashes between rival gangs of dealers were the first sign of increased tension but in August 2006 the party island was the scene of an unprecedented attack carried out in the midst of a busy clubbing area.

In the early hours of a Monday morning in August 2006 a BMW X5 carrying suspected dealers from Liverpool was chased along a main high street in San Antonio by a Seat Leon full of dealers from Morocco, thought to be linked to a gang from Newcastle. Guns appeared out of the windows of both vehicles and up to thirty shots were exchanged between them as they drove through an area packed with clubbers. One of the men in the BMW was hit, a bullet lodging in his spine. Two innocent bystanders who had just arrived from Northern Ireland for a two-week holiday were also caught in the crossfire. One was hit in the jaw and had to have a metal plate inserted in place of part of his bone; the other was hit in the chest and had a lucky escape when the bullet passed right through him without hitting any vital organs.

In the aftermath of the shooting the authorities on Ibiza attempted to crack down on the drug trade, issuing fines and temporary closure orders against several clubs which police accused of tolerating drug dealing and consumption. One venue was found to have 'snorting booths' complete with glass ledges and door locks. Cocaine residue, cardboard tubes and bloody tissues were scattered in each. The club's owners claimed the partitions were actually telephone booths, but could not explain why no telephones had actually been installed.

The clubs eventually reopened, the tourists returned and the drug market quickly returned to normal. In January 2009 police in Ibiza captured one of the biggest hauls of ecstasy in the island's history. More than 24,000 pills were found in the boot of a UK-registered car that had been parked just outside Ibiza Town. The car had been spotted the previous year and was known to have been used by one of the main drug gangs operating in the area. Checks on the car led to an empty apartment in San Antonio which was raided and found to contain £210,000 in cash, all of it in small bills. The twenty-six-year-old Welsh owner of the car and the apartment was not on the island at the time of the raid. He had returned to the UK for the winter and was arrested only when he returned to Ibiza in June for the start of the new party season.

The island's drugs gangs often make extensive use of branding in the hope that satisfied clubbers will seek out the same pills throughout their stay on the island in order to achieve a consistent high. The pills seized at the villa were all marked with a dollar sign and star on the front, a brand that had proved hugely popular the previous summer.

Soon afterwards police swooped again, this time arresting a twenty-five-strong gang of Britons, most of them from Liverpool. Thousands more ecstasy tablets were seized along with two guns, extensive accounts books and £50,000 in cash. Police later revealed that the gang had been under surveillance for some time and were arrested as it was believed they were about to flee the island. The dealers had based their operation in a pub in the heart of San Antonio's club-heavy 'West End' district which is hugely popular with young revellers. In a bid to attract a different class of customer, the drugs were being distributed in bars and clubs by the staff, including waitresses and go-go dancers. It was said to be the most active drug dealing operation in all of Ibiza.

In addition to the street-level dealers the raid also captured several of the middlemen who had been supervising the activities of the gang. They had based themselves in plush white-walled villas in the San Antonio hills, which they rented for up to £1,000 per week. Anxious to protect themselves from rival gangs, the middlemen had introduced substantial security measures to protect themselves. Baseball bats and machetes were in place behind every reinforced doorway. A high-powered rifle was also recovered from one property. Among those arrested during this latest crackdown was one of the men who had been present in the car during the shootout in San Antonio in 2006. He had only been recently released having received a three-year sentence for drug trafficking on the island in the aftermath of the shooting.

When I travelled up to the hills of San Antonio in search of any remaining gang members it was clear that the crackdown had sent many of them running for cover. Several properties appeared to be hastily abandoned and one neighbour confirmed that they had previously been home to groups of young men from Liverpool who only ever appeared during the height of the clubbing season.

The main Liverpool-based syndicate may now be irreparably damaged but the laws of supply and demand dictate that another firm will move in to fill the vacuum. It is highly unlikely that there will be any significant shortage of party drugs on the island during all the summers to come.

Back on the mainland Jake and I continue our quest to find the perfect bar, partly in a bid to drown my sorrows as I learn that neither of the men from Newcastle, one of whom is now facing charges of attempted murder for attempting to shoot two police officers, is Allan Foster after all. It later emerges that the international appeal for information about his whereabouts resulted in just two calls being made to the Crimestoppers hotline, neither of which provided any useful information. At the time of writing, he remains at large.

I'll soon be flying back to London and as I sip cold beer and flick through copies of some of the local English language papers evidence of the underworld links between Britain and Spain is everywhere. In April 2009 two men were snatched outside a curry house in West Yorkshire and tortured for two hours before being dumped near Crosby Marina in Merseyside. In the course of the terrifying journey, one of the men had one of his ears sliced off in a *Reservoir Dogs*-style act of retribution. It later emerged that a drugs package sent out from Spain and destined for the UK had gone missing somewhere along the way and the kidnappers had been trying to find out where it was.

The following month three middle-aged Britons, one of whom lived on the Costa del Sol, were jailed having been caught with 1.5 tonnes of cocaine after their yacht got into difficulties in the stormy seas off the Irish coast. The cash-strapped trio, none of whom had prior convictions of any kind, had become reluctant middlemen in the deal after having been hired by a smuggling gang and each offered a six-figure sum to make the journey across the Atlantic.

The three men had travelled to Trinidad and Tobago, via Spain and Venezuela, where one purchased the yacht, *Dances With Waves*, using a false Irish passport that had been provided by the gang behind the venture. The vessel had been due to land in north Wales but had foundered in high seas after suffering engine trouble. With little sailing experience between them, the men were actually relieved to have been caught and gave themselves up without a struggle. One had lost more than two stone in weight due to seasickness during the journey from the Caribbean.

A year earlier three Britons had been jailed for a total of eighty-five years in Cork for their part in a similar, equally bungled operation. Drugs worth £345 million were recovered from the sea off south-west Ireland after an inflatable dinghy being used to bring the shipment ashore suffered engine failure and capsized.

Operating on behalf of drug lords based in Britain and Spain, the hapless middlemen had been given the task of bringing 1.5 tonnes of high-grade cocaine ashore. A catamaran, the *Lucky Day*, had crossed the Atlantic from Barbados before rendezvousing with the smaller offloading vessel and transferring the drugs over. Rocked by strong winds and a three-meter swell, the heavily laden inflatable dinghy overturned, hurling the two men on board into the sea with the drugs. One managed to make it to the beach and raise the alarm, the other was pulled from the sea by a lifeboat crew. The two remaining members of the gang were arrested on land two days later after being spotted on the cliffs overlooking the bay.

Although Jake is reluctant to go into too many details, he points out that in both smuggling attempts, the first stage of the operation would have involved smuggling vast sums of money out of the UK and taking it to Spain in order to make a down payment on the shipment. I hear that much of this money is laundered through a network of dodgy bureau de changes throughout the Costas, something confirmed in July 2009 when at least ten people including one Londoner were arrested in a series of swoops on money-changing agencies in Fuengirola through which around £155 million was thought to have passed.

As we head to my car, walking in the beautifully warm evening, Jake and I pass through a residential area that backs onto the Puerto Banus development and he points to an apartment block on the other side of the street.

'You ever hear of a crim called —?' At this point Jake mentions the name of an extremely well-known north London villain whom, for legal reasons, I can only refer to by the pseudonym of 'Bob Coombes'.

I nod. 'Yeah, he's a legend, the guy that went on the run after that big drugs bust.'

'Right. Well that's where he was hiding out when they finally nicked him.' Jake pauses mid-stride, cocks his head to one side and looks at me quizzically. 'Actually, I've got some bits and pieces on him that you might find interesting. I don't think he'll mind – none of it will come as any surprise to him or his mates or the police, but you might like it. It'll give you a bit of an insight into the sort of things that people at his level, the middle level, get up to on a day-to-day basis.'

The next day Jake meets me in a small café in a remote corner of the Estepona seafront and with a big grin on his face, hands me a thick, dog-eared notebook. It is, he explains, a sort of diary kept by one of Bob's friends and fellow gang members who spent the best part of five years recording the activities of Bob and several other prominent criminals from the London underworld.

Working as an enforcer for the drugs gang, the friend was considered wholly trustworthy and was privy to virtually every deal, plan and scheme that Bob and his friends ever got involved with. The notebook Jake has given me is an incredible insight into the day-to-day realities of life on the wrong side of the law. More than that, it provides an extraordinarily detailed peek into two years of the life of Bob himself.

8
FACES

Bob Coombes is, in the words of one senior Scotland Yard officer, a premier league villain. Not a kingpin by any means without a doubt but a high-ranking member of the underworld elite. During the two years before the ill-fated drug bust for which he was finally arrested, Bob was completely unaware that one of his closest friends was faithfully recording almost every aspect of his life of crime.

Although many outside the criminal underworld imagine villains are generally incredibly discreet about their activities, the reality is that in order to foster contacts, expand their operations and maximise their chances of making money, gangsters are forever talking about their plans and activities. This is particularly true of those in the 'middlemen' category who will often find themselves in the role of facilitator, connecting one group with drugs to sell to another looking for drugs to buy.

Because of this virtually every criminal act Bob ever got involved in was at some point or another discussed with his friends and soon afterwards written down in his friend's notebook. The diary therefore provides an unprecedented glimpse into the life and times of someone operating at this level of the underworld and shows that success is dependent on contacts, tenacity and most of all sheer good luck.

As I work my way through the pages of the notebook I feel as though I'm almost reading the personal diary of Bob Coombes. The stresses and strains, ups and downs of operating in the modern underworld are all laid bare as, on occasion, are Bob's personal problems.

JUNE

8th

Bob hears from two separate sources that Kyle, a friend of his who went missing some time ago, has been murdered in Spain due to non payment of a drugs-related debt. The man was apparently taken offshore and thrown overboard a month earlier. It is not known exactly who was responsible.

16th

Bob arranges for three cars to travel to France to collect a consignment of cannabis resin. Each car is being driven by a single male. They will travel in convoy but they have been told not to associate with one another during the ferry crossing to avoid creating suspicion.

18th

One of the three cars was stopped by Customs, the other two got through. The drivers saw the car being stopped but assumed it had been let go and continued their journey. Bob met the vehicles at a transport café near Rickmansworth to collect the drugs. No surveillance was spotted at the meeting place so Bob is happy to use it for future trips.

AUGUST

7th

Bob and two friends spend a couple of days at an upmarket caravan site near Hastings. Bob tells the others that he found a tracking device in his car along with some kind of radio transmitter. The car – a brand-new silver Range Rover with a white leather interior – had been stolen a couple of weeks earlier and Bob is convinced that the police planted the device at the time. As a result of the find Bob and his friends agree that they will have their vehicles 'debugged' on a regular basis.

10th

An associate of Bob arranges for a husband and wife team to travel to Holland with a large quantity of cash. The pair then pack two kilos of cocaine in the woman's bag. They successfully make it through Customs. The cocaine was supplied by the same people that Bob obtains his own drugs from.

Bob introduces a rule that no one is allowed to speak about 'business' in his flat. Having been burgled the previous month he is now convinced that his flat has also been bugged by the police.

18th

Bob travels to Canada to visit the head of the major drugs gang he often works for. The man is being held pending extradition to Spain. He tells Bob that he will be released in the near future and that he is working on putting together the biggest deal he has ever brokered. Bob is told the deal involves a Lebanese man called 'Mohammed', some Colombians and involves stops in both Italy and Turkey.

Bob returns to England and announces that he intends to buy a house in Islington so that he can live next door to one of his criminal associates.

SEPTEMBER

5th

One of Bob's friends was at a horse race the previous weekend and was approached by two men claiming to be police officers. They asked the friend to become an informant and claimed they already had one inside the gang. As proof, they gave the friend the telephone numbers belonging to Bob and other key gang members.

Bob has told his friend to meet with the officers again and fake interest in supplying information to them in a bid to try to find out more about who the informant in the gang is.

21st

Bob returns from a trip to Spain and sells his beloved car. He feels he has no choice because the address where it is registered was raided by police the previous weekend and several people were arrested for drug possession.

He still intends to buy the house next to his friend but is having trouble raising a mortgage, having been ripped off by a bent broker who ran off with his entire deposit. He wants the home for himself and his new wife, having recently married for the third time.

NOVEMBER

4th

Bob learns that a friend of his, currently on trial, has managed to bribe several members of the jury in order to ensure they return a 'not guilty' verdict.

13th

Bob is looking for somewhere to store around 600,000 ecstasy tablets. Some associates of his were arrested in south London in possession of 500,000 tablets, all part of a much larger consignment that Bob had helped to bring into the country. He is now desperate to move the remainder of the drugs to a safe location before the police can get their hands on it.

Bob hopes to be able to sell most of the ecstasy that day to a Greek dealer living in the Finsbury Park area of north London.

22nd

Bob receives 250 kilos of cannabis that was recently imported from Holland. He is giving out samples to various people in order to find buyers.

FACES

JANUARY

7th

Bob has been attempting to distance himself from two mid-ranking members of his smuggling organisation who he believes have become 'careless' and are therefore putting the rest of the group at risk. Bob is involved in a deal to import forty tonnes of cannabis from Pakistan. Rather than having it sent directly to himself, Bob arranged for paperwork linked to the importation to be sent to his elderly uncle.

13th

Bob is certain that he is being followed. He spotted two vehicles that seem to be keeping an eye on him so he deliberately drove down a one-way street. Both vehicles followed him. He abandoned his car and went home.

24th

Bob hears that his forty-tonne load of cannabis was seized by the Pakistani authorities at the docks at Karachi.

At the same time, Bob is getting increasingly worried about the men who were arrested back in November with the 500,000 ecstasy tablets. Bob can't work out how they were caught and is attempting to get hold of the police papers for the case to see if he can find any clues.

28th

Bob travels to Amsterdam to see the head of his drug organisation who has moved there since being released from prison in America. They discuss various deals and Bob also hands over a new British passport for his boss in a fake name.

Soon afterwards Bob obtains a copy of the case papers regarding the 500,000 ecstasy tablet seizure. He had supervised the driver who delivered the drugs to the buyers and had made sure he was not followed to the drop-off point. He therefore believes his own vehicle must have been fitted with another tracker device allowing the authorities to swoop.

FEBRUARY

9th

Bob is on the warpath. An argument over a woman at a pub called The Marquis of Granby ended up turning into something of a brawl. Bob has arranged for four men to go with him to a restaurant in Highgate to confront the man he fought with. The men will all be armed – four handguns and a machine pistol. Bob says he is prepared to use them if the man does not apologise.

Later that day Bob met the man and they made up to the extent that they have agreed to do business together.

Meanwhile Bob heard from Amsterdam that the boss was furious with him because the passport he took over turned out to be a forgery rather than the real thing in a false name. The boss is particularly angry because Bob charged him full price for the item. Bob has apologised and promised to supply another passport as soon as possible.

13th

Bob now has a range of firearms at his disposal including a .357 magnum, an Uzi sub-machine gun and a 9mm Browning automatic. He also has a bulletproof vest. Bob is trying to obtain an anti-tank gun, which he hopes to use to rob a security van in the near future.

In the meantime Bob has been travelling to Scotland to meet with a dealer who is looking for someone to supply cannabis. Bob has assured him that he will have several hundred kilos available in the next few weeks.

MARCH

8th

Bob is flying to New York with his family. Once there he will meet up with a man called 'Tony', a leading member of the American mafia. Tony was previously convicted for his part in an armed robbery which Bob was also involved in. Tony has promised to arrange for Bob to receive cocaine directly from South America.

12th
Kyle, the man thought to have been murdered in Spain, has turned up alive and well. He had spread rumours of his death in order to avoid paying a debt. He is now re-establishing himself in the drugs business.

29th
Bob is planning to kill a business rival of his in the next few weeks. In order to facilitate this he will be taking delivery of a stolen car which has been fitted with false number plates. The vehicle will be hidden away and only brought out on the day it is needed. Bob has not yet decided whether he will carry out the hit personally or arrange for another person to do it.

Bob is flying to Malaga to meet a Dutchman called 'Rickey' who is the supplier of the cannabis resin Bob is expecting to arrive in the next few weeks. Apparently there is a problem with the cannabis but it is still expected in the UK on schedule.

APRIL

7th
Bob has obtained a red Peugeot. He intends to use this car when he shoots the man who owes him money and has refused to pay. He has said that he has previously attacked the man in order to get him to pay but this hasn't worked so he intends to shoot him 'as an example'. His friend agrees to look after the car for him.

15th
Bob will not need the car until the end of the following weekend at the earliest. He says he will send his wife away before he carries out the shooting.

27th

Bob will require the Peugeot 'within a few days' for use in the shooting. The proposed victim is believed to be a man named Smith.

29th

Bob no longer wants the stolen Peugeot for use in the shooting and it is free to be abandoned so it can be recovered by the police. Bob explained that the intended victim was currently under investigation by the police for a separate matter and it would be better for him to wait until they attacked him.

MAY

1st

Associates of Bob from the American mafia are arriving in London and will be staying for around ten days. They have sent their wives and daughters ahead and have booked into the Hampshire Hotel in Leicester Square. The men are coming over for further discussions about the new cocaine supply route direct from South America.

5th

Bob tells his friend that he is keeping his dealings with the mafia men secret from his main business partner. Bob has also obtained multiple kilos of high purity amphetamine powder which he is selling for £4,000 per kilo.

11th

Tony, the mafia man, is arranging for $100,000 to be sent to Bob by bank transfer. The money is to pay for someone in the UK to look for a man who ripped Tony off. The man apparently ran off with a multimillion pound sum belonging to Tony and his associates after agreeing to 'front' a company on their behalf.

Bob has been approached by two well-known south London gangsters and offered the chance to take part in an armed robbery they are planning. Bob has declined the invitation but introduced the men to someone else who he believes would be suitable. The venue for the robbery is a large post office depot in Essex where the gang have an inside man. They hope to come away with at least £1 million in cash.

26th

Bob is to travel to Spain with his family at the weekend. Once there he will meet up with his usual business associates. He will be overseeing the final stages of the transportation of a two-tonne delivery of cannabis.

Bob is also planning to take part in an armed robbery in Switzerland in August. The target will be a diamond exhibition in Basel. The job has been set up by the mafia men. They know where the diamonds are to be stored overnight and will attack the storage premises. Bob will be staying with his family in a villa in Spain and will travel to Switzerland on the day of the robbery.

JUNE

7th

Bob returned from Spain to find his new car, a Mercedes, had been broken into. The radio facia had been removed but no attempt had been made to remove the actual body of the radio. On closer examination Bob found several screwdriver marks in the passenger footwell and suspects the police may have broken into his car to plant a tracking device or bug. He plans to have the car carefully examined and scanned.

11th

Bob goes to see a female friend of his who lives in a flat above a shop in the West End. She is in possession of a large amount of stolen jewellery which she is attempting to sell. The items were stolen as a result of a tie-up robbery a few weeks earlier. One item, a diamond-encrusted gold watch, is being offered for £10,000.

14th

The Dutch drugs boss has announced a reorganisation of activities. Some members of the gang are to move to Spain permanently to supervise things over there. Bob has been given a new role and will now be responsible for finding buyers for the drugs when they arrive in the UK. He is free to continue working on his own 'side' projects at the same time. The firm intends to bring in one tonne of cannabis every fortnight.

JULY

24th

Bob has heard from one of his criminal associates that he is being targeted by the police. The associate claims to have access to police information and is hoping Bob will pay handsomely to get hold of the files. The associate says that police know where Bob stayed for his honeymoon and also the hotel where the mafia men stayed when they arrived in the UK. Detectives have taken away the itemised telephone bills for both rooms.

28th

Bob takes possession of a brand-new Lexus with a personalised number plate. Having briefly split with his wife the couple have now reconciled. Bob wants to buy a new house for them.

AUGUST

16th

The American mafioso have arrived in Nice in preparation for the robbery at the diamond exhibition in Switzerland. Bob still intends to join them.

22nd

Bob has hired a lorry driver, Darren, to collect between three and four tonnes of cannabis from Holland during the next week. The drugs will be available for sale a few days afterwards. The handover will take place at a motorway service station. The drugs are being supplied by a Moroccan man named Hasan.

26th

Bob says there has been a slight delay with the cannabis due to be collected from Holland. According to Hasan, the drugs have arrived in the Netherlands from Spain and are currently being repackaged. Delivery to London is still expected in the coming week. The drugs will be collected using a scaffolding lorry which is flat backed with high sides but no roof.

27th

Bob has decided not to send Darren to collect the drugs. Apparently he has been asking for too much money to do the run. Instead he will send a man called Ron. Although he has no lorry of his own, Ron has ready access to a hire company which will loan him a vehicle whenever he wants.

OCTOBER

6th

Ron has suffered a slipped disc and will not be able to collect the drugs. Instead Darren is being sent after all. The delivery is imminent. Possibly over the coming weekend.

Bob has spoken to the head of the gang in Amsterdam who said he had been told conflicting stories about what has happened to the cannabis, including one rumour that the load has been sold to another customer. The boss is not concerned and is sure the drugs will be delivered as promised, though Bob is unhappy because he is starting to run low on cash.

18th

Still no drugs. Bob travels to Amsterdam to see the boss who reveals that Hasan had told him that he had not even taken possession of the cannabis from his own supplier. Hasan has been telling lies to everyone about the anticipated delivery date. The boss is still not concerned because he has done similar business with Hasan before and it has always been successful. Hasan has received a payment of £1.8 million in advance for the shipment.

NOVEMBER

2nd

Still no drugs. Bob is becoming increasingly impatient waiting for Hasan to send the cannabis over to the UK. He was even considering going to Spain to meet with Hasan and get a realistic delivery date. The boss from Amsterdam persuaded him not to do so and again assured him that the delivery would proceed.

22nd

Still no drugs. Bob is very concerned that Hasan may have reneged on the supply of the cannabis. No one can get hold of him. The boss is frantically trying to placate everyone.

29th

The reason for Hasan's silence has emerged. He has been arrested and is now being held in custody in Spain.

JANUARY

12th

All members of the gang, including the boss, now accept that they are unlikely to get any of the cannabis they ordered and part paid for from Hasan while he is in prison. One of the gang went to visit him to see what could be done but Hasan lacks the necessary 'clout' with the rest of the suppliers to enforce delivery.

Bob is particularly upset having put £300,000 into the deal. To add to his problems, he is experiencing new difficulties with his wife and has chosen to take a break from criminal activities in order to sort them out.

29th

Bob has become embroiled in a dispute between a rival gang and two notorious brothers. He is extremely unhappy as the argument has little to do with him but he is being forced to carry a gun around with him all the time in case the brothers come after him.

MARCH

23rd

Bob's mother has died. Bob says he has no cash at the moment and is asking friends to help him out when it comes to paying the funeral expenses.

31st

At his mother's funeral Bob reveals that he is putting together a heroin importation of at least 100 kilos, part financed by the boss in Amsterdam. Bob did not say how he would obtain the rest of the money.

APRIL

13th

Bob and a friend rob a post office van in Norwich, coming away with £1 million worth of postage stamps. The pair had used ex-post office vans during the robbery. They have already passed the stamps on to a fence and received a down payment. In total they will receive £450,000 for their haul.

19th

Tony, the American mafia man, was refused entry to the UK on the day of the funeral of Bob's mother. Instead he flew to Italy where Bob joined him. The pair finalised the plans for their cocaine importations. Bob is to set up a company to import second-hand motorcycle parts from Sacramento and, once the company is seen to be trading normally, cocaine will be concealed in the car parts that are being sent over. Bob has already secured a warehouse in Croydon for the use of the new company.

The parts will be sent over in a half container. A legitimate export company, shipping agents and transport company will be used. The only people with knowledge of the true contents will be those at either end. Tony has in excess of 500 kilos of cocaine available, all of it originating in Venezuela.

When I reach the final page of the notebook, I look over at Jake who has been staring at me intently the whole time, enjoying my reactions to each startling new snippet of information the material has provided to me.

It's truly fascinating stuff but I feel like I've been reading a novel only to find that someone has torn out the final few pages, so I don't know how the story ends.

'So what happened next?' I ask.

The corners of Jake's mouth curl up into a sly smile. 'Well, after that, young Bob got himself nicked. And the rest ... well you already know the rest. He's doing fifteen years now.'

We spend the next couple of hours sharing a few more beers and looking out over the yachts of the marina. At one point something on the television in the upper corner of the bar catches Jake's attention. I turn just in time to see images of heavily armed police officers examining automatic weapons, huge quantities of drugs and fearsome hunting knives. I can pick out only a couple of words of the Spanish commentary and turn to my companion in the hope that he can fill in the details.

'Who got busted?'

It takes a few more seconds before Jake's eyes finally leave the screen and meet mine. '*Los Angeles del Infierno*,' he says softly. Then, picking up on the look of confusion on my face, he translates into English. 'The Hells Angels. And one of them's a Brit.'

9

BIKERS

They had chosen the location of the house with extreme care.

An isolated building protected by a major motorway to the north with a mix of scrub and arable land to the east and west, you can reach it only via a single unpaved track which snakes its way up from the narrow cobbled streets of the centre of Altea, a small town on Spain's sun-drenched Costa Blanca.

The two-storey hacienda-style home is also equipped with a sophisticated security system backed up by motion-sensitive flood-lights and several CCTV cameras, making it all but impossible for visitors to arrive unexpectedly. For this reason it took the officers from the organised crime unit of the Guardia Civil several days of careful planning before they were ready to launch their early morning raid in April 2009.

Officially known as 'Garage 81' the property they targeted serves as the official clubhouse of the Costa Blanca chapter of the Hells Angels Motorcycle Club (the eighth and first letters of the alphabet are H and A so the number 81 is regularly used by the gang and its associates as a kind of shorthand). When the heavily armed police team smashed their way inside they found a games room and recreational area complete with a polished wooden bar engraved with the club's copyrighted Death's Head logo and the letters AFFA – Angels Forever, Forever Angels. They also found a pistol and supply of ammunition along with numerous knives and offensive weapons. Several computers were taken away for further examination and three members of the club – one of them from Britain – were arrested.

Simultaneous raids took place on Hells Angels' clubhouses in several other provinces including Murcia, Barcelona, Malaga,

Valencia, Madrid and Gran Canaria. In all twenty-two members of the gang were taken in for questioning and police recovered several military-grade weapons, bulletproof vests, one kilo of cocaine and 200,000 euros in cash. It was the third time the authorities in Spain had hit the notorious biker gang in recent years and previous raids had uncovered similar drugs and weapons caches ultimately leading to numerous convictions.

Exactly why the HA chapters in Spain had been eager to amass so much firepower has not yet been established, but what is known is that the raids took place at a time of heightened tension between the Angels and their greatest rivals within the biker fraternity, the Outlaws. A year earlier, in what amounted to little short of a declaration of war, the rival gang had opened up a Costa Blanca chapter of its own. To allow such an incursion to take place unopposed would be a sign of weakness and the Angels were under pressure to take immediate action. Sources within the biker world told me that a strike had been planned but, due to the raids, had subsequently been postponed. A clash at some point in the future does, however, remain inevitable. The two gangs are like matter and anti-matter: they simply can't exist in the same place at the same time.

The Hells Angels are, without a shadow of a doubt, the premier back-patch motorcycle club in the world. They have more than 3,600 members in at least thirty countries, a proud history that can be traced right back to the end of the Second World War and, thanks to an ill-informed public at large who consider virtually all bikers to be Hells Angels, the club has a name that has become synonymous with the whole boozing, brawling, rule-breaking lifestyle.

Their ultimate aim is nothing less than global domination of the entire biking brotherhood. Back in 1969 a special edition of the controversial underground magazine Oz featured an interview with Crazy Charlie, then president of the newly formed London chapter. Speaking about the club's plans for the future he said:

'They're going to get bigger and bigger. There's no limit. One day it's not going to be Hells Angels London or Chapter California. It's going to be Hells Angels, Earth.'

The power of their legacy combined with the might of their marketing and public relations machine means that outsiders can easily be forgiven for assuming that the Hells Angels were the original driving force behind the creation of the alternative biker movement.

But the simple fact is that the Outlaws were there first.

The official history of the Hells Angels (a seamstress missed out the apostrophe while creating the first back patch and it has been officially omitted ever since) states that the club was founded on 17 March 1948 in the San Bernadino district of California. The official history of the Outlaws MC states that their club was founded in 1935 in the town of McCook, Illinois, just outside Chicago.

(Ironically, while the public generally see all bikers as Hells Angels, law enforcement agencies around the world see all such bikers as Outlaws. The US Department of Justice defines Outlaw Motorcycle Gangs as those whose members use their motorcycle clubs as cover for criminal enterprises. According to the FBI, five clubs presently have this designation: the Bandidos, the Pagans, the Mongols, the Outlaws and the Hells Angels.)

The two groups co-existed in relative harmony until 1969 when an Outlaw allegedly raped the wife of a Hells Angel. The woman's husband and several other Angels confronted the man in New York and beat him half to death. This sparked a revenge attack in which three Hells Angels were kidnapped and executed by being shot in the head at point-blank range, before their bodies were thrown into a quarry in Florida.

Soon afterwards the club adopted ADIOS – Angels Die In Outlaw States – as a second motto along with the longstanding: 'God forgives, Outlaws don't'. Since then the body count has grown and the conflict has slowly spread around the world. It was inevitable that one day the bloodshed would come to the UK.

*   *   *

By the early nineties, the vicious fighting between the
Wolverhampton chapter of the Hells Angels and the small, independent Birmingham club known as the Cycle Tramps had reached
its bloody peak. There had been literally dozens of assaults, numerous stabbings, the odd shooting as the Angels tried their best
to break up the smaller club, leaving themselves as the premier
biking fraternity in the area. There had also been a number of
mass brawls in which huge groups of both gangs would rush one
another, armed with motorbike chains, baseball bats and meat
cleavers. Many predicted the Cycle Tramps would soon be extinct.

In early 1993 a delegation of bikers from the Cycle Tramps
visited two smaller gangs in the West Midlands, the Pagans and
the Ratae, who had been at war both with one another and with
the Hells Angels for years. Exactly what was said has never been
made public but within the space of a few hours the rifts of the past
seemed to have been forgotten. Representatives of all three clubs
then travelled to Derby to visit another gang: the Road Tramps. At
the time the Road Tramps ran the Rock and Blues Custom show
held each summer and it was the largest event of its kind in the
north of England. The show has been going since 1983 and is well
respected in the biker community as well as a solid money spin-
ner. The Road Tramps, like the Cycle Tramps, had been involved
in a long-running dispute with the Wolverhampton Angels who
had expressed a considerable interest in taking over the Rock and
Blues show, with or without the Road Tramps' blessing.

A few weeks before the opening of the July 1992 show,
Derbyshire police received a tip-off that the Hells Angels would
mount an attack at some point during the proceedings. The police
promptly forbade the Road Tramps to allow any Angels on the
site and unwittingly cleared the way for the most crucial development of the biker war to proceed unhindered.

A few hours after the show had opened, members of the Road
Tramps, Cycle Tramps, Pagans (not affiliated to the American
gang of the same name), Ratae and several other gangs including
the Stafford Eagles and the Road Runners appeared and slipped

on new jackets. Emblazoned on the back was a patch design that no one had ever seen before. The logo was a skull with a kind of Indian headdress made up of different coloured feathers. One was blue and white – the colours of the Pagans. Another was red and blue – the Road Tramps – and yet another red and yellow – the Cycle Tramps. There were seven feathers in all, each representing a different gang. In the interests of self-preservation, the bitter rivals had come together to form a brand-new motorcycle club: the Midland Outlaws.

The newcomers made it clear that they existed in their own right and, despite their provocative choice of name, were not affiliated to the American Outlaws in any way. Despite this, a few weeks later two Angels kidnapped a member of a neutral gang who was known to be friendly with members of the Midland Outlaws. He was tortured until he told everything he knew about their reasons for formation and their plans for the future. The Angels, it seemed, were running scared.

And with good reason. The Midland Outlaws soon showed their support for another of the Angels' deadly rivals, the Bandidos, by sending a delegation to attend a party in honour of a new chapter opening in Scandinavia. The Bandidos were expanding rapidly in Europe to the point that in some countries they outnumbered the Angels. It was only a matter of time before the inevitable happened. The Midland Outlaws' return to the UK coincided with the outbreak of what would come to be known as the Great Nordic Biker War, a vicious conflict that would rage for the next three years, leave at least twelve dead and dozens injured.

The fighting began in 1994 when a Hells Angel was shot dead in the southern Swedish port of Helsingborg during a fight that also saw a Danish Bandido wounded. In March a Finnish leader of the Bandidos, Jarkko Kokko, was shot dead in Helsinki. Days later Bandidos leaders were attacked at airports in Oslo and Copenhagen. In July a Danish Bandido was shot near Drammen in Norway.

A week or so later an anti-tank missile – one of a batch of twelve stolen from a Swedish army base – was fired at the empty clubhouse of a Finnish Hells Angels affiliate. The building was reduced to a smoking pile of rubble. Days later two similar rockets slammed into Angel clubhouses in Copenhagen and Jutland.

In October 1995 several Hells Angels were dining at the Stardust restaurant in Copenhagen when they were set upon by a group of Bandidos. Two Angels had to make a humiliating escape via the women's toilet. The incident prompted the Angels to obtain missiles and explosives of their own and go about seeking revenge. Within a few weeks they had fired an anti-tank grenade at a prison in Copenhagen that housed a Bandido accused of an earlier missile attack against the Angels. The Bandido was wounded but survived.

In October 1996, during the annual 'Viking Party' of the Hells Angels in their heavily fortified headquarters in Titangade, central Copenhagen, the Bandidos fired an anti-tank missile from the sloping roof of a nearby building. It tore through the concrete wall and exploded in a ball of molten metal. Louis Nielsen, a thirty-eight-year-old prospect for the Angels was killed, as was twenty-nine-year-old Janne Krohn, a local woman who was only at the party because the Angels wanted to improve their image by opening the event up to neighbours.

In January 1997 a Hells Angel was shot dead in his car in Aalborg, Denmark and six months later a car bomb exploded outside the Bandidos clubhouse in Drammen, Norway. A female passer-by was killed as she drove past. The blast flattened the heavily fortified building, set nearby factories ablaze, and shattered windows three-quarters of a mile away. That attack was followed three days later by one in which one Bandido was killed and three wounded by a Hells Angels' associate who opened fire at them outside a restaurant crowded with holidaymakers in the resort town of Liseleje.

By this time both gangs were increasingly aware that the feuding could not be allowed to continue. The massive amount of self-imposed security, as well as the high cost of arms and explosives, had put a major financial strain on both groups. Soon feelers were being put out in an effort to restore peace.

Shortly afterwards, live television coverage captured the announcement of a truce between the Hells Angels and the Bandidos. Ultimately the killing ended not because of the cost in human lives but rather because of the potential in lost business. The resolution involved drawing up an agreement in which every town and city in Scandinavia was systematically split up to allow both sides to profit from criminal activities.

Meanwhile back in England the Midland Outlaws and the Angels both focused on increasing their numbers and recruiting new members, seemingly gearing up for a clash of their own. In June 1997, just three months before the truce in Scandinavia had been announced, the Hells Angels heard that a small but notoriously violent London-based club called the Outcasts were attempting to absorb an equally small Hertfordshire club called the Lost Tribe. Concerned that such a move would make the Outcasts too great a force to be reckoned with, the Angels jumped in and made the Tribe honorary members. They made approaches to several Outcasts and invited them to become Angels.

'It was more like a threat than an invitation,' one Outcast said later. 'The Angels had received orders direct from the United States which said that unless they maintained their position as the premier biker gang in the country, they would lose their charter. They made it very clear that if we didn't join them, they would destroy us.'

A couple of Outcasts took up the offer but the vast majority refused, determined to stand up to the might of the Angels by whatever means necessary. In November 1997 two members of the club were arrested in East London in possession of loaded shotguns, seemingly on their way to confront the Angels. There followed a series of minor clashes between the two gangs and it was clear that it was only a matter of time before things came to a head.

January 1998 saw the annual Rockers Reunion in Battersea. About 1,700 people attended the concert, which has traditionally been regarded as an Outcasts event and had been trouble-free for fifteen years. But this time up to twenty Hells Angels were involved in a brutal attack on two Outcasts.

According to eyewitnesses the Angels attacked 'like sharks', going in small groups, kicking and stabbing before retreating and another group taking over. Groups of four or five Angels, armed with knives, axes, baseball bats and clubs, swooped on their victims in wave after wave of attacks. Unarmed bikers equipped with headset microphones helped pick out the Outcasts from the crowd.

The first victim was thirty-three-year-old David Armstrong, a father of one known as Flipper because he had lost his right leg while serving with the Royal Irish Regiment. He was dragged from his bike and hacked to death with axes and knives. He was stabbed four times in his abdomen and left leg. His lungs were pierced and he suffered severe internal bleeding.

Armstrong's friend, Malcolm St Clair, raced to his aid but soon became the next target. Italian photographer Ramak Fazel who was passing by watched in horror as a bearded biker lay into St Clair with an axe. 'He was bringing his axe up over his head. The victim was lying with his head between his knees.' Fazel then saw another man pull out a ten-inch knife and continue the attack. 'The knife was thrust in on both sides. Then they calmly walked away. It was cold-blooded.'

Fazel then saw two of the attackers climb into a Volvo and made a note of the registration number on a napkin. The car was traced to Ronald Wait, vice-president of the Essex Angels – known as the Hatchet Crew. He was arrested after Mr Fazel picked him out at an identity parade.

Wait initially said he was drinking at a bikers' clubhouse in Reading, Berkshire, at the time of the killings. The alibi was supported by several members of the club but dismissed. Wait, who has had triple bypass heart surgery and suffers from angina and diabetes, then said he was too ill to have taken part in any attack. Despite this, he was taken to court to face trial.

During a brief spell in the witness box Wait, who gave his occupation as security guard, refused to talk about the incident explaining the Angel code of silence thus: 'The rules state that you are not allowed to make a statement to police or speak to them if it involves another club member. You have to seek permission to speak to the police.' Initially charged with murder, the prosecution decided not to proceed with the charge during the course of the trial. Wait was eventually found guilty of conspiracy to cause grievous bodily harm and jailed for fifteen years.

The weeks that followed the deaths of Armstrong and St Clair saw more clashes between the two gangs. In March a fertiliser and petrol bomb was found at the clubhouse of the Angels' Lea Valley chapter in Luton, Bedfordshire. A Kent motorcycle shop owned by members of the Hells Angels was the target of an attempted arson attack. Then two Outcasts were shot close to the clubhouse of the Outcast Family chapter in east London. Both victims survived but refused to cooperate with the police.

In June 1998 Outcast Richard 'Stitch' Anderton was arrested after officers from the National Crime Squad found a massive haul of guns and ammunition in his home. They believed the weapons were intended to be used as part of an assault on several properties owned by members of the Hells Angels. Detectives stopped Anderton in his car and found a loaded Smith & Wesson .45 revolver tucked into the waistband of his trousers. A search of Anderton's flat uncovered weapons including an Uzi sub-machine gun, an AK-47 rifle and a rocket launcher.

After his arrest Anderton claimed he had been told the Angels had drawn up a 'death list' containing the names of several Outcasts who were to be 'killed on sight'. Anderton had previously been a 'prospect' member of the Angels. He left for unknown reasons and was believed to have been placed on the 'death list' because he was considered a traitor. (The two men murdered at the Rockers Reunion were also former Angels associates.) Fearing for his life, Anderton moved from Essex to Dorset and armed himself with the handgun. He claimed the other weapons and the drugs were merely being stored at his property.

Around the same time, Warwickshire Police received intelligence that the Midland Outlaws were planning to plant a bomb at the Bulldog Bash, the annual bike show organised by the Hells

Angels that takes placed on private land considered to be within the territory of the Outlaws.

The festival passed without incident but the following year a Belgian club, 'Outlaws MC', which had existed as an independent organisation for more than twenty-five years, was patched over to become a fully fledged member of the American Outlaw Association (AOA). In 2000, the Midland Outlaws did the same. The Angels now had an enemy that was truly a force to be reckoned with, and eager to make its mark.

In August 2001, a group of French-Canadian Angels who had been enjoying the festivities at the Bulldog Bash, the annual four-day biker festival organised by the Hells Angels on a piece of privately owned land near Long Marston, were heading towards London on the southbound carriageway of the M40 in a three-bike convoy when they came under attack.

A dark-coloured saloon that had been following them for a short time suddenly accelerated and moved into the middle lane alongside them. Several handguns appeared at the windows and a number of shots were fired before the car raced off. One of the bikers was hit in the leg but managed to stay in control of his machine long enough to pull over to the hard shoulder. His injuries were not life threatening and he refused to make a complaint or provide a statement to police.

Although investigated as an act of attempted murder, the incident was treated as an indiscriminate, motiveless attack and not linked specifically to bikers or to the Bulldog Bash. That connection would not be made for another six years.

By the time we finally meet up, more than a year has passed since Scott first got in touch to ask whether I would be interested in speaking to him. As a senior figure in the biker gang world virtually every aspect of his life is governed by a code of conduct and series of rules that among other things strictly forbids him talking about club business to the police, to members of rival gangs and, of course, to 'civilians' like me.

Scott's motivation for speaking is his concern about the future of the biker movement that has been a major part of his life for the past twenty-five years. He has been involved at the very highest levels of the organisation and at the highest levels of criminality in the UK, in Europe and beyond. He has taken part in large-scale drug trafficking, bought and sold lethal weapons by the carload and been at the front line during episodes of physical violence resulting in serious injury and even death.

Scott feels enormous loyalty to his club and his many tattoos attest to the fact that it will always be a part of his life, yet he is willing to risk expulsion and death threats from his former comrades because he believes it is important for the public at large to understand the motivations behind the seemingly mindless acts of deadly violence that are fast becoming a day-to-day reality for those in the biker world.

We spend much of that first meeting putting our heads together to try to work out how, in the event that Scott decides to go ahead and give me an unprecedented view into the inner workings of the biker world, we can protect his identity, at least in the short term. We eventually decide that, despite his loyalty to the patch he wears on his back, it is better if I do not identify which of Britain's two biggest biker gangs he actually belongs to: both adhere to the same military-style structure, both are involved in a similar range of legal and illegal activities, both take their lead from 'mother' chapters based in America.

I agree to do my best to 'edit' his words to ensure there are no specific references that could betray his allegiance and after several more meetings to iron out other details, Scott begins to open up. I have been writing about the world of Britain's biker gangs for almost fifteen years and thought I'd heard it all, but as Scott begins to tell me about some of the things he has witnessed and taken part in, I find my jaw dropping with shock.

'The ultimate goal was always to kill one of the enemy and take their patches,' he explains. 'We would go out in small groups in a couple of cars and head deep into their territory, heading to pubs and bars that they were known to frequent. What we wanted was to find one or two of them on their own. It might sound cold-blooded but we were fully aware that the enemy were doing exactly the same thing, going out and looking for members of our club. But this wasn't like the old days when a bunch of you would ride out looking for a bunch of them and then have a bit of a punch up. When we went out, we were looking to do murder.

'There were times when I really felt as though I should go and get my head examined, times when I was heading towards situations where I was likely to end up dead or seriously injured and the obvious thing to do would be to take off my patches and just walk away. But nobody ever does. You have to be prepared to die for your patch, that's how much you have to believe in it. And when you come through something like that, it bonds you to the club and your brothers in ways that just can't be described.

'I remember reading *Black Hawk Down* a few years ago. At the end, when the American soldiers make it back to safety after having gone through this horrific battle in which half of them have been killed or wounded, the first thing a load of them do is sign up for five more years of service. I remember reading it and thinking, yeah, too right, but if you've never been through something like that, it's impossible to understand why you'd ever want to put yourself in that sort of situation.

'One time, during the Nordic Biker War, I was at one of the big shows looking after a couple of senior figures from one of our European chapters when news came through one morning about a missile attack on a clubhouse in their home city. I went into his tent, woke him up and told him what had happened. His face just fell, he was so sad, so concerned. Then I said: "There's one bit of good news though, it was our lot that did the attack and the other lot who are dead." After that he got up and started dancing around the outside of the tent in his underwear and singing at the top of his voice. A few people came over to ask what was going on. When I told them you should have seen the looks on their faces. They thought we were animals.'

Scott goes on to talk about robbing drug dealers at gunpoint, providing protection for other dealers during exchanges of cash or money and occasionally getting involved in the drug trade himself. Unfortunately much of what he has to say is so specific that I am unable to repeat it without breaking the terms of our agreement.

The truth is that the primary reason the big biker gangs do battle is in order to protect their business interests. And these days, almost exclusively, that means the drug trade. Across the world biker gangs are involved in drug dealing and trafficking on a massive scale. The Angels and the other biker gangs involved in the drug trade protect themselves from police 'buy and bust' operations by restricting themselves to selling to those on a list of 'approved' customers. Particular deals are coordinated and run by individual bikers using a few associates, mostly prospects or hang-arounds (the two ranks below full membership of the club) to do the actual legwork. That way even if they are caught, the club is unlikely to be implicated.

For this reason prosecutions involving large numbers of bikers or attempts to prove the club as a whole is involved in a conspiracy are rare.

'Criminality is down to individual choice,' Scott says. 'You don't have to be a criminal to be in the gang. The idea that the Angels or the Outlaws are some kind of mafia is a joke. But at the same time, no one has ever been kicked out of either gang because they've broken the law. The only rules that matter are the club rules, fuck everything else.'

A study of biker gangs in Australia found that the forty-six members of one club had 1,800 criminal convictions between them. Another club with forty-eight members shared 750 convictions. Local police noted that the only place it would be possible to find individuals with a higher number of antecedents would be inside a prison.

'The important thing is to make sure that whatever you do will not reflect badly on the club itself. From the moment you join, everything you earn is said to be at least partly due to your association with the club. After all, if you're buying drugs or weapons, you're gonna say it's for the gang, not just for you, so that people know that if they try to fuck you over, they're going to be in a world of shit. It means people can also expect certain standards. If they buy a load of coke and it turns out to be crap, there is a whole structure and hierarchy they can go and complain to.

'The flipside is that if you leave or get kicked out, everything you have actually belongs to the club. They say without the club you wouldn't have any of it. Once you're out of the club, they come round and strip your house clean. You're not allowed to have any of it.'

This notion was confirmed to me a few weeks later when I managed to persuade the wife of a dead Hells Angel who was known to be heavily involved in the drug trade to speak to me about his experience. 'He always put the club first,' she told me. 'He did terrible things on their behalf. I never knew the details but I'd see the weapons, the drugs and the injuries. One time he came back wounded and the next day there was a story in the paper about an incident that matched his injury exactly. It was obvious he'd been involved. A few months after that he fell out with some of the leaders and knew they were planning to kill him. He started carrying a gun around with him all the time but it was no good. A few days after he died – they made it look like an accident – about twenty of them came to the house in a convoy with a couple of vans and took absolutely everything. They never said a word to me the whole time.'

The role of women within biker gangs has always been that of second-class citizen. One long-suffering wife complained about the fact that her husband was never able to celebrate her birthday as it coincided with an important club anniversary. 'One year he made it back in time for midnight. I thought to myself, this is what I've got to put up with for the rest of my life.'

Bikers are notoriously sexist. They have moved on a little from the days when female partners were expected to wear belts with 'Property Of' followed by the name of the biker to whom the woman 'belonged', but not much. A T-shirt still popular in many circles bears the legend: 'If you can read this, my bitch fell off.'

Wives and girlfriends are not allowed to attend meetings that involve official gang business. This is partly for security reasons but also an excuse to allow members to freely indulge in 'patch snatch' – women of easy virtue who are attracted to biker gangs. Such mistresses, along with official 'old ladies' are not supposed to be told anything about what is going on with the club, though in reality many are party to highly sensitive information.

Another source tells me the story of what happened when one group of wives and girlfriends decided to rebel. Fed up with constantly being left home due to their men always being out on 'club business' the women decided to form a club of their own.

Better organised, less given to bouts of drunken rowdiness and with great taste in nicely customised bikes, the gang quickly thrived. At first the men paid little attention – the fact that the women were no longer giving them such a hard time was all they cared about. But then the women decided to take things a step further and organise runs and rallies of their own. In order to do this they would need permission from the main gang in the area so they arranged a formal meeting.

The women had organised themselves along identical lines to the men so that at the meeting their president, treasurer and sergeant-at-arms sat down at the clubhouse table and made their request. The men said no. The women tried putting things a different way, even allowing a small element of compromise. The men still said no – the rally could not go ahead.

Convinced the objection was being made purely on the basis of gender, the sergeant-at-arms could not control her temper any longer. 'For fuck's sake, all we want is to be treated the exact same way you'd treat us if our club was full of men.' With that the president of the men's club got up, walked up to the female sergeant-at-arms and punched her in the face knocking her out. 'Anyone else want to be treated like a man?' he asked. The female club disbanded soon afterwards.

Ultimately the female gang could not be tolerated because it threatened to become too much of a distraction and therefore reduce the amount of time male members could spend fulfilling their two main goals: finding new recruits and making money. According to the FBI, Outlaw motorcycle gangs earn at least $1 billion a year, the vast majority of it from the illegal drug trade.

Virtually every fight, every shooting, every stabbing and every bombing that has taken place between biker gangs in the UK and further afield in the past twenty-five years is ultimately connected to a desire to protect the highly lucrative drug business from which the gangs derive the vast majority of their income. Although they are also involved in several other areas – prostitution, theft and extortion among them – drugs are considered the core business.

Although there is plentiful evidence of the involvement of biker gangs in the UK in large-scale drug trafficking, the links are nowhere near as obvious as they are within similar clubs in Europe, America and Canada. One reason for this is that British gangs, and the Hells Angels in particular, are able to make huge amounts of money from legitimate ventures such as the Bulldog Bash. Thought to generate well in excess of £1 million each year, it is not known how much of this money finds its way back to the 'mother' charter in California.

The Bash is therefore by far the most significant event in the Angels calendar, a fact that has made it hugely vulnerable to enemy attack. It is clear that if the Bulldog Bash were ever to be shut down, it could mark the beginning of the end of the Hells Angels in the UK.

Gerry Tobin never knew what hit him.

The thirty-five-year-old mechanic was riding his bike along the M40 motorway at speeds of up to 90mph, eager to get home after having enjoyed the festivities at the Bulldog Bash. Just after 2.15 p.m. on Sunday 12 August 2007, Pawel Lec, who was riding one of two other motorbikes travelling with Tobin as part of a small convoy, pulled into the middle lane to allow a dark green Rover 600 to pass. He then watched in horror as the vehicle manoeuvred into position just behind Tobin and a pistol appeared out of the car's left-hand window. Before Lec could react two shots were fired in quick succession.

'The car drove off and it looked like nothing had happened to Gerry,' Lec said later. 'We were driving as if nothing had happened and after a very short time – two or three seconds – I noticed that Gerry let off the handles of his bike and fell underneath the wheels of my bike.'

The shots had come from two separate weapons. The first bullet had smashed through the metal mudguard at the back of Tobin's Harley-Davidson and skirted through his rear wheel; the second skimmed the base of the biker's helmet and lodged in his skull, killing him almost instantly.

Yet despite the seemingly precise nature of the murder, Gerry Tobin was simply in the wrong place at the wrong time and became the target that day by pure chance. He was killed for one reason and one reason alone: he wore a Hells Angel patch on his back.

The car that pulled up behind him was being driven by Dane Garside, vice-president of the South Warwick chapter of the Outlaws. The shots were fired by president Sean Creighton and sergeant-at-arms Simon Turner. Close by, another full-patch member of the gang Dean Taylor was in a white Range Rover with probationers Karl Garside and Ian Cameron while a final member, club treasurer Malcolm Bull, was patrolling the area in a Renault Laguna, acting as a link between the other two vehicles.

It was Creighton himself who had first proposed the deadly plan several months earlier during a club meeting at Supreme Harley Supplies, a small garage close to one of Coventry's busiest suburban shopping areas which operated as a legitimate custom shop during the day and served as the chapter's clubhouse by night. Leaving nothing to chance, Creighton had spent weeks practising his marksmanship on a tailor's dummy that he kept at his home. Numerous contingencies and back-up strategies were in place so that in the event that their chosen survived the initial burst of gunfire, other members of the club would step in and insure that his survival was only temporary. Whatever happened, at the end of the day, at least one Angel had to be dead.

He and the rest of the chapter had spent the previous three days carrying out reconnaissance on the network of roads around the Bulldog Bash. On the day Tobin was shot they had been up since 5 a.m. looking for a suitable victim, parking in a lay-by on the A46 waiting for someone to come past. After spotting Tobin's convoy they had followed him for thirty miles, waiting for the right moment to strike.

Once the deed was done the killers sped back to Coventry, abandoning the Rover in a quiet country lane and then torching it. Five days later the Outlaws met up at the Tollgate Pub in Coundon where they bought no drinks but took extensive notes during an intensive debriefing session.

Fully aware that the members of motorcycle clubs famously do not cooperate with police, regardless of whether they are the victims or the perpetrators of a murder, detectives believed they were in for a long and difficult investigation. But while the hit itself was incredibly professional, aspects of both the planning and the cover-up left a great deal to be desired.

With eyewitness reports and CCTV footage of the vehicle as it travelled along the motorway, police knew they were looking for a Rover. When a burned-out model was reported in the area just a few hours after the shooting, they quickly set about looking into its background. The name and address of the registered owner turned out to be fake but incredibly, the previous owner was listed as none other than Sean Creighton.

After that the clues came thick and fast. Creighton and Dane Garside were seen on CCTV at a nearby petrol station wrapped in hats and warm clothes despite it being a hot summer's day and later a search of the clubhouse in Coventry turned up two shotguns in a bag with Turner's fingerprints on them. Police also found the dummy used for shooting practice. Within the space of a couple of weeks the entire chapter had been rounded up and charged with murder.

As the seven defendants waited on remand, other members of the Outlaws travelled to Spain in order to help celebrate the launch of the newly formed Costa Blanca chapter. After a week of hard partying, the Outlaws arrived at Alicante airport in early January 2008 for their flight back to the UK only to find a similar number of Hells Angels getting ready to board exactly the same flight.

Both groups had already passed through security and had no weapons on them. With each side hoping to gain the upper hand, a series of frantic phone calls were made to the UK calling for reinforcements to meet the flight and bring as many weapons as they could get their hands on.

By the time flight ZB499 landed at Birmingham airport, the Outlaws and the Angels each had around fifteen members ready to do battle. The fight took place in a linkway joining the two airport terminals close to where the passengers emerge after clearing Customs.

With virtually no warning, the two groups who had got off the plane met up with fellow gang members who had made it to Birmingham, took hold of their weapons and charged into each other. Knives and meat cleavers as well as iron bars, knuckledusters, hammers and even a tyre iron were all put to savage use as terrified passers-by ran for cover. Witnesses even reported one man wielding a samurai sword. Although the airport is patrolled by heavily armed police officers, they felt it was not safe for them to intervene and kept their distance. Remarkably only one of the bikers was critically injured in the clash.

Twelve bikers were eventually brought to court but perhaps the most interesting thing about the fight at the airport was the ages of those involved. Biker gangs have, for the most part, fallen out of fashion and the average age of their membership has been rising as a result. The average age of the seven Outlaws in the dock was forty-seven, the eldest being fifty-one and the youngest forty-four. However, in the case of the five Angels, the average age was forty, the eldest being fifty-two and the youngest just twenty-eight.

It turns out the Angels had spent the months before the battle recruiting heavily from the local underworld. The new members were not necessarily bikers at heart but had enough of an interest to allow them to be fast-tracked into the club. Many of these new members are said to be involved in drug dealing, all part of an effort by the Angels to establish themselves further in the UK market and to boost their fighting strength in the aftermath of the murder of Gerry Tobin.

In March 2008 David Melles, another member of the Outlaws, was arrested after police found an armoury of illegal guns at his home. The fifty-two-year-old grandfather had hidden a sawn-off and pump-action shotgun, dum-dum bullets and a Derringer pistol at his house near Stroud. Police believe the weapons were to be used in a planned confrontation between the Outlaws and their rivals. Melles was later jailed for twelve years.

In the months that followed biker violence flared all round the world with dozens of tit-for-tat incidents taking place between the Hells Angels and their rivals. In March 2009 in a terrifying echo of the events at Birmingham airport, a group of Hells Angels battled with a group from rival gang the Comanchero inside the terminal at Sydney airport. A twenty-nine-year-old member of the Angels was killed after being repeatedly smashed in the head with a metal bollard.

Later that same year Sean Creighton and the other members of the South Warwickshire chapter of the Outlaws were due to go on trial for the murder of Gerry Tobin. Shortly before proceedings began, Creighton changed his plea to guilty, insisting that he alone had been responsible. It was a brazen attempt to try to get the charges against the remaining club members dropped but was doomed to fail. Although the others subsequently claimed they had been unaware that a shooting had been planned and that they were merely carrying out a surveillance operation, ample evidence existed to show that they had been aware of the conspiracy from the start.

Their cause was not helped by the chapter's treasurer, Malcolm Bull, breaking a cardinal biker rule by making a statement to the police that helped clarify his own role in the club as well as that of his fellow defendants. Bull was promptly separated from other defendants in the dock and had to be transferred to a different prison. He now risks retribution not just from Hells Angels but also from other Outlaws.

While in the witness box Simon Turner told the court: 'Everything about Mr Bull is disreputable to me. Mr Bull has turned on everything that we are – he has brought us to this junction in our life. He has turned his back on everything he was by speaking to the police.'

Despite the negative PR generated by the case and the fact that it was unclear whether the killing had been sanctioned by the American Outlaw Association, the governing body for Outlaw chapters worldwide, the gang put on an impressive display of strength outside the courthouse with up to one hundred Outlaws in full regalia turning up daily throughout the duration of the trial, all under the watchful eye of armed police. One source suggested that, despite this show of support, the chapter was believed to have gone 'rogue' and that Creighton and the others were becoming increasingly addicted to crystal meth in the months leading up to the murder. All seven bikers were found guilty of murder. Their combined sentences totalled 191 years.

In the aftermath of the Tobin murder Warwickshire police repeatedly tried to ban the Bulldog Bash, partly over fears of violence and partly because their inquiries had established clear links between the biker gangs and organised crime. With the Bash generating cash profits of up to £1 million over its four-day run, senior police officers became extremely concerned about just what the Hells Angels were getting up to with that kind of money.

Stratford-upon-Avon District Council's licensing committee granted the event a new ten-year licence in 2008 but the following year Warwickshire's Assistant Chief Constable Bill Holland asked the panel to review the event's licence due to 'heightened' tensions between the Hells Angels and the Outlaws.

In his statement to the committee Holland said: 'I am satisfied that the Bulldog Bash Limited is made up of "full patch" members of the Hells Angels and their close associates, and that the Hells Angels are involved in serious and organised crime. There has previously been serious, including fatal, violence connected to the event and this poses a serious risk.'

According to Holland, the Warwickshire force had spent around £1.4 million policing the event but organiser John 'Bilbo' Britt claimed this was a complete waste of money. 'They have tried three times to stop this show and have failed each time. Certain people in the police think us bikers are in some kind of war but we are not. It is discrimination, because we are in a fight with the police, to stop them ruining part of our lifestyle. We are not just going to sit back and let them do that. If the police have the evidence that we are involved in organised crime, take us to court. We've been doing it for twenty-three years and never had any trouble in the festival. Under our leathers we're just lovely big cuddly teddy bears.'

In his closing submission to the committee Michael Bromley-Martin QC, representing the organisers of the event, said: 'There is no evidence whatsoever that the Hells Angels organisation, as opposed to individual members of the organisation, are involved in organised crime.' The committee agreed, stating that it had been presented with no evidence that the Bulldog Bash was 'anything other than a well-managed public event' organised by law-abiding individuals.

In reality the Bulldog Bash is far too big a money-spinner for the Angels for them ever to allow any serious criminality to take place at it or to be in any way linked to it. In the meantime both gangs have returned to the serious business of making money and expanding their membership in any way that they can.

The Angels are now said to be focusing their attention on producing crystal meth, also known as ice, an intense stimulant that has swept across America and is becoming increasingly popular on this side of the Atlantic. According to the DEA it is now the most popular hard drug in the Midwest and West, ahead of cocaine and heroin.

Crystal meth produces an intense euphoria that allows people to work or party or engage in sexual activity for days at a time without rest. It is said to be significantly more addictive than crack cocaine. Although it remains relatively unknown over here, its use is spreading fast. A study by the Association of Chief Police Officers found that crystal meth 'is being produced, sold or used in every area of the UK.'

The bikers involved in producing it are believed to be learning manufacturing and distribution techniques from Angels based in America and Canada who dominated the trade there until recently when it became so lucrative that the notoriously violent Mexican drug cartels stepped in and took over.

In recent years members of the Hells Angels in the UK had become increasingly involved in the trade in marijuana, particularly that grown in South Africa, which sells for a premium. However, the international trade in that drug has collapsed due to the massive growth of the domestically produced product.

Angels in Canada also used to make much of their money from the cannabis business until they too were ousted from the trade by another gang. A gang that has since firmly established itself in the UK.

10
HOME GROWN

With its eight bedrooms, four bathrooms, five reception rooms, extensive grounds, servants quarters and lengthy gravel drive, Field House is without doubt the quintessential English country home in the midst of the quintessential English country village.

The £2.4 million mansion can be found in the most fashionable part of Hoole Village, a tiny parish just outside Chester, with a mostly wealthy, socially elite population of around 220. The village is too small to have a local newspaper of its own, but then nothing much happens here anyway. In August 2009 a faulty junction box led to a minor power cut; the following month the main slip road to the village was partially closed for resurfacing, and in October police raided Field House and found one of the largest cannabis factories ever uncovered in the UK.

Thousands of plants were growing throughout three of the building's four grandiose storeys. The ground floor had been converted into makeshift living quarters for the team of 'gardeners' and the basement was used as a drying room but the rest of the house was devoted to cultivation. All the windows had been sealed and blacked out, holes had been bored through the floor to help with ventilation while a cumbersome system of hosepipes snaked up the stairs around the banister and carried water to all parts of the house from the downstairs kitchen sink. Power for the operation had been diverted directly from the National Grid.

According to Inspector Phil Hodgson who led the raid, the plants his officers found were unlike any he had ever encountered – a 'mutation of normal cannabis which matures and grows extra rapidly. They were fed by a fast-growing fertiliser and the result was a plant that grows many heads, something none of us have seen in our lives,' he said. 'Some of the plants were actually fifteen feet tall.' The street value of the haul was estimated to be in excess of £500,000 and Hodgson believed the set-up was capable of producing a new crop every three months.

No one was inside the house when it was raided and, judging by the half-eaten rotting food that had been left behind, the occupants had departed in something of a hurry. 'There's not been anybody here for a couple of weeks. Because it was linked to other addresses that we searched, they probably knew we were coming,' added Hodgson. Police had been tipped off about Field House a month earlier after raiding another cannabis factory some thirty-five miles away in Nether Alderley, one of Britain's wealthiest villages. There, in a home worth more than £1 million, they found plants worth around £150,000. The sole occupant – a fifty-year-old Vietnamese woman – was arrested and taken into custody. She was later charged with producing cannabis and abstracting electricity dishonestly.

In 1997, just 11 per cent of cannabis consumed in the UK was actually grown here, the balance being smuggled in from abroad. By 2007 the proportion of domestically farmed product had climbed to more than 60 per cent and the figure continues to rise to this day.

This dramatic shift is due almost entirely to the arrival in the UK of organised gangs from Vietnam who have rapidly achieved near total domination of Britain's marijuana business. The gangs employ a high level of expertise and operate a tried and trusted business model that is capable of generating vast profits in a short space of time.

The know-how and methodology was imported direct from Vancouver where, in the mid-nineties, Vietnamese gangs took over the cannabis trade that was previously being run by none other than the Hells Angels.

Thousands of refugee 'Boat People' had arrived in Canada during the seventies and eighties. One of their main destinations was Vancouver and the surrounding province of British Columbia which already had a large South East Asian population and, because of its position on the country's west coast, was known as the 'Gateway to the Pacific'.

Canada has always had a relaxed attitude to 'soft' drugs and those caught growing small or even relatively large, potentially commercial quantities often manage to escape jail. The Angels had exploited this to the extreme, establishing pot plantations in barns in the rural countryside and smuggling the drug across the border into the United States where it sold at a significant premium.

But such premises were easily located and regularly raided, leading to spectacular seizures and costly losses for the biker gang. Criminal elements among the newly arrived Vietnamese community spotted a gap in the market. Instead of operating on an all-or-nothing mammoth scale, they focused on turning networks of rented houses in busy residential areas into clandestine grow-ops.

Far more difficult to uncover, these operations would be staggered so that a new crop was ready for harvesting every couple of weeks. If one house in the network were to be raided, profits from the others would more than cover the loss and it was a simple matter to establish a new farm in a new home.

In only a few years, the Vietnamese gangs had all but pushed the Hells Angels out of Vancouver, prompting one police officer to describe them as 'the most tenacious, extraordinarily focused criminals ever introduced into Canada'. After some sporadic violence between the rival groups, a compromise was reached: the Vietnamese gangs would continue to grow their high-quality marijuana while the bikers would handle distribution and end user sales.

Vietnamese-style grow-ops then began to appear in other parts of the world. Some of this was down to senior figures from the gangs looking to expand their business but there were also cases in which individuals – often extended family members – travelled to Canada and paid handsomely to learn the secrets of cultivating marijuana in a kind of franchise operation.

The grow-op gangs were soon a force to be reckoned with in Australia, followed by Sweden, the rest of Europe and also the

United States, but it was in the UK that things really took off for them. The first such set-up was uncovered in Sheffield in late 2003, just a few months before the downgrading of cannabis from a Class B to a Class C drug in January 2004. With many people mistakenly believing the drug had been legalised – in fact, the penalties for trafficking remained the same – demand, particularly for high-quality varieties, slowly started to rise. Concerned about this growth, and also the rising potency of the product, the government would later restore the drug to Class B status, but by then it was too late.

I first became aware of the impact of Vietnamese cannabis gangs in 2005. While attending a murder trial at London's Woolwich Crown Court, I noticed that five cases being heard that day all featured defendants with the same surname – Nguyen. I thought I'd stumbled across some massive conspiracy but soon learned that each of the cases was separate, that all involved homes that had been converted into cannabis farms and that none of the defendants were related to one another.

(Nguyen – pronounced so that it sounds similar to 'win' – is by far the most common family name in Vietnam. Around 40 per cent of Vietnamese people have the surname. By contrast Smith, the most common family name in both the United Kingdom and the United States, is shared by just 1 per cent of the population in each of those countries. To add to the confusion, Nguyen can also be a first name.)

It was a pattern that had been repeated time and time again in the preceding weeks and one judge even complained that he was having great difficulty telling one case from another, having dealt with so many in such a short space of time.

Although separate, the cases did indeed appear to be mirror images of one another. Typically the conspiracy began with a well-dressed, well-spoken individual, often a woman, approaching an estate agent with a view to renting a property and offering to pay at least six months in advance.

Once the lease had been signed the property was transformed into a cannabis farm virtually overnight. Windows were sealed and blacked out, walls were covered with foil to retain heat, tonnes of soil was spread across the floors throughout all the main rooms and large holes were cut through the ceiling and roof to help vent the toxic fumes released by the fertilisers. In some cases entire internal walls were completely demolished.

Under cover of darkness a high-tech lighting and irrigation system would be sneaked inside. Electricity to power the enterprise would invariably be drawn directly from the national grid, bypassing the meter, to avoid drawing suspicion from the utility companies – a typical farm uses £30,000 of electrical power each year.

Once all the modifications were completed, the house would be occupied by a recently arrived illegal immigrant who would be paid to look after and nurture the plants. Under no circumstances would he or she be allowed to leave.

The gangs have concentrated on cultivating strains that grow quickly and have a high THC content – the main active ingredient in cannabis – to give them a product that carries more bangs per buck and can therefore command a higher price. They briefly experimented with hydroponic systems where the plants were grown in nutrient-rich water rather than soil, but this turned out to be too complex for the gardeners.

Every few months a team of harvesters would appear to collect the crop but otherwise the 'gardener' would have no contact with the outside world. With no transportation costs, no border controls to evade and an eager customer base literally right outside the door of each operation – cannabis is by far the most popular and widely consumed illegal drug in the UK – the Vietnamese grow houses make sound economic sense. According to the police the set-up costs for a typical operation seemed to vary between around £15,000 and £50,000 while annual profits on a single grow house ran from £200,000 to £500,000.

Eager to learn more, I spent the next few months desperately trying to cultivate contacts in a bid to find someone involved with the cannabis farms, but got absolutely nowhere. The grow-ops, I would later learn, are intimately entwined with the shadowy figures involved in large-scale people smuggling. As a result the levels of fear and intimidation within this world are astonishingly high.

One of the keys to growing cannabis in this sort of set up is to be able to provide the plants with round-the-clock care. Thanks to the seemingly endless supply of desperate illegal immigrants, the Vietnamese gangs have found a way to achieve this that is still economically viable and did not take kindly to inquiries that threatened to disrupt the enterprise.

I had several doors slammed in my face, I was unceremoniously turfed out of numerous community centres, telephones were suddenly disconnected and people who were happily chatting away one minute would lose the power of speech as soon as I brought up the subject of the cannabis gangs. More than once, I was greeted with a cheery 'Hello, how are you' only to find that moments later the person I was talking to had lost all ability to speak or understand English.

Eventually I made the acquaintance of a young Vietnamese woman, Lam, who was employed as a translator by various solicitors. Her work brings her into regular contact with those inside the houses as well as some of those considerably higher up the chain. Fearful of reprisals from within her tight-knit community, she would speak only on condition of absolute anonymity.

'It works the same way as it does with the Italian gangs,' she told me. 'They only trust their own, they only trust other Vietnamese. I've been here for three years now and I get offers at least once or twice a month to go and work with them.

'Because I speak good English and I don't look like a criminal, they have offered me thousands of pounds to go to estate agents and sign up some properties which they can take over. They said I would have false documents – everything from a passport and driving licence to bank statements and utility bills – so nothing could ever be traced back to the real me.'

The gangs also pay estate agents a handsome commission to look out for properties that might be suitable – the main criteria being that they are easily converted and have landlords who never go round to check on their tenants.

'There is no one leader. Each of the gangs operates separately though they sometimes cooperate with one another if they think it means they can make more money. Some of the gangs have only four people, others have more than one hundred. Some have one house, some have twenty. They also work with other gangs who buy the cannabis from them and distribute it.

'Ninety per cent of the translation work I do now is related to cannabis,' Lam continued. 'It starts in Vietnam. People get offered something like a package deal with the snakeheads, to come over here for two or three months all inclusive and tend some of the grow operations. At the end of that time they are told they will go home with maybe three or four thousand pounds. That's enough to set them up for life. More money than they could get from doing anything else.

'The gardeners are called ghosts because no one is ever supposed to see them, no one is supposed to know that they even exist. They are told never to open the door to anyone, not for any reason. Some of the houses even have traps – like door handles wired up to the mains – in case people try to break in.

'Because they are here illegally the gardeners are easy to control. The gangs also use a lot of children aged about fourteen or fifteen for the same reason. They promise money but many of them don't get paid at all. If they try to leave they are told their families back in Vietnam will suffer.

'I worked with one woman who was smuggled into the UK where she had worked in a restaurant. She had built up big debts from gambling and was offered the chance to pay off her debts by tending to some plants. When she refused, the gang threatened to kill the children she had left behind.

'She was only supposed to work as a gardener for a month but that soon became two months. She was a prisoner in the house. She was never allowed to leave for any reason. Every now and then someone would come and bring her food and check the plants. Apart from that she never saw anyone, never saw daylight. They kept saying they would let her go but then a week before she was going to be set free, the police raided the house and she was arrested. Now she's in prison and when she finishes her sentence, she'll be deported.'

Conditions inside the cannabis farms are usually horribly cramped and extremely dangerous, with the 'ghosts' at risk of injury or death due to fire or electrocution. Police have found children living in cupboards and lofts to maximise space for plants, in houses powered by electricity running from makeshift connections to mains supplies. Each year dozens of farms are uncovered not through police or community action but because they catch fire due to faulty lights or substandard rewiring. In one case a farm was found to be drawing its entire electricity supply from a nearby street lamp.

'If someone has a background as an electrician, the gang will force them to work on their behalf using whatever means necessary,' says Lam. 'It's an absolutely vital part of the operation and you need to know what you're doing. At the same time, no electrician would willingly do the job because of the risks involved.

'A lot of the people who end up doing the gardening don't fully understand what they're letting themselves in for. The others, for them it's a calculated risk. In Vietnam we have the death penalty for drug crimes. They execute eighty or ninety people each year. If people are desperate enough for money they will do anything and it's impossible to put them off. Everyone knows drugs are a crime but everyone also knows that they mean big money. Compared to what they might get back home the punishments here are seen as a bit of a joke.

'When they get arrested they always say they earn almost nothing but that's not the case. If they were not getting what they consider to be decent money they would simply throw open the doors, sell the stuff on and make a run for it.

'They used to always say they thought the plants were for medicinal purposes and that they were shocked when they learned they were illegal drugs. For the first couple of years it worked but now the courts have got wise to it. The judges say: "I've heard this same story too many times" and send them to prison for a long time.

'Yet many of them still feel this is the easy way to make money. They have language problems and cannot get high-paying jobs and they go to do this because of the easy cash. But I feel bad for my people. Now every time I say I am Vietnamese people make jokes about cannabis. They think we are all involved.

'This is big business. The bosses take the whole thing very seriously and keep meticulous records about the number of plants in each property and what stage of maturity they are at. They know how much money they should be making and get angry if profits are not what they should be. They protect themselves from prosecution by making sure that everyone is so terrified of them, they are unwilling to say anything to the police.'

One such boss has the distinction of being the only person connected to Vietnamese cannabis gangs to make it onto *Crimewatch*.

Along with his Chinese colleague he has been linked to more than one hundred cannabis factories discovered in the Bradford area in recent years. Arrested in Nottingham in 2007, he failed to answer bail and has not been seen ever since. Also going by the names Mr Hong and Mr Khan, he is known to be able to produce fake British passports which he uses to convince landlords to rent properties to his subordinates.

Starting out in city centres, the man was one of the first operators to begin setting up farms in more rural areas because of police pressure. In London, for example, between 2005 and 2007 the Metropolitan Police uncovered more than 1500 cannabis factories.

The clampdown in London and other big cities actually proved to be a boon for the gangs. Suburban areas meant lower rents, larger houses with more space to cultivate drugs and therefore higher profits.

'They are getting cleverer now. They won't put any plants in the living room, they'll leave the curtains slightly open and have a television on inside. It's all about giving out the impression that this is just a normal family home, that nothing untoward is going on inside.'

All too aware that their activities can make sharp-eyed neighbours suspicious, particularly in well-heeled areas, the gangs are doing all they can to keep on the good books of those around them.

When the next-door neighbours of a house in Gateshead that had been converted into a cannabis factory began to complain about the odd smells, the Asian woman who claimed to be living there apologised saying it was due to 'burnt coffee'. A few days later she presented her neighbours with a box of expensive festive biscuits and wished them a Happy Christmas.

With a commodity worth tens of thousands of pounds hidden in secluded locations and virtually unguarded, opportunities for rip-offs and double dealing are all too plentiful. There have been literally dozens of cases where violence has been involved.

In April 2008 a gang of Chinese and Vietnamese criminals met up at the Saigon Saigon restaurant in Edinburgh to discuss just who was responsible for stealing part of the crop at one of the many grow houses the gang was running. One name came up time and again: Zang Hou.

Within the space of a couple of hours, fifteen members of the gang had stocked up with weapons and made their way in three separate cars to Hou's Ellen's Glen Road home, arriving just before 1 a.m. They smashed their way inside, punching and kicking their terrified victim and dragging him out into the street.

A neighbour, woken by the commotion, looked out of his window to see a group of men outside Hou's home holding clubs and baseball bats. When Hou emerged, it looked as though he was 'fighting for his life', the neighbour said. He was being hit in the face and on the body and dragged along the street to a nearby car. The neighbour made a note of the registration and called the police.

In the meantime Hou was driven to a house in Castleview Grove and taken into a room where his hands were tied and he was threatened repeatedly. It was only when he overheard the things the gang were talking about that it became clear to him that he was not the person they were looking for – although he worked in one of the cannabis grow houses, he hadn't stolen so much as a single leaf.

It took Hou another half hour to convince his captors of this and they eventually agreed to let him go, giving him a few hundred pounds as 'compensation' for what they had done and putting him in a taxi home.

Not all such incidents end so amicably.

When twenty-two-year-old Hung 'Vi' Tran, a lowly member of a West London-based cannabis growing syndicate, was found to have stripped the leaves off several plants growing at a house in Gresham Road for his own use, the boss of the gang, Hoang Le, ordered his co-workers to execute him.

Manicurist Dinh Nguyen picked up Vi in his car along with another member of the gang known simply as 'Te' who worked as an enforcer for Hoang Le. The trio were heading towards Elephant and Castle when the accusations began. 'Suddenly Te asked Vi about the theft. He gave hints that Vi was involved. He started with a soft voice saying: "Just tell me."

'Then Vi reacted angrily. He denied it totally. I said something like: "It's already happened, don't talk about it anymore." Both men were exchanging swear words and then suddenly I heard a noise like "kop". I turned around and Vi was bleeding from his forehead. I reached round with my right hand to keep them separated but Te said: "You don't want any trouble, just keep driving."'

According to Nguyen the fight then escalated in the back seat and he caught glimpses of it in his rear-view mirror.

'Te was crazy. He pointed a knife at my back and I was scared. The night was dark and raining so sometimes I could not see what was happening. At one point I saw Vi lying against the door. I heard Vi saying: "I wasn't involved, don't hit me." Then he screamed "My God, my God." At first Vi was resisting then he just stopped. Te took a jacket and he placed it over Vi's head and body. He covered him then he kept on hitting him.'

Nguyen panicked and took a wrong turn, ending up on a side road on Barnes Common where Te ordered him to stop. 'Te used both of his hands to grab Vi round the chest and pulled him out of the car. I didn't see what happened next.'

Drivers spotted Vi's body as they drove past the common the following morning. A post-mortem revealed he had been struck on the head with a hammer and then received multiple stab wounds to his face, mainly around his eyes.

'Te' has never been found while Hoang Le committed suicide in jail while awaiting trial. Dinh was cleared of murder but convicted of conspiracy to produce class C drugs.

Although internal disputes are commonplace, the biggest threat to the grow-op gangs comes from outside.

In 2007 Wayne Walters, the head of a London drugs gang, was convicted of murdering a Vietnamese drug dealer. Hai Son Nguyen had met up with Walters along with his friends, Jermaine Fyves and Conroy Pitter, in order to sell them £7,000 worth of cannabis.

With his friend Van Pu waiting outside the flat in Comet Street, Deptford to keep watch, Nguyen handed over the drugs but when he asked for payment Walters refused. Instead he produced a handgun and shot Nguyen twice in the stomach.

The three men escaped with a bag and a suitcase containing £7,300 worth of cannabis weed. Mr Nguyen was left lying on the floor with two bullet wounds to the stomach and was taken to University Hospital, Lewisham, for emergency surgery. But the bleeding kept returning and he finally died the following month.

Across the country, whenever large quantities of herbal cannabis are suddenly being sold by members of street gangs, local police know a cannabis factory has been found by another gang and raided. From the street gang's point of view it is, of course, the perfect crime as the victims can do nothing to draw attention to themselves. At least four gardeners have been murdered as a result of raids by other gangs.

When police in Aspley, Nottingham, received an urgent call to go to the aid of a man being attacked in his home they arrived to find that he was a gardener for a cannabis factory and that his attackers were thieves trying to steal his crop.

Quang Vo had first seen the men a few days earlier when they came to the house and peered in through the kitchen window. When they returned they kicked in the door and threatened him with a knife and sword in an attempt to steal the drugs he had been paid to look after.

In late 2009 six men – three Vietnamese, three British – appeared in court in connection with a mass disturbance that had involved up to twenty men. A Ford Transit van carrying eleven large laundry bags full of freshly cut cannabis was found nearby. Police believe the Brits had been attempting to steal the cannabis from the gang.

I ask Lam if it would be possible to speak to someone working inside one of the houses and perhaps gain access to one. She tells me it is extremely unlikely. 'They are all so paranoid about being robbed that they keep the locations as secret as possible. It's one of the reasons that gardeners are not allowed to go anywhere, at least not until there has been a harvest.'

Lam explains that even if I did find someone willing to talk, they would get into enormous trouble if their bosses found out what they had done.

I drop the idea and focus instead on other aspects of my investigation. Then, a month or so later I unexpectedly hear from Lam. She has been speaking to a contact who spent time at a cannabis factory but got sick and had to be moved out. Although he himself won't talk to me, I might be able to go and look at the factory itself.

She doesn't have an exact address – the 'ghost' was never allowed outside and therefore never saw the number on the front of the door – but the house is located on a quiet residential road in Sheffield and sits on the corner of another road. The house has a garden with high hedgerows and is opposite some kind of park.

I drive up to Sheffield the following day and fear at first that my journey has been wasted. Bawtry Road, as luck would have it, turns out to be nearly two miles long and has parkland along much of its length. But then I remember what Lam said about the hedgerows – most of the houses here have their front gardens paved over.

It takes only a few passes up and down before I am certain I've found the right place. I have come prepared with a stack of leaflets from a relatively local pizza delivery firm which I intend to use as an excuse for walking up the path and poking my nose through the letterbox.

I open the gate and make my way towards the front door. It's a bright afternoon but all the curtains are drawn. I fold a leaflet and push it against the letterbox. Nothing happens. I fold the leaflet again, making it extra stiff. Again nothing happens. The box, it seems, has been sealed. I look down and see a cardboard box with a slot in the top on which the word 'post' has been scrawled in what looks like a child's writing.

Undeterred, I press the doorbell and then rap my knuckles against the door. If anyone is home they do not answer. I feel certain that the house is being used for cannabis farming but I have no proof. My suspicions are confirmed a few months later when this property and four others are raided as part of a major operation.

According to the police, the gang behind this particular grow-op is said to be run by a middle-aged couple, the woman being the true powerhouse. According to Lam's source, a significant number of grow-ops in the UK are being run by women.

Twenty years ago it would have been unusual to find any females anywhere above the very bottom level of the criminal career ladder but today they play an increasingly key role and have shown time and time again that they are more than capable of matching and often outdoing their male counterparts when it comes to ingenuity, cunning and sheer brutality.

11
THE FAIRER SEX

The murders followed one another in quick succession.

The first came at around 6.15 a.m. on a bleak New Year's Eve morning just outside the centre of the Danish capital of Copenhagen. A bleary-eyed John McCormick, dressed only in T-shirt, underpants and socks, opened the door to his second-floor apartment in the city's Nørrebro district to find himself staring down the barrel of a 9mm handgun. A split second later a single bullet slammed into the centre of his chest and he fell back into the hallway. Dead.

Less than four weeks later, during the final week of January 2002, the killers struck again. The body of fifty-four-year-old Colombian Arturo Rodriguez Miranda was pulled from the water at the harbour village of Hou, a popular tourist destination in Scandinavia's Åarhus region. Miranda's hands had been tied behind his back and his throat had been cut so deeply that he had almost been decapitated. As if that were not enough, Miranda had also been blasted through the back at point blank range with a shotgun.

Both victims were known to have been heavily involved in the drug business.

John McCormick left his native Middlesbrough in the mid-1990s and ran a bar in the Spanish resort of Fuengirola as a cover for his drug activities. He soon earned himself a reputation as a man not to be messed with. In 1996 his brother, Barry, was jailed for twelve years at Teesside Crown Court for ecstasy trafficking after detectives tailed him on dozens of trips to the Costa del Sol, ostensibly to visit his brother. Although John McCormick was not involved in the court case, Judge Roger Scott described him as a 'very violent drugs baron'.

After ripping off several British dealers in Spain, McCormick fled to Denmark using a false passport in the name of Ronald Carey. He was soon back in business. In the weeks leading up to his death his apartment had been as busy as a train station; a steady stream of visitors calling at all hours of night and day in order to purchase drugs.

Like McCormick, Miranda had also come to Denmark to get away from his enemies, having fallen out with members of high-level cocaine cartels trafficking the drug between South America and Spain. And just like McCormick, he made the mistake of trusting the wrong people.

The two brutal executions made headlines across the country, shocking a populace used to having one of the lowest per-capita murder rates in Europe. But what made these deaths particularly chilling was that the main suspect in both was not some hardened mobster but rather an unassuming, middle-aged British woman.

In the early nineties a new generation of high-stakes drug smugglers entered the Spanish scene. Instead of joining forces with the established networks – mostly run by former British armed robbers – they operated in small, independent units and worked with others only as and when needed. Among this new breed of trafficker, Beverley Storr was one of the leading lights.

Storr had not only held her own in the male dominated world of organised crime but had managed to rise to the top. Ruthless and determined, she had spent years successfully arranging for large quantities of drugs to be smuggled from Spain into Britain until she was caught in Malaga with one and a half tonnes of cannabis worth £3 million. Jailed in 1997 she was freed in January 2001. She returned briefly to Britain before heading back to Spain and then on to Denmark, part of a wave of international smugglers who chose to base themselves there at the time.

Arriving in Copenhagen with her long-time lover, Reginald Blythin, a convicted drugs trafficker and former armed robber, she quickly established new contacts that put her back at the centre of a lucrative smuggling enterprise.

One of her early customers was none other than John McCormick, but after the first few deals, relations suddenly turned sour. The exact reasons for the breakdown may never be known but it is thought that, through Storr's contacts in Spain, McCormick's past had caught up with him. Although McCormick had a fearsome reputation, something about the situation seemed to unsettle him. Friends reported that in the month before he died he had become increasingly ill at ease and confided that he had run into trouble with acquaintances on the drug scene.

Soon after McCormick's death, Storr and Blythin moved to Hou where they rented a holiday cottage close to the harbour. Within a few days, Arturo Miranda had come to visit and soon became a permanent houseguest.

Around the end of January, Miranda suddenly vanished. Neighbours reported seeing Storr cleaning the house with a sense of 'great urgency' before she too disappeared. A forensics team discovered traces of blood, leading investigators to conclude that Miranda had been tortured and killed inside the house before his body was dumped in the sea.

A few days later Storr's car, a red Volvo 240 with British number plates, was discovered abandoned at a railway station near Kodling, close to the German border. Storr and Blythin were then added to Interpol's most wanted list leading to the pair being dubbed the 'twenty-first-century Bonnie and Clyde' in the press.

It was around this time that I first began receiving anonymous tip-offs claiming to know Storr's location. I followed these up with phone calls and other inquiries but, although in one case a woman matching her description had been seen at the hotel I had been directed to, she had long gone by the time I made contact. She and Blythin had, it seemed, vanished into thin air.

It turned out that Blythin, originally from Chester, had a vast network of underworld contacts throughout Norway, the Netherlands, Belgium and France as well as Spain. From that moment on he and Storr used that same network to keep one step ahead of the police.

For a few months it worked like a dream but in July 2002 Storr was surrounded by armed police acting on a tip-off as she tried to board a flight at Schiphol airport, Amsterdam, using a fake Spanish passport. Blythin was nowhere to be seen.

Storr was charged with Miranda's murder and remanded in custody. However, in October 2003, she was suddenly released.

Henrik Madsen, a journalist on *Århus Stiftstidende*, the newspaper that covers the village where Miranda's body was found, told me that Storr had to be freed, even though she was charged with murder.

'The Danish police wanted to try Storr and Blythin together, but he had disappeared. You can't keep people in custody for ever, and time went on and on. The Danish legal system says the police must give a judge good reasons to keep holding someone. They simply ran out of arguments.'

Instead of waiting for the court to order her release, the Danish police made a special request for her to be allowed to go on the grounds that they had obtained all the information they needed from her. It was, of course, a ploy aimed at getting Storr to lead them to Blythin. He was known to have visited Britain several times since going on the run, despite having had his name added to Scotland Yard's Ten Most Wanted list.

Storr returned to London and moved into a dingy flat in Newington Green Road, Islington, with a new boyfriend.

Six weeks later he returned home one evening to find the place unusually quiet. 'I unlocked the door and called out to Bev. I thought it was strange because the lights were off and she always leaves them on. I saw her lying face down on the floor and I noticed a bucket next to her head with sick in it. I tapped her on the shoulder and tried to find a pulse. Her legs were swollen and there was no colour. I called for an ambulance. I went to the sitting room and then I noticed the pills on the table.'

The first police officers to arrive on the scene found Storr dressed in a white towelling robe surrounded by bottles of antidepressants and assumed her death was just a regular, tragic suicide. It was only when details of her background emerged that police launched a more thorough investigation, fearing that she might have been silenced by underworld enemies. She was just forty-three years old.

Although Storr was being treated for depression shortly before her death, it was not clear how many – if any – of her pills she had taken. The Danish authorities, who were believed to have been keeping Storr under surveillance, were concerned that her medication may have been tampered with, or she could have been forced to take an overdose to stop her from talking.

Although Blythin was a potential suspect, Storr's criminal record and high-level connections with organised crime meant that many other people could have been just as keen to kill her.

An inquest was opened at the time of her death but adjourned while detectives examined whether she had been coerced into an overdose. It wasn't until April 2007 that St Pancras coroner Dr Andrew Reid ended all speculation by announcing that Storr had taken her own life.

'I am satisfied that Beverley Storr consumed alcohol and Dothiepin in circumstances where she was possibly going to be found by her friend or partner when he returned,' he said. 'Unfortunately, he returned late in the day and it's not clear when she took the pills. It's not clear whether it was a cry for help or done with the intention of ending her own life. There were no suspicious circumstances although she had been involved in an incident in Denmark. There's no reason to link the two events.'

Dr Reid returned an open verdict because he could not decide if her overdose was a cry for help or intentional. She died after ingesting a concoction of pills prescribed for depression and at least one bottle of vodka. No suicide note was found.

In the introduction to *Gangland Britain*, my first foray into the UK's underworld published back in 1995, I apologised to anyone who might have had issues with the book's overly male bias explaining that: 'despite occasional media interest in girl gangs and the fact that there have been female-run mafia and triad syndicates, most crime is male-dominated and women are most often relegated to the role of accessory.'

This is no longer the case.

Although women are statistically far less likely to be involved in crime than men, that gap is narrowing rapidly. Ministry of Justice figures from 2009 showed that annual arrests of teenage girls and women had reached record levels with more than 250,000 detained by the police.

Youth Justice Board figures show that the number of personal violent attacks by girls dealt with by youth offending teams rose by 48 per cent from 10,412 in 2003 to 15,413 by 2008. They also show sharp increases in the number of public order offences, up 37 per cent to 5,852, and racially aggravated crimes, up 113 per cent to 758, committed by girls under eighteen over the same period.

A report by the Institute of Criminal Policy Research suggested that the increase was due to women being more willing to commit and admit offences because society had changed its expectations about their behaviour.

Although this may be more apparent within the 'ladette' and binge-drinking culture and the anti-social behaviour associated with it, women are also increasingly involved in crime at a far more serious level.

Mother of two Karen Stott ran a charity called The Fair Project, which toured schools teaching children about the dangers of drugs, racism and gangs. Stott knew her subject intimately because when she wasn't working for the charity, she was busy running a twenty-four-hour cocaine operation. As if that were not hypocritical enough, Stott also employed her two sons, Khan and Vidal, to help make deliveries.

Their main clients were clubbers in London's West End. Drugs were available around the clock and the service was so slick it was compared to a pizza delivery company.

All customers would have to do is call Karen Stott's mobile phone and within about half an hour, one of the three would arrive at their home or a rendezvous spot and hand over the drugs in return for cash. Customers would pay fifty pounds for a gram but Stott demanded a minimum order of two grams for each call-out.

Stott enjoyed a glamorous lifestyle with the thousands she made from her drug empire, driving a £30,000 Mercedes SLK convertible and buying designer accessories including a Louis Vuitton handbag and a Gucci watch. She took frequent holidays to exotic destinations including Egypt and the Caribbean.

She soon attracted the attention of the police who launched an undercover operation during which officers brought drugs from the family to secure evidence against them. On one occasion Stott went into a school to give a talk on the dangers of drugs the day after she had unknowingly supplied cocaine to an undercover police officer.

Despite her wealth Karen paid her sons only minimally for their assistance. After his arrest Khan Stott, who was technically homeless, told officers he made £1,800 during a fortnight in August while his mother was in Barbados and that he only helped her to help pay off his girlfriend's £8,000 debts.

Vidal Stott who worked as a gym instructor told officers he would take over from his mother at night and when she was on holiday. He drove to do a deal at 1 a.m. with his eight-month-old daughter in the back seat.

As well as becoming more active in the drug business, women operating at this level of criminality are increasingly getting involved in other areas, and seldom shy away from the violence that seems to go hand in hand with the underworld. In some cases they can be even more ruthless than the men.

When Constance Howarth was arrested at gunpoint in May 1997 and three Mac-10 Ingram sub-machine guns capable of firing 1,100 rounds per minute were found in the boot of her car, she immediately played the 'dumb blonde' card.

'I'm just a girl,' she told the officers. 'I don't know anything about guns. I was just running an errand for a boyfriend. He's now disappeared – he is a bit of a rat, the situation he has got me into.'

In reality Constance Howarth had spent almost her entire adult life rubbing shoulders with some of Britain's most notorious criminals. Among her closest associates were Glasgow Mr Big Paul Ferris, London-based old-time godfather Henry Suttee and Salford underworld legend Paul Massey.

It was Ferris who had bought the guns, nicknamed 'Big Macs', from a dealer in Islington and asked Howarth to drive them north as a favour. He got seven years for the haul while Howarth got five, reduced to three on appeal.

After her release from prison Howarth briefly got into trouble again when she was accused of attempting to nobble a jury in a murder trial, but she soon settled down and took a job at PMS, the Salford company founded by notorious villain Paul Massey. At the time Massey was serving fourteen years for a gangland stabbing, so the company was being run by his friend Bobby Spiers, a man with a string of convictions stretching back to his youth.

Soon after Howarth started working for the company, Spiers had a falling out with an up-and-coming business rival named David Totton. He and Totton had both been queuing up to get into the same Manchester nightclub. Spiers was allowed in but Totton was refused. He then told the bouncers that he was with Spiers, expecting his fellow security firm director to show him a degree of respect. Instead Spiers came out of the club, took one look at Totton and announced that he had never seen him before in his life.

To add insult to injury, Totton then began drinking at Spiers' local pub, the Brass Handles on Salford's Langworthy Estate. Spiers decided that Totton had to be dealt with but was unable to take action directly because he feared Totton's popularity would lead to a backlash against him.

Instead Spiers hired the boss of another security outfit, IMAC, to carry out the hit. IMAC was run by Ian McLeod, head of Moss Side's infamous Dodington gang. No stranger to violent crime, he had served a ten-year prison term for drug dealing and was once dubbed the 'leader of the pack' by a judge during his gang's war with the rival Gooch Close mob. Spiers offered McLeod £10,000 to take care of his problem. McLeod readily agreed.

He in turn recruited two young members of his gang, Richard

Austin, nineteen and Carlton Alveranga, twenty, both from Moss Side, to carry out the actual hit which it was decided would take place at the Brass Handles itself.

Neither of the would-be hitmen had any idea what Totton looked like and, being from outside the area, neither knew the layout of the pub. This was where Constance Howarth came in.

Spiers knew that Howarth was also a regular at the pub and asked her to help out by providing confirmation that Totton was inside on the day of the hit and guiding the two young gunmen to their target. Howarth, he explained, was ideal for the job because no one there would ever suspect her of being involved. Like McLeod before her, she eagerly joined the plot.

Regulars at the packed pub were watching a live soccer match on TV – Manchester United vs Newcastle – and thought she was sending harmless texts and gossiping on her mobile phone – but in fact she was giving deadly details to the hit team outside as to where their target was sitting.

On Sunday 12 March 2006 McLeod, Austin and Alveranga arrived outside the Brass Handles in a Ford Mondeo just after 2 p.m. In the minutes that followed there were a flurry of phone calls and text messages between McLeod and Howarth who was already inside the pub.

At around 2.20 p.m. Austin and Alveranga got out of the Mondeo on Highfield Road. A witness told the police that the two men appeared reluctant and were being forced to get out of the car. They then made their way over the grassed area in front of the Brass Handles and into the vault of the pub.

As Austin and Alveranga came though the door, their faces partially covered, Howarth calmly nodded towards Totton who was sitting in a corner watching the game with friends, then went to the Ladies. As all hell broke loose in the main bar, she refreshed her lipstick.

The two men walked over to Totton and fired six shots at him, hitting him in the face and chest. Fellow regular Aaron Travers, twenty-seven, attempted to intervene and suffered gunshot wounds to his chest.

But during the shooting, Alveranga's gun suddenly misfired and Travers and others took the opportunity to try to overpower him. There was a brief struggle during which Alveranga's gun was fired towards the floor. The weapon was then used to shoot both Austin and Alveranga who ran out clutching bullet wounds to their chests but collapsed on a grass croft outside.

McLeod's dark-coloured Mondeo was waiting with its doors open when the pair ran outside. McLeod shouted 'Is he dead?' before running over to Austin to check his body. He then screeched off in his car while an angry mob from the pub appeared and began kicking and punching the two men as they lay dying on the ground. In the meantime Howarth slipped away out of a back door unnoticed.

Totton and Travers were taken to Hope Hospital with gunshot wounds but miraculously both survived. They refused to assist the police with their inquiries and made no statements about what had happened to them.

Immediately after the shooting the shutters were pulled down inside the Brass Handles and CCTV from inside the pub was wiped before police could get hold of it. Despite the pub being busy due to the football match, no one inside admitted to having witnessed the killings.

Much of this is believed to be due to the man who took Alveranga's gun and used it to shoot both him and Austin. He was, according to sources close to those involved, a senior member of the Gooch Close gang who just happened to be in the pub at the time. He is believed to have made sure that everyone who witnessed the events of that Sunday afternoon – Totton and Travers included – knew exactly what would happen to them if they ever spoke about what they saw. Police are said to know the man's identity but have no evidence against him. It is highly unlikely that he will ever be convicted.

Initially faced with a wall of silence, police only began to make progress when witnesses outside the pub helped identify McLeod as the man who had sent the hitmen inside. By tracing all mobile phone calls made and received in the area, detectives were soon able to build up a vivid picture of what had taken place. They found that more than forty calls had been made between the mobile phones of McLeod and Howarth in the time leading up to the hit.

During the month-long trial at Preston Crown Court in March 2007, Howarth claimed she did not know Totton and said she had no idea the shootings were going to happen but said she had got two phone calls saying: 'Is this trouble down to you – have you set them up?' She admitted lying to police by saying she had not made any phone calls but said: 'If you know Manchester and Salford you can't talk to the police. It's like grassing somebody up – you don't do it even though they threatened me – you just can't go to the police. Your life is not worth living if you go to the police.'

Austin's mother Bridget told how she tried in vain to get her son out of Moss Side, before he became a hitman. 'My son was aware of the gangs in Moss Side and that it was just a way of life,' she said in a statement. Bridget desperately wanted Richard and the rest of her family to move away from Moss Side because she could see how bad the area was. 'I moved to Wythenshawe, but Richard continued to visit his father and friends in Moss Side. I worried every time Richard would not come home as he would probably be in Moss Side. I had no idea who he was with. I am sometimes angry that he allowed himself to get himself in that situation.'

McLeod, forty-five, was jailed for life with a minimum term of twenty-one years while Constance Howarth was given life with a minimum term of twenty years.

Bobby Spiers believed he had the perfect alibi. He was at the football match being watched by those in the pub at the time. But officers linked him to the crime through his mobile phone. The logs confirmed that he had been in regular contact with McLeod and Howarth the whole time. He fled to Spain, but was extradited and sentenced to life with a minimum term of twenty-three years.

12
WAREZ

'By conservative estimates, more than 200 million people around the world download music, movies, television shows, video games and other electronic entertainment. Music alone accounts for more than a billion downloads a week. Yet most people who share files have no idea where they come from. They have no idea there's an entire world, a massive global infrastructure, that exists solely to acquire and disseminate new content. At the highest level of this machine is a place where virtually all these files that spread all around the world originate. It is a place where deals are struck, where identities and access are jealously guarded and where an elite group of technocrats silently works the controls. Those of us who haunt this place have a name for it. We call it "The Scene".'

So begins the very first episode of an innovative web-based drama series that rapidly achieved cult status by providing a startling, fictional glimpse into the workings of a true-life, secretive, organised international criminal network like no other. Members of The Scene utilise some of the most sophisticated technology on the planet, trade in a commodity worth thousands of millions of pounds and collaborate closely for weeks or months at a time, yet the vast majority of those involved, even those in the same country, have never met and have no idea of each other's true identities.

But what makes most of the men and women of what is more properly known as the 'warez scene' – a corruption of the word 'software' and pronounced 'wares' – really stand out from the crowd is that, unlike those involved in all other forms of organised crime, they are not in it for the money. 'These groups exist solely to engage in piracy and compete with each other to be the first to place a newly pirated work on the Internet,' a spokesman for the

Serious Organised Crime Agency told me. 'They want the kudos, they want the bragging rights. Getting their releases online before anyone else is the only thing they really care about.'

Each individual member of a warez group has a specialist role. At the top of the hierarchy are the 'suppliers'. Their role is to obtain copyrighted software, video games, DVD movies and MP3 music files as soon as they become available. Once obtained, the material is passed on to 'crackers' – gifted programmers who are able to compress large files or remove copy protection. The 'cracked' program is then put back together and tested for bugs before being passed on to a 'courier' who handles final distribution.

The journey from the warez scene to the general public via the World Wide Web begins with one of the thirty or so 'topsites' – highly secretive, underground computer servers where some 90 per cent of pirated and unlicensed material originates. According to law enforcement authorities the websites where the films are posted are invitation-only affairs that operate in secluded online zones known as the 'darknet'.

Utilising state-of-the-art technology, topsites have massive storage capacity and ultra-fast connection that make them capable of transferring the contents of an entire DVD in less than a minute. Topsites are the highest point in the distribution pyramid and the speed with which new files can reach ground level is astonishing.

Within minutes of a new file appearing on a topsite couriers will begin copying and redistributing the file on to as many other servers as possible. One file becomes ten, ten become one hundred, one hundred becomes a thousand and so on. Within the space of seventy-two hours literally millions of copies of the most popular files will have filtered their way down to the publically accessible peer-to-peer (P2P) file sharing sites like Limewire and Kazza.

A seminal article in *Wired* magazine on the warez scene explained just what this means for the average person: 'It's a commonly held belief that P2P is about sharing files. It's an appealing, democratic notion: consumers rip the movies and music they buy and post them online. But that's not quite how it works. In reality, the number of files on the Net ripped from store-bought CDs, DVDs, and videogames is statistically negligible. People don't share what they buy; they share what is already being shared.'

The scale of this 'sharing' is mind-boggling. One single machine taken during a piracy raid contained more than 65,000 individual pirated titles. In the three years prior to being broken up, one warez group, DrinkOrDie is estimated to have pirated more than $50 million worth of movies, software and music. Members of the groups admitted that there were simply not enough hours in the day for them to look at or use even a tiny fraction of the material they had stolen. While this material starts out only being accessible to each group's inner circle, the work done by the couriers means the files find their way to the Internet where they can be found by anyone capable of typing the name of a band or film into a search engine.

With warez groups competing to be first past the post, the ultimate goal of all those on the scene is to have a zero-day release – one that hits the Internet before the product is commercially available. One of the most famous incidents of this kind occurred when DrinkOrDie – whose key members were based in the UK – made copies of Windows 95 available two weeks before the software was officially released by Microsoft.

Software piracy has been around almost as long as the personal computer: in 1976 William Henry Gates, the then twenty-one-year-old general partner of the fledgling company 'Micro-Soft' wrote an open letter in the *Homebrew Computing Newsletter* complaining that the fruits of his labours were routinely being stolen. 'As the majority of hobbyists must be aware, most of you steal your software. Hardware must be paid for, but software is something to share. Who cares if the people who worked on it get paid . . .'

Virtually every high-end business software package, some of which can cost hundreds or even thousands of pounds to purchase legitimately, has been cracked and uploaded to the Internet where anyone can download it for nothing. If the software cannot be obtained through the usual sources, it will often be purchased using stolen credit card numbers – tens of thousands of which are traded across the darknet every day – so that no one in the group is left out of pocket. Though the value of these losses from business software piracy runs into tens of millions of pounds, it has been the multi-billion pound profits generated by the seemingly unstoppable rise of the DVD film – now accounting for two thirds of Hollywood's total income – that has led to the warez scene being thoroughly infiltrated by figures from more traditional forms of organised crime.

For a long time no one in the warez scene cared about money. There was an unwritten rule that no one involved would ever sell any of the programs or other forms of entertainment they had acquired for money. But ultimately everyone has their price.

In the drama series *The Scene* a fictional warez group called CPX acquires early copies of Hollywood blockbusters from a variety of sources and competes with other groups to release them on the Internet first. The main story arc charts one member of the group as he crosses a huge taboo by selling a film to a group of DVD pirates based in Asia known as 'silver sellers' after finding himself deep in debt. Within hours, and crucially before CPX has even managed to upload the file, bootleg copies of the film are available on DVD throughout the streets of Singapore, Hong Kong and beyond. Although the story is fiction, it is squarely grounded in reality.

In the summer of 2009, the science fiction alien film *District 9* was released at the cinema in the United States. Made for just $30 million – a paltry amount compared to most modern-day action flicks – the film would go on to gross almost $120 million at the US box office alone, with a further $15 million earned in the UK. Although a huge success there is no doubt the film could have earned even more but for the existence of the warez scene.

District 9 first appeared in theatres in the USA on 14 August 2009. Two days later a warez group called Camelot released a 'CAM' copy of the film onto the Internet. For anyone living in the UK it meant that not only would they not have to pay to see the film, they could also see it more than a month ahead of its official UK release. For anyone choosing to download Camelot's offering the experience might not have been quite what the filmmakers had envisioned. A CAM version of a film is the lowest tech version available. Quite literally someone will sit in a cinema with a camcorder and record the movie from their seat. The sound quality can often be terrible and if the person doing the filming is forced to move to another part of the cinema, the picture can jerk around or cut out completely.

Two days later another warez group, Spool, released their own version of the film on the Internet. An information file attached to the file said the following: 'Enjoy this true homemade Cam! We made a mistake of giving this to a friend a day ago, now he has sold this to Asia silver sellers. Shame on him. Hence Camelot's cam.'

Although selling films to piracy gangs is a lucrative business, the big money is not made online but in the real world. Asia is piracy central and the vast majority of the world's pirated discs are replicated there, usually at the behest of major organised-crime groups who can afford to spend more than $1 million on a replication machine.

The disks themselves are sold at markets and on the streets through a network of illegal immigrants that stretches right across the world. A new film can be out in a lookalike DVD box within a day of the gang receiving the Internet file. And with such films more popular than ever, the need to recruit new people to help sell the product is on the rise.

'It used to be that everybody could always find a job working in a restaurant,' says Bobby, a case worker for the immigration service specialising in the rights of those smuggled into the country illegally. 'But in recent years there has been a massive crackdown on people being employed illegally. A restaurant faces fines of ten thousand pounds for each illegal they are found to have on their staff. No one can take the risk any more so all the restaurants have had to let their illegals go.

'The people who got sacked from their jobs, they still had to live, they still needed money to buy food. More importantly, they still needed money to pay back their debts to the snakeheads. The amounts are huge and because they earn so little, the debt never seems to go away. But the payments are still due every week whether you are working or not.'

In desperation, increasing numbers of illegal immigrants from China and Vietnam have begun selling counterfeit DVDs, products supplied by the bottom end of the chain that is fed directly by the warez scene. Working alone and often carrying dozens of DVDs potentially worth hundreds of pounds, such sellers are incredibly vulnerable. Robberies and assaults are common. Sometimes the results are even more tragic.

Twenty-nine-year-old Xiao Mei Guo sold pirated DVDs outside various tube stations in London to pay back the gang that had smuggled her into the UK during an epic four-month journey that took her halfway around the world. She travelled at night on foot or cramped in the back of a stifling lorry during the heat of the day.

Xiao arrived in London with her husband Jin in August 2006. They set up home in Cannon Street Road, Whitechapel, in a house with other Chinese immigrants. What little extra money she had left at the end of each week she sent back to China for the benefit of the two sons they had left behind. Jin was jailed after being convicted of hawking and Xiao was having to work much harder to repay the money they both owed. He was still in prison in August 2007 when Derek Brown approached Xiao and offered to buy a large batch of DVDs from her. There was, however, one condition. Brown said he had been ripped off in the past and wanted to make sure the films worked. She would have to go to his flat so he could check the quality of each film in turn.

What Xiao didn't know is that Brown, a portly middle-aged man from Preston, was a convicted rapist who had bragged to friends that he wanted to become known as a top serial killer. Brown borrowed Nigel Cawthorne's *Killers: The Most Barbaric Murderers of Our Time* from his local library three weeks before he began his murder spree. He pored over pages of information on killers like Peter Sutcliffe, the Yorkshire Ripper, who murdered thirteen women between 1975 and 1980, and Dennis Nilsen, who killed fifteen men and boys in a five-year stint in north London.

Brown is thought to have deliberately chosen Whitechapel as his hunting ground to emulate Jack the Ripper, who claimed five prostitute victims there in 1888.

Before heading to London Brown, a newspaper delivery driver, bragged to a close friend the press would soon be 'hounding' her for information about him. On the last occasion he saw her he made the chilling boast: 'You will hear of me.' He chose Xiao as his first victim because he believed no one would miss her.

CCTV captured Brown chatting with Xiao on the morning of her disappearance on 29 August 2007 at Whitechapel underground station, before both headed for the tube. She was last in touch with friends when she sent a text message from Rotherhithe station saying she was to show a customer some DVDs before he bought them.

Kola Owolabi, who lived below Brown in Laburnam Court, Rotherhithe, heard a woman's cries from the flat as he chatted to a friend on the day Xiao disappeared. 'It was female. It sounded like a young voice. I didn't hear any words. There was a scream, a thud, then silence.'

Three weeks later, Brown killed Michelle Barrett, mother to a six-year-old boy and a drug addict who scratched a living by working on the streets to fund her crack addiction.

Several sex worker colleagues interviewed after Barrett vanished knew Brown as a client and had been to his flat. They also revealed he had hired Miss Barrett several times in the past. Barrett spent the weekend before she disappeared in a drugs and sex binge with a senior member of the Australian Hells Angels, who was in London for a funeral.

On 18 September 2007, after going out to work in Commercial Street, Michelle Barrett never returned to the flat in Boxley Street she shared with a friend. Brown, who had been caught on CCTV loitering in Whitechapel that day, had picked her up and taken her back to his flat, this time using his company van, before killing her.

The murder inquiry began when Ms Guo was reported missing and police found the crucial CCTV footage of her at the station. Brown was arrested on 6 October 2007 after he walked in to a local Londis shop where officers were making routine inquiries and showing pictures of him. Officers watched him leave before stopping him outside. Forensic teams moved in to his two-bed flat two days after he was arrested and found every room was spotted and smeared with the blood of both women.

Xiao's blood was found near the front door, suggesting she may have tried to escape from the flat before she was dragged back inside. There had been attempts to clean up the flat. Blood was found on a packet of scourers in a cupboard, on a pair of industrial gloves and there were drip marks and spots on the hallway wall and carpet. Brown had torn out bloodstained carpet and tried to give furniture away to neighbours.

It is believed Brown hacked up the two women, wrapped them up and made repeated trips to the nearby River Thames to throw the pieces into the water. The large rucksack he was seen with in the Whitechapel CCTV has never been found and dumbbell weights are also missing from the flat. Police believe he may have filled the rucksack with body parts and thrown it into the river using the weights to make sure the bag went to the bottom.

Xiao may have been wary of Brown but she was under enormous pressure. At first glance, DVD-selling looks like an easy job. The illegals buy the DVDs for £1.75 a disk and sell them on for £3. But it isn't that simple. What starts off as a simple business transaction soon develops into something far more sinister. There are strict sales targets and punishments for those who fail to meet them, including threats to family members back home. Getting away from the gangs once you have fallen into their web is almost impossible.

The British–Chinese writer Hsiao-Hung Pai decided to go undercover among Britain's 200,000 undocumented Chinese workers for her book *Chinese Whispers*. She found that many people do not survive the journey here. Some are abandoned on freezing mountaintops crossing into Europe; others suffocate in lorries. In the book she tells the story of an ordinary Chinese man called Ah-Hua. He started selling ten DVDs a day for a notorious gang known as the Dong Bi, which operates all over Britain.

But soon they were making impossible demands on him. When he couldn't take the pressure any more, Ah-Hua told them he wanted out. Pai explains: 'That night, five Dong Bi gang members pushed their way into his flat. They beat him up until he lay helpless on the floor. Then they dragged him out of the flat, blindfolded him, and drove off into the night.'

He was held captive for three weeks. His captors told him that they had located his family in Fuqing by going through his mobile phone. They would release him if he could pressure his family to come up with £12,000 to 'buy' his freedom. Within a week, his wife had borrowed the money at sky-high rates of interest. Today he works in Chinatown as a kitchen porter, paying off the price of his freedom and regretting the day he ever got involved.

Meanwhile the part of the warez scene that ultimately supplies the raw material for the films that the likes of Ah-Hua sell continues to go from strength to strength. Because of the links to the online world and the high levels of technical skill of some of those involved, the scene sits on the edge of the far larger cybercrime community.

Online theft currently costs $1 trillion a year and the number of attacks is rising sharply as many people do not know how to protect themselves. Traditional cybercrime – committing fraud of theft by stealing somebody's identity, their credit card details and other data – is growing the fastest. Rather than geeky individuals working from their basements, much of the work is carried out by large, well-organised gangs, often led by highly intelligent professionals. In one recent case a lawyer who saw great potential in cybercrime assembled a gang of around 300 people, many with a high level of technical skill, each with a specialised role.

What is increasingly apparent, however, is despite the enormous level of skill that many of those involved in this kind of criminality often possess, the greatest threat to an individual's passwords, identity and private information is one which does not require a computer at all. Just a friendly face.

13

CYBERCRIME

The woman with the cut-glass accent on the other end of the phone line turns the charm up to eleven as she waxes lyrical about how much she enjoyed my last book. She has called to commission me to write an article for the glossy upmarket magazine that she edits and suggests we discuss the matter further over dinner at a plush Mayfair restaurant. I accept eagerly, not because I need the work, not even for the chance of a slap-up meal, but because I can't resist the opportunity to meet the slick and accomplished confidence trickster once described as: 'London's most dangerous woman' face to face.

Exotic, beautiful and always immaculately dressed, Farah Damji first rose to prominence in the latter half of 2003 when details of her affairs with two married men – one a best-selling travel writer, the other a high-profile newspaper journalist – became public. Both relationships ended acrimoniously and soon afterwards an anonymous character called 'Ms Equaliser' sent emails containing detailed accounts of the affairs to the men's wives and hundreds of prominent figures in the British media.

The story soon found its way to an even wider audience when Damji, the daughter of a multimillionaire property developer, wrote a lengthy article for the *Daily Mail* giving her side in an ill-fated attempt to elicit sympathy. But within a matter of days, a rather different picture of the Ugandan-born Indian socialite had emerged.

A decade earlier Damji had been rubbing shoulders with the New York elite, running four art galleries in Manhattan that showed the works of some of the city's most sought-after painters and sculptors. Her shows drew an exclusive crowd – Edward

Albee, leading fashion designer Carolina Herrera, ABC news anchor Peter Jennings and photographer Kelly Klein, former wife of designer Calvin. When the galleries found themselves in financial difficulty, Damji could have chosen to go to her wealthy father for help. Instead she chose fraud and identity theft.

Sent a cheque for $38, she altered it to $38,000 and paid it into her account. A few weeks later she sold a painting to a collector who immediately sent her a cheque for $12,000. When Damji complained that the cheque had not arrived the collector promptly sent another. Damji then cashed them both. Unable to pay her landlord the rent on her fancy mid-town apartment she handed him a cheque she had received for $20, which she had altered to $20,000. The cheque bounced, of course, so the landlord obtained an eviction order and seized her belongings. Damji then forged the signature of the judge assigned to the case and amended the order so that she could get her belongings back.

Desperate for a new home, Damji then began writing cheques from a closed bank account and hiding from past creditors behind a variety of aliases. When the authorities finally caught up with her she pleaded guilty in Manhattan Supreme Court to five felony counts of grand larceny, possession of forged instruments and tampering with official records. She was sentenced to six months incarceration and served part of her time at the notorious Rikers Island prison.

After her release she opened yet another gallery in the Hamptons district of New York using a fraudulent lease. When an arrest warrant was issued she promptly vanished. During that time she is believed to have befriended the members of several leading families from the New York mafia, consorted with top underworld figures, worked for a drug dealer and run a high-class escort agency. In between she found time to have two children by different fathers and allegedly 'terrorised' several ex-lovers with a *Fatal Attraction*-like intensity.

In 2002 she resurfaced in England having reinvented herself as a journalist and social commentator. She began writing for the

Observer, the *New Statesman* and had a regular column in the *Birmingham Post*. Next she launched *Indobrit*, a quarterly magazine for British Asians that later changed its name to *Another Generation*. The third issue of the magazine had just been published when the scandal about the affairs, followed by the revelations about Damji's criminal past, finally emerged.

Damji brushed it off, dismissing it as ancient history. But by the time the magazine reached its fourth issue, dark rumours had begun to circulate that the beguiling editor-in-chief's predilection for financial shenanigans had followed her across the Atlantic.

'When you first meet her, she comes across as incredibly cultured, businesslike and totally believable,' one of Damji's former associates, who asked not to be named, told me a few days before I was due to meet with her. 'But it's all a sham. It's smoke and mirrors. She's a first-class confidence trickster. You can't believe anything she says. You can't trust anything she does. She reinvents herself all the time. She's dangerous. She doesn't do anything without having some or other scheme in place. You have to watch her like a hawk. And for God's sake, whatever you do, don't let her get hold of your credit card.'

I arrive at the restaurant on the edge of London's Berkeley Square a few minutes early but Damji is already at the table waiting for me. She is wearing a low-cut, short summer dress which shows off her smooth, toned legs, a neat navy blazer and low-heeled shoes. Her luxuriously thick and impossibly shiny dark hair hangs around her shoulders like an expensive wrap. Her eyes are a rich, deep chocolate brown and dance and sparkle with delight as she speaks. When she smiles her entire face seems to glow. There is something undeniably appealing and seductive about her.

The conversation flows as easily as the wine and we prattle on about nothing in particular. She name drops a lot, asking if I know this person or that person before giving me her opinion of them or some juicy titbit of gossip. She tells me about her homes – a swish apartment in trendy Chelsea, a detached home in Hampshire and a further property in New York.

During the main course we talk about my work and about the article she wants me to write for her. During dessert we discuss the controversy surrounding her affairs with the two men, one of whom I happen to know. We skirt over her experiences as a convict in America but she tells me, 'One day I'll write a book about it all.'

When the bill arrives I hesitate momentarily, unsure of what to do. Even though she has invited me to dinner I feel I should at least offer to pay, but at the same time I feel far safer with my credit card hidden deep inside my wallet. Only a second or two passes before Damji herself snatches the bill and reaches for her designer handbag. She reaches into her purse and retrieves a gold credit card, placing it down on the silver dish and covering it with the bill before I can make out the name. The waitress returns a moment later with a slip for her to sign – this was just before the introduction of chip and pin – which she does with a flourish.

I promise to deliver my copy to the magazine in the next few days. Damji promises to write my cheque out the moment she receives my contribution. 'We can do a direct swap, money for copy,' she laughs. She grips my arm as we kiss cheeks to say goodbye.

I email her my article a few days later. 'It's fantastic. I'm writing the cheque right now,' she tells me when I call to confirm she has received the piece. 'I'm literally writing it out as we speak and it will go in the post today.'

The money never arrived, of course. It soon turned out that I had got off lightly.

'I first met Farah when I replied to an advert looking for someone to layout her magazine,' says designer and cartographer David Wenk. 'I called her up and asked if I could come by her office. She told me the BBC were about to interview her there and that it would be better if she could come to my house.

'She turned up in a limo a few hours later with a computer that I was to use to layout the magazine.' Wenk had initially been told that only a few pages needed work. It soon emerged that the entire magazine needed to be done. 'She told me it was an emergency because her previous designer had left her in the lurch. Over the course of the next week I worked more than 105 hours to get it finished. She virtually moved into my flat over that time. When the magazine was done I billed her for £3900. She never paid.

'During the time we were working, she had bought in loads of takeaways to help keep me going. It seemed pretty decent at the time. It was only later that I found out she'd charged it all to one of my credit cards. She took my gold card and used it to wine and dine other members of her staff at Selfridges and then used the change to buy a pair of Jimmy Choos. She had my name, my card and my address. She could do whatever she wanted.'

Wenk was not alone. Dozens of other writers, photographers and contributors were either not paid for their contributions to the magazine or given cheques that ultimately bounced. Others suffered even more.

Damji stole a credit card from her children's nanny and used it on sixty separate occasions during a day-long, £4,000 shopping spree in Birmingham. Too exhausted to head home afterwards, she used the card one final time to book herself a room at the Crowne Plaza Hotel. Back in London Damji tried to use the card again in Peter Jones but was arrested when staff became suspicious. During her police interview, Damji claimed she had simply been trying to collect air miles and blamed her au pair for the misunderstanding.

Released on bail, she soon stole a credit card belonging to Darshika Mahavir, a marketing assistant who had gone to Damji's house after being invited to make a sales pitch. Damji bought more than £1,000 worth of clothes from Harvey Nichols before being arrested again and bailed again.

Less than a month later Damji took a card from publicist Rakhi Gokani who had been organising a photo shoot for the magazine. Gokani only discovered her card was missing from her handbag after it had been used thirty-four times.

Nothing in Farah Damji's life was quite what it seemed. Although she travelled everywhere by limousine this was because she had obtained the car account number of a major television company and used their vehicles. In the space of a few months she clocked up rides worth almost £20,000.

Although she remained a regular at top social functions, she was struggling to hide a growing addiction to cocaine and an increasing reliance on alcohol and prozac, all of which was pushing her deeper and deeper into debt. 'I was probably spending £800 a week on cocaine,' Damji confessed later. 'I was going through a really hard time and I was just taking more and more. Eventually I couldn't operate without it.'

In January 2005 Damji phoned upscale jewellers Boodle and Dunthorne posing as the assistant of the *Daily Mail*'s showbiz correspondent and asked if she could have the use of two diamond and platinum rings worth more than £10,000. The rings were never seen again.

With the net fast closing in, Damji's schemes became ever more elaborate. Due to stand trial on theft charges, Damji phoned the main prosecution witness against her and posed as an official from the Crown Prosecution Service. She explained that because of a change of plea, he would no longer be required to attend the case. The following week Damji turned up at the court but the witness against her did not, leaving the judge no option but to postpone the hearing.

Damji then got hold of the Crown barrister's home phone number from his chambers by claiming to be from the CPS. She told him a record of her previous convictions was 'unreliable', her solicitors were 'very good and therefore, she was likely to win'. She advised that he dropped the case. She also called the CPS pretending to be a secretary to the then Home Secretary David Blunkett, and said it was not in the public interest to go ahead with the trial.

When all this failed Damji simply failed to turn up at her pre-trial hearing, causing her mother to lose the £10,000 security deposit she had lodged with the court. Damji went on the run with a credit card stolen from freelance journalist Ambarina Hasan. Damji used the card to open a savings account and obtain a loan of £18,000. She also stole two credit cards and a driving licence belonging to her osteopath 'friend' Nazia Soonasara, who began receiving letters from the Nationwide Building Society and the Carphone Warehouse thanking her for opening accounts.

Damji was finally arrested on 14 May 2005 after tracker dogs found her hiding in her garden in Hampshire. Initially she pretended she was Hasan – and even had documents to prove it – but her real identity soon emerged.

With her total thefts now exceeding £50,000, bail was finally refused and Damji was remanded in Holloway before being found guilty of six counts of theft, eleven counts of obtaining property or services by deception, two counts of perverting the course of justice and asking for a further twenty-five offences to be taken into consideration. She was sentenced to three and a half years. All went quiet on the Damji front for the next few months until, in July 2006, she found herself back in the headlines. She had been transferred from Holloway to Downview Prison in Surrey where she signed up for an Open University sociology degree. Given temporary leave to attend a tutorial, Damji never returned.

Never one to do anything by halves, the following day Damji became the first ever fugitive to write a blog about life on the run. 'Seems I am the cause for great consternation because I have apparently "absconded",' she wrote on her MySpace page. The following day in an entry entitled 'Sea Air' she wrote of how much she was enjoying life outside prison walls. 'It's so peaceful; the sound of seagulls replacing the screaming police sirens streaming up and down King's Road. Blue skies, sea air. Some of the prison pallor is leaving me; I'm starting to feel awake again. Gonna go for a long walk this morning.'

Her freedom ended five days later when a national newspaper tipped off police as to her whereabouts, which they had discovered with the help of her blog. Damji served the rest of her sentence without incident, spending her time studying and working on her autobiography, a book she finally completed soon after her release.

The former associate continued: 'I have known Farah for about three years. We were very close. She abused the trust of my friends, not just one or two but several. And then she tried to do the same thing with me. That was incredibly upsetting. It wasn't a complete surprise because I knew what sort of person she was but still, I didn't expect her to treat me that way.

'I enjoyed her company. She is a very intelligent and charming woman but there is no doubt that there is something wrong with her.'

Farah Damji is no master criminal and her illicit earnings only barely qualify her for 'middleman' status, but she is, however, a superb example of the power of social engineering, perhaps the most important tool at the disposal of modern hackers, cybercriminals and identity thieves. At its most basic level, social engineering is the process of manipulating a victim so that they become an unwitting accomplice in the crime being committed against them.

In March 2009 Lord Hugh Rodley, a prominent member of the British aristocracy, was convicted of playing a leading role in an attempt to carry out the world's biggest bank raid in which a gang of international criminals and hackers tried to steal £229 million.

The plot began not online but in the 'real world' when the head of security at Sumitomo Mitsui Banking Corporation was forced to let two hackers into the Japanese firm's City of London headquarters after threats were made to his family. The men promptly installed spy software on the executives' computers to steal their log-ins and passwords giving them access to the bank's accounts at the highest possible levels.

Rodley's role, working with the assistance of his business partner Bernard Davies, was to create a web of international companies, stretching from the Seychelles to Spain, that would be used to launder the proceeds of the raid. With his aura of sophistication and perpetual refinement, Rodley was the perfect front man for the plot. He enjoyed all the trappings of the rural aristocracy, with a £2 million Gloucestershire home surrounded by five acres of gardens, riding stables, a Rolls-Royce and an office in Mayfair.

Rodley, his wife known as 'Lady' Pamela, and their daughters, Natasha and Natalie, were prominent figures in the British Morgan Horse Society and frequently took part in riding competitions. When Rodley contacted accountants with a view to creating new companies or opening bank accounts, they virtually fell over themselves to help. But behind the respectability was a lifetime of fraud. Rodley wasn't a lord at all. His name wasn't even Hugh. Born Brian McGough in Ireland in 1947, he was a bankrupt with a long criminal record for offences including forgery and obtaining property by deception. As key as it was to the success of the operation, Rodley's role relied heavily on his ability to use social engineering to get what he wanted and what the rest of the gang needed.

But while the plot was underway, Rodley could not resist a little fraud on the side. Using fake cheques he tried to steal £45,120 from the English National Ballet and £35,399 from Casio. He even scammed another member of the gang, spending more than £27,000 on credit and store cards by stealing the man's identity. One account at Harrods was used to buy riding tack for his daughters.

Ultimately the plot failed because of mistakes made in the electronic forms members of the gang had to fill out before the money was able to be transferred to the first of the companies Rodley had set up. Soon afterwards the alarm was raised and all those involved were rounded up. When Bernard Davies, Rodley's long-term business partner, realised he had been used by the man he considered to be his friend, he killed himself three days before the start of the trial, leaving a letter to detectives giving extensive details of the Sumitomo plot.

Davies wrote: 'When a partner has done the dirty on you, you put him in the frame.' Signing off, the wealthy serial conman wished investigating officers well: 'Thank you for the way you have treated me, I am very tired, I have lost the will to fight. Good luck.'

* * *

Ultimately people will trust other people more than they will trust computers so social engineering remains remarkably effective. In the early days of chip and pin credit cards, thieves who stole a card would locate and phone the owner using a credible-sounding voice saying 'Are you the owner of credit card number X? We are the police and can inform you the card has been recovered and is in safe keeping. Please will you confirm your ownership of the card by giving us your PIN number?'

Few people would fall for that one any more so cybercriminals have changed tactics. Today they direct their efforts towards social-networking sites and launch their attacks from there. If you get a message from a Facebook friend suggesting you check out a web link, you're far more likely to do it, based almost entirely on the fact that you have a relationship with the person who sent the message. And once you hit that link, your machine is infected.

Many such attacks go unreported, sometimes because the victims feel ashamed to have been caught out but also because in many cases the victims are not aware of what has happened. In December 2008 it emerged that an international identity theft ring used social engineering to steal more than $2.5 million. Kevin Mintick, at one time the most wanted computer criminal in the world, has said repeatedly that social engineering was a key part of his success and that it is far easier to convince someone to give you a password than to attempt to crack it. Once a password has been obtained the cybercriminal will often find it opens many, many doors. According to those involved in phishing, most passwords are used in more than once place 50 per cent of the time.

Finding a cybercriminal online was the easy part. Once you know where to look, the chatrooms, forums and websites where they congregate and exchange their wares are everywhere. However, finding a cybercriminal who was actually prepared to talk to me about their illegal activities seemed at times to be an almost impossible quest. Rip-offs and sting operations by law enforcement officials from all over the world are so common that no one involved in crime on the Internet trusts anybody else or anything they say. It's a wonder anything gets done at all!

Internet Relay Chat rooms – an untraceable form of instant messaging – are filled with hackers advertising their wares, from keystroke loggers and password cracking programs to stolen credit card numbers and banking details. 'The more you get into this world, the more amazing it gets. Back in the day, the only way to acquire this kind of detailed knowledge about how to be a successful criminal was to go to prison. Now, for those who know where to look, it's all available online.'

After being ignored, frozen out of conversations, 'flamed' and deluged with spam (luckily I had created a separate email address just for the purpose of this part of the book) I finally came across someone who seemed both genuine and interesting. Wary of exposing himself to the authorities, he has decided that for the purposes of this book only he will call himself SC5000 – the model number of a popular chip and pin-card-reading terminal which is key to one of his major streams of income. Now in his mid-twenties, SC5000 started out hacking for fun but while poking about in the most remote regions of the net quickly stumbled across money-making opportunities that seemed too good to be true.

What quickly became clear from my conversations with SC5000 is that the demographic of the cybercriminal is changing. The stereotype of a bedroom-bound geek is no longer true. Many are long-time bank and identity thieves in the offline world who have become acquainted with the riches that carding sites promise. At the top of the pyramid are sophisticated hackers – many of them East Europeans – with the technical skills to hack databases and online bank accounts. Furthermore, many of those making money from this field are equally likely to be involved with drug trafficking or armed robbery. Part of the reason for this is that the level of technical skill needed to steal tens of thousands of pounds is far lower than most people would think. With only a rudimentary knowledge of computing a criminal can make more money than they would from dealing drugs and never have to leave the house.

When the level of potential profits are compared to the risk of being caught, it is little wonder that cybercrime is the fastest growing activity in the underworld.

The rise of cybercrime is inextricably linked to the rising number of credit card transactions and online bank accounts. If you can get hold of this financial data, not only can you steal silently, but also – through a process of virus-driven automation – with ruthless efficiency. For those who don't possess the skills to obtain card and account information themselves, it can be bought 'off the shelf' from a wide range of online sources. The cost varies according to the amount of cash or credit available but is often surprisingly small.

A recent survey by a financial services company found that the majority of people in the UK estimate that their personal information would be sold to a criminal for a sum of up to £1000. In fact, individual credit card numbers can sell for as little as 4p each. Email addresses and bank account details can be bought from as little as 5p whilst a full identity is often only worth around £45.

Even for an account with a six-figure balance, the necessary information to have full control costs only around $400 (dollars are the most common currency of the online underworld). One reason for this falling value is that, in the same way that much manufacturing has been outsourced to countries where labour costs are cheaper, much of the technical side of online crime takes place in third-world countries where smaller sums of money go much further.

Phishing – the use of a fraudulent but convincing-looking website to get people to divulge their financial details – remains the most common form of social engineering and, despite increasing public awareness, remains hugely effective. The basic tools of phishing – a convincing scam email and website page, a stolen credit card with which to register the fake domain, a fresh spam list and so on, can be obtained extremely cheaply. The total costs of sending out 100,000 phishing emails can be as little as $60. In the very worst-case scenario, such an investment will produce a return of around 300 per cent. In reality, the average returns are far, far higher.

'The simple truth is, the reason that people like me exist and are able to make a living is that most people simply haven't got a clue,' says SC5000. 'They tend to think they're only vulnerable if they're shopping online or using their computer to do banking, but a lot of the information I use comes from Facebook and Bebo. I've even got stuff from people who play online games.

'You might only get $500 off a phishing victim perhaps one time in every thousand, but that's still fifty cents per password. When you look at the volumes we are dealing with, it's easy to see how the money can really start rolling in. A lot of the time there is more volume coming in than I know what to do with. I literally don't have time to look through the stuff. I just shift it wholesale, sell the live addresses to spammers. I can easily earn $1,000 a day just doing that.'

Only a tiny proportion of spam is successful but with individuals easily able to send out tens of thousands of messages on a daily basis, those incremental profits soon add to a good living.

You don't even need to be a computer expert to make money from cybercrime. Enterprising hackers have set up dozens of sites to service the needs of those wishing to enter the business. There are subscription services that send regular email updates with details of the latest security vulnerabilities and how to exploit them, others which supply 'tools' to allow you to build your own virus. Yet others provide a bespoke service – you let them know what you want and they will build you a virus to order. You can even buy 'hacking kits' on eBay at a cost of just $20.

Such is the level of sophistication that simple precautions which would have guaranteed someone's safety in the past are no longer enough. Infecting your computer with a virus used to be about getting an email and double clicking on the attachment. Now there are programs which will download a malicious 'script' into your computer simply because you have opened a page of a particular website.

'It all happens in the background, you don't have a clue,' says SC5000. 'The next time you open up your browser, you get directed to a different home page, a particular set of pop ups come up.' The most sophisticated attacks of this kind are not lures to fake sites that try to steal your bank-account login and password, but sites that redirect you to log in at your real bank but piggyback in with you and make transactions while you are logged in.

Increasingly credit card details are also being obtained via compromised chip and pin terminals. The machines are secretly switched over by corrupt staff at petrol stations or restaurants for models that are identical but contain additional electronics which wirelessly send the customer's card number, expiry date and PIN to a place where the gang can access it at their leisure.

While such information cannot be used to manufacture more chip and pin cards, it can be used to clone traditional magnetic stripe cards. This can be used in places where the technology has not yet been upgraded. Where would that be? Astonishingly, the USA has not yet introduced chip and pin technology and has no plans to do so. 'I know some people who go over there for a month and travel around, withdrawing money from ATMs or buying things like laptops and reselling them,' says SC5000. 'You get your picture taken at cash machines but it's easy to get around. And if you're from another country, there's no chance you're actually going to get caught.'

Rarely standing still in the search for new ways to cash in, criminals have also begun to perfect botnets – collections of compromised computers ordered by a hacker remotely to send spam, launch denial-of-service attacks or host phishing websites.

According to my source: 'You can make good money from spam. People think the only way people earn money is if someone actually buys the rubbishy diet pills or penis pump that is being advertised, but just having that page up on your computer counts as a "hit". When people click on an "unsubscribe" link [in a futile effort to stop getting spammed] you can make money from them the same way you would if they clicked on a web page for more information about a spamvertised product. This is also the reason that spammers will commonly use a series of linked web pages – as you try to close one, another will pop up to replace it. Most spammers send out anything from one million up to a hundred million spams every day. If only a fraction of those generate hits, you're still making good money.

'It's not all jam. You have to be online all the time. If you're not people don't trust you, they assume something is wrong. You get accused of being a copper or having sold out to the authorities. It happens like three, four times a week. People say things about themselves and other people but you have no idea if it is true or not. And of course the biggest problem is that anyone could be behind that email address or that IM id. You could think you're talking to one person but it's really ten different guys, all in different countries, working through the same proxy server. I know because that's the way that I operate and I'm not alone.

'Sometimes it's almost too easy. Everything from televisions to fridges is connected to the Internet these days, and it's surprising how much information you can glean from all sorts of devices if you put your mind to it.'

Many cardholders use their mother's maiden name as a standard security question but social networking sites mean such information is often a breeze to obtain. 'You send someone an email suggesting they play the porn-star name game, you know where you take the name of your first pet and add it to your mother's maiden name,' says SC5000. 'It's so funny and innocent, no one thinks twice. Works every time. They think they're all friends together. But anyone who has more than a hundred Facebook friends, there is no way they actually know all those people.'

Social networking sites are, according to SC5000, the way of the future. 'Because of the level of trust involved I make a lot of money through CPA – cost per action – deals. It means you can get paid each time someone looks at a web page, clicks a link or fills in an online form.' You might only get a fraction of a cent for each incident but if you can generate enough volume, you soon start to see healthy returns.

Honour among thieves has always been something of a myth but in the online world it has never even existed. Since cybercrime began, novices have been scammed by more advanced criminals, often falling for an offer to sell them credit cards or stolen identity information that turns out to be fake or false. Another common scam is to sell the same batch of credit card numbers to several different people all at the same time.

Although websites buying and selling identity information are easy to find on the Internet, the vast majority will be scams, ripping off customers on the basis that the victims won't be able to go to the police to complain. The 'real' sites tend to stay below the radar of most search engines. Finding them takes a little more effort and a rudimentary knowledge of Russian language.

Thinking big is also important. Buying (or selling) individual credit card numbers one at a time is almost impossible. Instead most transactions involve batches of tens or thousands or hundreds of thousands at a time and pushes the price down considerably.

SC5000 takes me step by step through the process of buying stolen credit card numbers online. It is a long and drawn-out process that ends with a delicate and scary procedure, very much akin to the moment when drugs and money are swapped over by more traditional organised-crime gangs. Once you have selected your cards and negotiated the price, you still don't know if the numbers actually work. Trying before you buy is out of the question so it is down to the seller to provide evidence that the cards are still within their limits and have not yet been cancelled. This can often mean he or she taking a few cards (or cloned cards) and carrying out several high-value transactions that are immediately cancelled. Receipts for the transactions are emailed to the buyer moments before the monies are sent across.

With so much money seemingly there for the taking, it is not surprising that a wide range of people are rushing to get involved. One recent case involved a lawyer who realised that he could make more money though cybercrime than his legal practice. He went on to assemble a gang of about 300 people with specialised roles.

Certain lawyers have always worked hand in hand with organised crime but, thanks to the rise of new technology, those inclined towards the underworld can now adopt a far more lucrative and senior position within such an enterprise.

With the links between cybercrime and traditional organised crime becoming stronger, the techniques of the latter are appearing in the former. There has been at least one case of someone who was kidnapped after spending too much time talking online about the activities of the group he was involved in.

Had Lord Hugh Rodley pulled off his little scam he would have become one of the richest criminals in the country. Despite his failure, the evidence points to the fact that many of those involved in the higher echelons of cybercrime are earning the sort of sums that would put even upper middle-level gangsters to shame. It is only a matter of time before one of them moves up the career ladder further still until they are able to enjoy the company of the world's most elite criminal masterminds.

PART THREE
KINGPINS

14

D COMPANY

Each and every year since the start of the new millennium the US Treasury Department has published a list of what it believes to be the world's leading drug barons.

Under the auspices of the Foreign Narcotics Kingpin Designation Act, the named men and women are immediately subject to a series of sanctions aimed at 'denying such persons, their businesses and their agents access to the US financial system and to the benefits of trade and transactions involving US businesses and individuals'. Anyone falling foul of the Act by trading with such a person risks a fine of up to $5 million and thirty years in prison. The kingpins themselves face immediate arrest if they try to enter the USA.

Ten or so new names are added to the list each year and, as such, it provides a fascinating insight into the upper echelons of international organised crime. These are individuals operating at the highest possible level of criminality. They are the chief executives and managing directors that all the foot soldiers and middle-management types below them aspire to become one day. All are believed to have become millionaires many, many times over as a result of their illegal activities.

Some of those featured were known to a wider public even before their official 'kingpin' designation: Burmese opium warlord Khun Sa, psychopathic Mexican outlaw Ramon Arellano-Felix of the Tijuana cartel, shot dead by police in 2002 and Cumhur Yakut from Turkey, said to control most of the heroin shipped into Western Europe and beyond.

Then there is Joaquin 'Shorty' Guzman, ruthless head of the Sinaloa Cartel who in 2009 made it to 701 in the *Forbes*' list of the world's richest men with a net worth of $1 billion. A fugitive since escaping from prison in 2001, he has become an almost mythical folk hero in Mexico with dozens of songs and poems written about his exploits.

Other 'kingpins' are more obscure but equally fascinating: husband and wife smuggling team Oluwole and Abeni Ogungbuyi, who fled the US in the nineties after being arrested for heroin smuggling and have remained on the run ever since, and Jamaican businessman Leebert Ramcharan, one of the wealthiest people in the island's resort town of Montego Bay.

As part of my ongoing research, I check additions to the list as a matter of course, partly to keep up to date with the who's who of top-level drug trafficking but also to look out for links to the British criminal underworld.

It was during one such check after ten new names had been added that I discovered that Leebert Ramcharan, number forty-five on the list, had been a regular visitor to England and the source behind dozens of major cocaine and marijuana shipments that were being brought into the country and distributed by 'Yardie' gangs.

In 2004 Leebert's brother Norman flew to the UK to have a stomach operation at a private hospital in the north of England. After convalescing, he booked into a plush London hotel, and was immediately placed under surveillance by Customs officers who had been monitoring him since his arrival.

Norman Ramcharan, who operated several businesses in Jamaica including fishing, lumber, hardware and shipping, had a long history of drug trafficking. He had two previous convictions after being arrested in Florida in 1994 following a massive cannabis seizure while using the name Donovan Marshall.

He served two years in prison and in 1987 he was arrested along with his brother Leebert in Maine, near the US–Canadian border, while transporting over 150 kilos of cannabis oil by foot across a river in an attempt to get it to Florida.

He was filmed and recorded meeting with his 'right-hand man' Everton Dennis, a law student and former Jamaican immigration officer. The pair were monitored in and around the hotel as they discussed various schemes they intended to use to launder the proceeds of cocaine trafficking between the West Indies, the Netherlands and the UK.

A few days later Dennis travelled to Manchester where he was observed buying a large black suitcase. He returned to Euston Station where officers moved in and arrested him. More than £69,000 was found in the case and also in his pockets. Ramcharan was arrested two days later at Heathrow Airport as he was about to board a plane for Jamaica.

A torn receipt in a rubbish bin in Ramcharan's hotel room led the authorities to a package containing vast numbers of false cheques that had been sent from London to Jamaica in a further laundering scam.

Released on bail, Ramcharan immediately tried to flee. He was found hiding under a sheet of chipboard in the back of a transit van at Folkstone which was about to head to Europe via the Channel Tunnel.

At Blackfriars Crown Court that November, Ramcharan was sentenced to seven and a half years after pleading guilty to laundering a total of £1.7 million. Dennis was given five years.

In March 2008 Leebert, who had been captured and extradited to the United States, was sentenced to thirty-seven years for drug trafficking offences. He was believed to have smuggled as much as fifteen metric tonnes of cocaine from Columbia into Jamaica from where it was transported around the world.

The next addition to the Foreign Narcotic Kingpin list after Leebert Ramcharan is Fernando Zevallos, described by the DEA as the 'Al Capone of Peru'. Once the owner of Aero Continente, the country's largest airline, he is currently serving twenty years for drug trafficking offences. Although his story is fascinating – prior to his incarceration he had been the subject of more than thirty DEA investigations, not one of which had produced a conviction or even any evidence of a crime – his activities had no link to the UK so I move on.

The name that follows belongs to an Indian national, Iqbal Mirchi, and I am immediately intrigued. Indian organised crime is one of the rising stars of the global underworld and second only to the Italian mafia in terms of the depth to which it has penetrated its domestic society, yet Mirchi was the first Indian ever to face the kingpin sanctions.

The entry carries little background information on Mirchi. It lists three separate dates of birth, four of the assumed names he most commonly uses and carries details of the three different passports he is believed to possess.

One thing is certain though: if Mirchi is indeed a major figure in the Indian underworld, he must somehow or other be connected to the global criminal network known simply as the D Company.

India's largest and most successful organised crime syndicate takes its name from its enigmatic and fearsome yet diminutive leader Dawood Ibrahim.

The son of a police constable, Dawood's ability to successfully combine high-level criminality with global terrorism has led to him being described as: 'the most dangerous man in the world'. Details of his early life are vague and hard to verify but it is generally accepted that, after dropping out of school, the young Dawood got his start by working as a mob hitman for a Mumbai underworld boss.

He ruthlessly made his way to the top of the food chain by literally executing every one of his rivals. By the mid-1980s Dawood was at the head of an organisation making vast profits from gold smuggling, prostitution, gambling, counterfeit currency, diamond trading, contract killing, extortion and, of course, drugs. Under pressure from the police and rival gangs he moved to Dubai in 1986 but continued to reign over Mumbai from afar.

Despite his extensive criminal antecedents Dawood managed to acquire a curious brand of respectability, not dissimilar to that enjoyed by the Kray twins during the sixties or Pablo Escobar two decades later. Prominent Bollywood stars and politicians were regulars at the lavish parties he hosted from his Emirates home and Dawood himself invested heavily in the film industry. At one point his stake was said to be as much as 60 per cent – enough to give him the power to decide which films got made and which actors and actresses starred in them.

Such is the appeal of the Dawood 'legend' that at least five movies have been made about his own life, all of them massive hits at the Indian box office.

In 1993 Dawood was accused of being the mastermind behind a series of bombings in Mumbai in which 257 people died and around 700 others were wounded. The bombings were believed to have been carried out in revenge for the deaths of hundreds of Muslims in riots in 1992, blamed on the right-wing Hindu Shiv Sena party.

Dawood, raised as a devout Muslim, is also known to have met Osama Bin Laden and, in the aftermath of 9/11, allowed his smuggling network to be used to enable senior al-Qaeda operatives to flee Afghanistan. More recently Dawood is said to have provided vehicles and weapons to the terrorists involved in the 2008 attacks on Mumbai.

The criminal portfolio of the D Company extends further still: Dawood is also a leading figure in the highly lucrative, shadowy world of cricket match-fixing.

A Pakistani judicial report in 2000 into the game, which found repeated incidents of corruption, made mention of Ibrahim. Internationally renowned fast bowler Wasim Akram described taking a call from Ibrahim during a tournament in 1999. During one particular match in which a highly favoured Pakistani side suddenly collapsed against England, Akram stated that he talked 'to someone called Dawood Ibrahim on the phone, who told him the match was fixed'.

The manner of Pakistan's collapse against England – losing their last five wickets for just six runs – immediately made ex-captain Rashid Latif, who has repeatedly campaigned against corruption, cry foul. 'I suspect match-fixing,' he said later that day. 'The way they lost the match, it's obvious something fishy has again started in the team.'

Any source of inside information or connection to key players is highly prized as even seemingly innocuous data about the team, such as selection policies or tactics, can be incredibly valuable. In the meantime Dawood and another prominent player, Javed Miandad, a leading batsman who went on to become coach of the Pakistan team, are particularly close: in July 2005 the gangster's daughter, Mahkukh, married Miandad's son in a lavish ceremony in Dubai. The pair had met while studying in the UK.

Two years later former England International Bob Woolmer – brought in to replace Miandad as coach of Pakistan after a series of losses – died in mysterious circumstances in Jamaica during the cricket World Cup, soon after his team unexpectedly lost to Ireland. Foul play was suspected and Dawood Ibrahim was said to be behind it.

Dawood was known to have sent several minions to the West Indies to look after his gambling interests in the games. These included one heavyweight figure, a former tax inspector turned underworld fixer and bookie. Soon after news of Woolmer's death, another notorious Indian gangster, Babloo Srivastava, went on TV to point the finger at Dawood. 'The Pakistan–Ireland match must have been fixed,' Srivastava said. 'The D Company may have lots of money at stake. Woolmer may have got an inkling of the fixing and hence he was killed.'

Woolmer was found dead in his room at the Pegasus Hotel and the initial report was that he had suffered a heart attack. Four days later Jamaican police launched a murder investigation after their pathologist reported that Woolmer had in fact been strangled.

In June, three months after Woolmer's death, the police closed their investigation concluding that he had died of natural causes. However, in November 2007 coroner Patrick Murphy asked for further tests to be carried out due to discrepancies between the toxicology tests carried out in the UK and those conducted in the Caribbean. The twenty-six-day hearing ultimately returned an open verdict, the jury refusing to rule out the possibility that Woolmer had been murdered after all.

Dawood's cricket-related scams are said to have earned him millions over the years but the true lifeblood of his business is the drug trade and in particular the heroin trade.

Both al-Qaeda and the Taliban are known to use the D Company's smuggling infrastructure to ship vast quantities of heroin out of Afghanistan and into the UK and Western Europe – all thanks to a financial arrangement said to have been struck by bin Laden himself. But they are not the only terrorists that Dawood allegedly deals with.

He is said to owe a large part of his success to assistance from an organisation officially named the Liberation Tigers of Tamil Eelam but far better known as the Tamil Tigers. The separatist group, which fought a long bloody campaign to create an independent Tamil state in the north and east of Sri Lanka before being defeated by the nation's military in May 2009, received a significant portion of their funding as a result of their ties to Dawood.

Despite being defeated on their home ground, the Tamil Tigers remain strong abroad. In the UK their support and funding network is almost entirely intact. Rival Tamil factions in London like the East Ham Boys and the DMX have fought regularly, battling to control fundraising and extortion territory. There have been ten murders since 2000 linked to the Tamil gangs and it makes me wonder if the D Company has some hand in the violence. But as I was about to discover, the links between Indian organised crime and the UK are far stronger than I could ever have imagined.

As I started to research Iqbal Mirchi's background the first thing I learned was that Mirchi isn't his real name at all. Born Iqbal Memon, he acquired the nickname because he owned a spice shop in his youth – *kali mirchi* is black pepper while *hali mirchi* is green chilli.

A 1993 report by the then Indian Union Home Secretary N.N. Vohra on India's criminal networks and their links to politicians named Mirchi as a typical example of someone who started out as a petty smuggler of cigarettes and alcohol and then became fantastically wealthy in a short space of time. Because of Mirchi's links to the upper echelons of government, the report said, he had become too powerful to be taken down.

'The growth of Mirchi is due to the fact that the concerned enforcement agencies did not at the time take action against him and, later, this perhaps became difficult on account of the enormous patronage he had developed. If Mirchi is investigated, the entire patronage enjoyed by him and his linkages will come to light. Director Central Bureau of Investigation has observed that there are many such cases, as that of Mirchi where the initial failure has led to the emergence of mafia giants who have become too big to be tackled.'

That same year Mirchi was accused of playing a part in the terrorist bombing campaign that Dawood instigated. A few months later, India issued an Interpol Red Notice arrest warrant against him after uncovering a huge illegal drugs factory in Pune, India's eighth largest city.

Police seized 1,600 kilos of methaqualone, a substance used in the manufacture of mandrax tablets, and 110 kilos of mandrax powder. Also known as quaaludes or just 'ludes', mandrax was a prescription sedative that became a massively popular recreational drug in the late sixties and seventies. Increased illicit use caused so many fatal overdoses that the drug was withdrawn in the 1980s, but it continues to be manufactured illegally, especially in India, and remains a widely abused street drug in South Africa to this day.

Mirchi is believed to have sold nearly five million mandrax tablets before the factory was discovered. After the case against him was registered, Mirchi never returned to India and instead based himself in Dubai.

I also found a United Nations report that linked Mirchi to Dawood and a number of references in the Indian press to Mirchi being Dawood's 'right-hand man' and India's 'number one drug lord'. Mirchi was also said to be linked to an ancient form of money transfer called *hawala*.

Based totally on trust, *hawala*, which means 'transfer' in Arabic, has seen a resurgence in recent years as it is the ideal way of moving money from one country to another without leaving any kind of paper trail.

Originally a merchant travelling overseas took with him a letter of credit issued by a *hawala* banker in his own country, which would be honoured by a *hawala* banker in another country. The money doesn't physically move from one place to another, it is simply paid out by agreement between the two bankers.

A few weeks later I stumble across a year-old edition of *India Today International* magazine that happens to have a cover story all about Dawood.

Inside there are several articles about the man's global crime network and a map of the world covering two pages with red circles in the countries where D Company has 'offices'. Although the map includes a red circle over the south-east of England, nowhere in the articles themselves is there any mention of the UK. However, to the right of the map, under the heading 'Chief Operators', the magazine has listed the names of 'some of the key men who help run the Dawood empire worldwide'.

The penultimate entry, accompanied by a small picture, reads as follows: 'Iqbal Mirchi: Handles drug trafficking, money laundering mainly in North America and the UK.'

From there everything moves rapidly. I learn that Mirchi has spent a considerable amount of time in the UK over the years, that he owns both property and businesses in this country. Using that as a setting-off point I soon manage to track down an address in the most unlikely of locations – the Essex town of Hornchurch – where Mirchi is still registered as being resident.

Almost without thinking I grab my notebook and head over there. I arrive at the end of the quiet road in an exclusive suburb and find the large, detached six-bedroom house that matches the address. A large iron gate sits across the entrance and two brand-new luxury 4x4 Lexus motorcars sit in the drive.

As my finger pushes against the doorbell the excitement of tracking down a man who has been named as one of the fifty biggest global drug barons, who is wanted for murder, terrorism and drug trafficking and is the right-hand man of one of the world's biggest crime gangs fades as the reality of the situation suddenly dawns.

He's probably not going to be very happy about me turning up like this.

The door eases open and a large man in a cream, open-neck shirt, pale grey trousers and bare feet stands in front of me.

'Mr Mirchi?' I ask.

The man looks at me as if I am speaking a foreign language.

'I'm looking for Iqbal Mirchi, also known as Iqbal Memon.'

The man, who bears a startling resemblance to the picture printed in the magazine clipping that I have in my bag, cocks his head to one side and eyes me suspiciously. 'Who are you?'

I explain that I'm a writer investigating the fact that Mr Mirchi's name has been added to the list of global foreign kingpins. The man's face falls a little and I fear he's about to shut the door on me so I decide to play my ace. I tell him that I've already started my story on Mr Mirchi and have been given lots of information from the US State department. I say the only reason I have come to seek Mr Mirchi out at home is to give him a chance to put his own side of the story across.

There is a pause as the man thinks while looking down at the floor. 'Mr Mirchi is not here right now,' he says softly. 'But I think you'd better come inside.'

I step into the hallway and immediately two more men appear. There is a rapid exchange of words and everyone looks at me. I look down at the ground and see that I am the only person wearing shoes. I dutifully remove mine and place them next to a pile of others. When I look up the man who opened the door indicates for me to move further into the house and then take the door on the right.

We enter a living room finished with dark wood floors and walls, furnished with two cream leather sofas and dominated by an enormous running machine. We both sit down. For the next twenty minutes, on the pretext of waiting for Mr Mirchi to arrive, we talk about every subject under the sun just so long as it has nothing to do with drugs, murder or terrorism.

My instinct is that the man is trying to suss me out, to see exactly what my agenda is and I seem to be right because just when I'm starting to run out of topics to discuss, the man leans towards me and stares intently into my eyes. 'I am Mirchi, I am the one you have come to see.'

'Pleased to meet you,' I say, and hold out my hand.

Mirchi then begins to systematically and passionately deny everything the Indian government has ever accused him of. 'Everything they say about me is total bullshit,' he tells me. 'The drugs, the murder, the terrorism. All bullshit. My first crime is that I am a Muslim. My second crime is that I am a successful Muslim businessman.'

According to Mirchi, his problems began soon after the 1993 bombings.

'A senior police officer told me that my name would be attached to false charges unless I paid millions of rupees in bribes. I refused and moved to Dubai. In my absence they made charges against me and claimed I had absconded. That mud has stuck to my name ever since.'

In April 1995 officers from Scotland Yard raided Mirchi's home and arrested him on an extradition warrant covering drugs and terrorism charges in connection with the 1993 blasts. By the time the case came to court, those charges had been dropped and replaced with a charge relating to the murder of a man named Amar Suvarna who had been shot dead in Mumbai in 1994.

In a Mumbai court in November 1998 two men were convicted of Suvarna's murder. The prosecution case was that Suvarna, a police informer, had previously worked as the manager of the Eden rice mill in London, which was owned by Mirchi. When the mill was raided by the British authorities, Mirchi suspected Suvarna of having provided the tip off. Suvarna quit his job and moved to Mumbai. Soon afterwards, Mirchi's business interests there were raided too and a furious Mirchi allegedly threatened Suvarna over the phone.

According to Special Public Prosecutor Rohini Salian, Mirchi put out a contract to kill Suvarna, which was subcontracted twice until it reached a notorious hitman named Abdul Gafoor and his associates.

Mirchi allegedly provided photographs of Suvarna and his address. The hit took place in a Mumbai shopping district on 24 February 1994. With his dying breath Suvarna claimed Mirchi was responsible for the attack, a claim that was accepted by the judge in the case.

Gafoor, who admitted his involvement in eleven other murders, and one of his henchmen were sentenced to life imprisonment.

An extradition request against Mirchi was made in respect of the Suvarna murder but turned down when magistrates at Bow Street decided there was no case to answer. India did not appeal, and actually paid Mirchi's legal costs. Despite this, all the terrorism and drugs charges against him remain on file in India and Mirchi will be arrested and tried if he ever returns.

Scotland Yard's own investigation of Mirchi, which ended in 1999, found no evidence of involvement in criminal activity in the UK. In 2001 the Home Office granted him indefinite leave to remain, yet the US Treasury Department had, despite all this, decided to add his name to the list of global narcotics kingpins.

'I now realise that I made a mistake,' Mirchi continues. 'I should not have fought the extradition, I should have stood trial. Then I would have cleared my name and I would be free to go about my business. I have offered to return to India but asked for a guarantee that I would be given judicial protection.'

The Indian government has refused Mirchi's request so he has stayed put. In the meantime several of his properties in India were seized and the passports of his wife and children were restricted, allowing them to travel only between Mumbai and Dubai. Mirchi moved to Dubai in order to be with them but was forced to leave and return to the UK when India made it clear that they would attempt to extradite Mirchi from there.

Since his return to the UK, India has shown no sign of bringing new charges. Mirchi has written to the US State Department expressing outrage about his name being included on the kingpin list. Although Mirchi seems genuinely mystified about why his name should have been added, I later learn that he had apparently been trying to gain entry to the US with a view to setting up

262

D COMPANY

a business there. This is believed to have prompted Washington officials to study his case, which in turn led them to blacklist him.

As for links to Dawood and the D Company, Mirchi dismisses all talk of his being a senior figure within the organisation as the result of people putting two and two together and getting five. In Dubai, Mirchi admits meeting Dawood Ibrahim. 'He is from Mumbai, I am from Mumbai. There was some contact but I have never worked for him. It was social. These people are the mafia, they kill people. I have never hurt anybody in my life.

'The bottom line is that I have never made any secret of where I am,' Mirchi says. 'The British police, the Indian police, the American police all have my address because I have written to them and told them. If I am a kingpin and they want to arrest me, they know exactly where to find me.'

In the meantime Mirchi continues to attract controversy. In 2005 his name cropped up during the trial of Hemant Lakhani, a Briton accused of smuggling a shoulder-launched missile to the US, who was said in court to be an associate of the 'drug lord and terror suspect' Mirchi.

In 2007 he made headlines once more when a huge bungalow that he owned in the Indian city of Bhopal was seized by the Central Excise and Customs Department under the auspices of the Narcotics Drugs & Psychotropic Substances Act and converted into a guest house for the use of government officials.

In May 2009 his name cropped up yet again, this time in connection with an assassination attempt against Indian billionaire and ardent Newcastle United fan Anil Ambani, whose helicopter was sabotaged while standing outside a hangar at Mumbai Airport the month before.

When I returned to Hornchurch to find out Mirchi's response to the latest allegations against him, I found that he had moved on and was supposedly living in Canada. But while Iqbal Mirchi may no longer be on the scene, there are plenty of undisputed kingpins of organised crime who remain much closer to home.

15

THE A-TEAM

He is seated directly opposite the entrance so I spot him the minute I push open the door to the café. His huge hunched shoulders twitch slightly as he leans forward in his seat and slowly lifts a mug of tea to his lips. His cold, unblinking eyes stare directly at me until I'm forced to look away.

There is nothing in his body language or demeanour that suggests this is the man I have come to meet and, while this is in part a huge relief, I can't help finding his presence here extremely disturbing. Out of the corner of my eye I see him replace the mug on the yellow Formica table and, as his heavy jacket falls forward, I'm sure I see a flash of something black and shiny tucked into his belt. My heart shudders.

I thought I had come to this slightly run-down greasy spoon joint on the outskirts of Hackney, east London, to meet a former senior associate of one of London's most notorious crime syndicates. Now I find myself wondering whether I have walked into a trap.

The man – Harry – agreed to talk to me after being told by a mutual friend that I could be trusted not to reveal his true identity. Normally that friend would be here to make the introduction but for various reasons he has been unable to attend leaving me on my own. By talking, Harry will be betraying secrets the gang would much rather keep quiet. Could someone be planning to silence him? Or me?

I'm only just inside the doorway but it's already too late for me to turn around and walk out. For one thing, the spiral-bound reporter's notebook in my hand is a dead giveaway. More importantly though, Harry, sitting across to the right, has spotted me and casually raises an arm to summon me over.

264

I head towards him, ultra-conscious of the fact that I now have my back to the man at the table opposite the door. From a distance Harry doesn't look anywhere near as scary as I'd imagined, especially considering the level at which he has been operating and the degree of violence I've heard he is able to employ. But as I get closer his gnarled knuckles and scarred face tell a different story.

He is sitting in the corner looking out towards the door, his back pressed up against the wall. It's a classic gangster set-up and allows him to see everyone who comes in and everyone who leaves. It means I have to sit with my back to the rest of the café, which I don't much like at all.

I'm about to speak when he holds up a hand to silence me and asks for my mobile phone. I hand it over and he deftly removes the battery, placing it down on the table between us alongside the handset and back cover.

I lean forward a little and lower my voice to a whisper. 'There's a guy at the table by the door, big guy, he was giving me the eye when I came in. I think he might have some kind of weapon on him.'

Harry doesn't miss a beat. He doesn't even peer over my shoulder to check who I'm talking about. 'What makes you think that?' he asks.

'I think I saw something tucked into his belt.'

Harry exhales slowly and shakes his head. 'Fuckwit.' He looks up. 'Not you, mate. Him! I'll have a word later.'

The truth of the situation slowly dawns on me. 'He's with you.'

Harry nods. 'The eyes in the back of my head. I don't leave home without him, but he's a dozy cunt sometimes. Now, let's talk about Tel.'

Harry and I are meeting a week after Terry Adams, the so-called godfather of the notorious London criminal syndicate, was jailed for seven years after pleading guilty to conspiring to hide up to £1 million of illegally gotten gains.

GANG LAND

Of the eleven children born to lorry driver George and Florence Adams that were raised in a council flat on the rough Barnsbury estate in Islington, it was the eldest, Terry, assisted by his younger brothers Patsy and Tommy, who would go on to form a gang that would achieve near mythic status in the annals of British organised crime. At its height their empire included pubs, clubs, restaurants, jewellery shops and dozens of other interests. Their net worth was said to exceed £100 million and the gang, also known as the A-Team, was linked to at least twenty-three murders.

Although the gang's wealth was said to have come from three decades of armed robbery, extortion, racketeering and drug dealing, Terry himself was not found guilty of any of those particular offences. He had, according to prosecutors, mastered the art of distancing himself from the actual criminality while still profiting from it. Despite being incarcerated he remains, according to Harry, a role model for villains everywhere.

'Terry was always the most level-headed one out of the bunch,' says Harry. 'Tommy was a bit wild and Patsy could be crazy at times. A lot of the people who are involved in this kind of business don't have a lot going on up top. But Terry and his brothers were different. They were a real class act. You could take them anywhere, mix them with any kind of company and they would always know when to behave themselves.

'Terry in particular was always nicely turned out, well dressed in his own way – someone once said he looked like a cross between Liberace and Peter Stringfellow. He wasn't a joke though, he was always totally in charge of whatever was going on. When he walked into a room, everyone stood up. He was treated like royalty.'

Harry began working for the A-Team when Terry, still in his early twenties, acquired a huge load of stolen Krugerrands that he arranged to have melted down and then sold back to the jewellery business.

'They'd started out as simple football hooligans, going out every weekend to follow Arsenal and look for a fight,' says Harry. 'But they've come a long way since then. They started running protection on the market stalls then did a few armed robberies and made a bit of cash, which they invested very, very wisely. They split things up between them, playing to their strengths. Terry was the brains, Tommy dealt with financial matters, and Patrick, who did a bit of time for armed robbery in the early days, was the muscle.

'It wasn't just that – the thing that made them so strong is that they were brothers who stuck together. While other gangs might have the occasional falling out over money or women or some other kind of disagreement, the Adams were always bonded together. It was like if you cut one of them, all the rest would start bleeding too. You take on one, you've got the rest on your back as well. That made them truly formidable to go up against.'

They were also lucky. Terry's dealings with the Krugerrands had given him valuable contacts in the precious metals business, contacts that would prove to be quite literally worth their weight in gold in the aftermath of a notorious robbery that for ever changed the face of gangland.

Just after 6.40 a.m. on 26 November 1983, six armed men burst into the Heathrow depot of the security company Brinks-Mat. The robbers seemed to know their way around and easily disabled the sophisticated alarm system. The few guards on duty were tied up, doused with petrol and threatened with being set alight unless they revealed the combinations to the final locks.

The thieves escaped with three tonnes of gold bullion worth £26 million. While it may have all seemed incredibly well organised and professional at the time the truth was very different.

'That job had been punted around south London for a few weeks,' says Harry. 'Mickey McAvoy, a young hardman, and an old blagger called Brian Robinson had put the word out that they were looking for a couple of sensible lads to help them with an inside job.

'They had heard there would be £3 million in cash in the vault and the plan was to split it five ways. It was only when they got there that they found the gold. They hadn't expected it at all. They were so disorganised that they didn't even have a big enough vehicle to deal with it. They had to go and get a van. They were supposed to be in and out within minutes but the job ended up taking nearly two hours.'

Until Brinks-Mat, London's underworld had been a strictly cash business. No one within the robbers' immediate circle had any experience of dealing with gold and the desire to turn the bullion into hard cash meant the call for help had to be put out far and wide.

McAvoy had worked for a man nicknamed The Fox, a shadowy character who for more than thirty years has been one of the most senior figures in British organised crime. The pair quickly became good friends. At the time of the robbery, The Fox was engaged in lucrative business deals with virtually all of London's gangs, including an up-and-coming firm called the Adams family.

When The Fox was asked to help find people willing to smelt the gold, they naturally sprang to mind. The Adams boys, then involved in running protection and smuggling cannabis, eagerly signed on. The gold was re-smelted by Terry's main contact – a Hatton Garden jeweller called Solly Nahome.

Two years later Tommy Adams stood trial at the Old Bailey accused of handling some of the proceeds of the Brinks-Mat robbery. He was acquitted. His co-defendant, a certain Kenneth Noye, had less luck with the jury and was jailed for fourteen years.

Under Terry's direction the gang took the money they had made from the gold and invested into the drug business, shipping vast quantities of cannabis and later cocaine into the UK.

Within a year Patsy had been arrested in connection with a three-tonne drug shipment but he too was acquitted. Rumours began to circulate that the family were able to nobble juries, had senior police and court officials in their pockets and were more or less unstoppable.

By now Tommy had forged links with Colombian and Yardie groups, enabling the gang to get their product at the lowest possible cost and have it distributed with remarkable efficiency. The money began to flow into their coffers with the force of a tidal wave.

Always on the look out for new business opportunities, Terry steered the family towards investing in nightclubs, a move which only consolidated their power base even more. Many of his business deals were brokered by none other than Solly Nahome, who had graduated from being a minor figure in the gang to become a trusted financial adviser. With him on board the gang rapidly went from strength to strength.

'A nightclub is a goldmine, especially with all the drugs around,' says Harry. 'If you control the club you control who goes in and out. That means you can control who sells the drugs inside and make sure you get a cut of the profits.

'Terry definitely has something of a criminal genius about him. He's a real thinker. They had board meetings and he'd be like the CEO. Getting that first London club was the best thing they ever did. Once you have a club, it's a public place, so it doesn't matter who you get seen with. You can go about your business and the Old Bill can't make a big deal out of it.

'The Old Bill tried sending a few people down there to see what was going on but they always stood out like sore thumbs. Just imagine, you've got a bunch of blokes knocking back the champagne and snorting Charlie, then a couple of blokes in cheap suits at the end of the bar sipping orange juice. You could smell them a mile off.

'Me personally, I worked with the Adams, either directly or as part of another firm, for more years than I care to remember. There were times when they'd indicate that they wanted things done, people taken out of the game, but I never got involved in any of that because I didn't see the point of doing other people's dirty work for them.

'Being part of their team was the best thing that ever happened to me. We were feared but we were also respected by other villains. The Adams had a reputation for being some of the best money earners in the business and they always made sure everyone got their fair share.'

When the Reillys, a rival criminal family from the same Irish-Catholic background as the Adams challenged their dominance of Islington, all three brothers knew what had to be done. In early January 1990 Patsy, always the most physically imposing of the trio, walked into a pub controlled by the rival firm and sat down for a drink – the modern-day equivalent of a gauntlet around the face. Word spread and the Reillys sent a car carrying four armed men to the pub to take Patsy out of the game.

But it was a trap. As the red BMW turned into Huntingdon Street, a team of Adams associates and possibly the other brothers let rip with an assortment of shotguns and pistols. Although dozens of shots were fired, not one person was hit. It didn't matter – the message had been received. Islington was Adams territory and the Reillys quietly sank into the background.

'When it came down to violence, they were always very strict about it,' says Harry. 'They never let their emotions get in the way. I remember one time I was with the brothers in Ra Ras, a north London club they owned, and a bloke, a villain, came in through the main doors. One of the brothers nodded in the man's direction and said: "That one, he's got to go." That was all there was to it. Nothing more than that ever needed to be said. Later that night the bloke was taken on a detour on his way home and stabbed to death.

'If they said someone had to go, nobody questioned it. It would be done. That was that. They would point a person out and you just knew that in a few days' time, they wouldn't be around any more.'

Another time, Harry witnessed a vicious attack on a man called David McKenzie, a financier who offered to invest money on behalf of the family but ended up losing them £1.5 million. McKenzie was invited to a house in north London where John Potter, the brother-in-law of Adams, lived.

'McKenzie didn't stand a chance. A few people put the boot in and then the knives came out. When it was over McKenzie had loads of broken ribs, he'd been stabbed in the face, his arm and nose and one of his ears had been cut to shreds.

'There was blood everywhere. I thought the main guy who was attacking him had lost it, I thought he was going to kill him there and then at the house and I didn't want any part of that, but it broke up just in time.'

When the case came to court an Adams family associate called Christopher McCormack was accused of carrying out the attack. However, the jury accepted the defence claim that a complete stranger had been responsible. McCormack claimed to have got McKenzie's blood on his jacket from an earlier meeting, when he had broken up a fight between the financier and another man. McCormack was acquitted of all charges. He thanked the jury profusely and offered to buy them all a drink.

Over the years police, Crown Prosecution Service staff and jurors were said to have been bribed and intimidated leading to not-guilty verdicts against members of the gang that were said to quite simply beggar belief. 'Funny thing about the Adams,' says Harry. 'Witnesses tended to forget a lot of stuff like names and faces where they were concerned. If they liked you, life was good. If you fell out with them, your life was over pretty quick.'

In the past thirty years the Adams have been linked to at least twenty-three gangland murders. Although the classic family hit involved two men on a motorcycle, the shots being fired by the pillion passenger, their victims were despatched in a wide variety of ways.

One such death involved the former junior British high-jump champion Claude Moseley, who was killed with a samurai sword swung with so much force that it virtually sliced him in half. The family apparently felt Moseley had to be disposed of because he had attempted to short change them over a drug deal.

The execution was believed to have been carried out by Gilbert Wynter, a Jamaican-born gangster who came to the UK in 1982 and quickly became a main enforcer for the Adams family. Broad-shouldered and immensely strong, Gilbert walked with a slight limp after being run down by the Flying Squad during the course of an armed robbery in the mid-eighties. Close to Terry in particular, Gilbert was arrested and charged with Mosley's murder but the Old Bailey case collapsed when the prosecution's chief witness refused to testify against him.

Wynter walked free while the witness, Wayne Martin, was jailed for three months for contempt.

Another man who experienced a sudden fall from grace was pub accountant Terry Gooderham. He was found shot to death in the front of his Mercedes along with his girlfriend Maxine Arnold. Gooderham is believed to have crossed the family while dealing with some of their finances.

According to underworld folklore, the moneyman begged: 'You can't kill me in front of my girlfriend.' The hitman – believed to be Wynter – turned to Maxine, shot her dead, and said: 'You're not with her now.' Then, having granted the man his wish, he pulled the trigger for the second time.

'About £150,000 went missing and Gooderham was thought to be responsible. A few of us who were known to be in with the Adams got pulled in by the police after he got killed and questioned,' says Harry. 'One of the coppers said: "we know your lot done it", but they didn't have any proof so it never went anywhere.'

Yet another victim was a drugs dealer known as 'Manchester John' who borrowed £100,000 to finance a deal and couldn't pay up on time. He was beaten up and made to sign over the deeds of his flat. When its value was found to be less than the accumulated debt, Gilbert Wynter is believed to have taken him 'up north', killed and buried him.

'They would not tolerate disloyalty. If there was a million pounds on the table, Terry would always make sure that everyone involved got their share of the loot. The quickest way to fall out with them was to try to take away what they believed was rightfully theirs.'

No one was safe, they simply weren't scared of anybody. In 1991 'Mad' Frankie Fraser, a gangland veteran and former enforcer for the Richardson gang, was shot in the head outside a London club in another attack attributed to the Adams gang. He was lucky to survive.

The gang hated publicity. When armed robber turned journalist John McVicar wrote about them in 1987, he received a visit from a friend of the family politely requesting that he refrain from doing so in the future.

When McVicar broke his promise in the aftermath of the Frankie Fraser shooting he received yet another visit. 'I hope it won't go any further,' he was told, 'but if I were you I'd purchase some portable insurance, get in some target practice and be very careful of big trail bikes in your immediate vicinity.'

Another journalist was sent a pig's trotter through the post after writing a critical article.

While working at *Time Out* in the late eighties I too managed to incur the wrath of the family. Deciding that I should be given a 'good hiding', they instructed a well-known gangland figure, since deceased, to pay me a visit. Fortunately for me, the person they chose happened to be one of my contacts and found the whole thing hilarious. 'Don't worry, Tone,' he said after spending half an hour winding me up about it, 'I'm not going to hurt you. But you need to be careful because next time they'll just get someone else to do it.'

Their troubles with the press were soon forgotten as the gang got back to the business of making money. Says Harry: 'The Adams started out being old school. But as the years went by they quickly learned that you have to adapt. When all the younger, newer gangs started appearing on the scene, a lot of the old guys didn't want to have anything to do with them. But the Adams and Terry in particular, welcomed them with open arms. He would never focus on just one thing. Anything that could make money, he would see as an opportunity.

'They moved with the times. They weren't localised like the Krays and despite the fact that they were always being written about in the papers, they didn't go looking for publicity. They ran their business like a modern-day multinational company. They had liaisons and contacts with groups all over this country and abroad. As far as I'm concerned, they were the closest thing Britain has ever had to the mafia.'

According to Harry, the key to the success of the Adams was their willingness to work with gangs from a wide variety of backgrounds. 'When they were at the top of their game, they were operating like a franchise. They wouldn't have to get their hands dirty because there were always people lining up wanting to do it for them.'

Such was the power of the Adams name that the gang were actually able to charge others for the use of it. The cost was £250,000 a time and payment had to be made in seven days. No exceptions.

'If you were doing a job and you had the Adams behind you, even just the name, it meant no one was going to fuck about with you, everyone would know they were going to get paid and everything would go as smoothly as possible. It sounds like a lot of money, but it would be worth every penny. Think of it like starting up your own business and being able to say one of those blokes from *Dragons' Den* is backing you up. It's priceless.'

As their wealth and status grew, so did the pressure within the police force to bring them down. Every attempt seemed to end in failure. At one point in the nineties there were seven separate law enforcement teams simultaneously examining their activities, but none of them were able to bring the brothers to justice. Once again, rumours circulated that the gang had police officers and civil servants in their pay. They were, it was said, untouchable.

The only fly in the ointment was the Inland Revenue. In 1995 the Special Compliance Unit, which investigates cases of illegal tax avoidance, finally got around to looking at Terry Adams and realised that he had never, ever paid a single penny of income tax. His initial explanation – that he didn't actually have a job – carried him only so far. The problem was, his lifestyle had little in common with the rest of the unemployed.

Terry's north London home had been bought for £1 million in cash and furnished with antiques and paintings – some of which were stolen – including nineteenth-century Meissen figures, a Tiffany silver cup, a Chinese lacquered Davenport, a Queen Anne gilt mirror, Picasso still-life linocuts and Henry Moore etchings. In case this made anyone doubt his true nature, above his mantelpiece

Adams also had a life-size poster of Al Pacino in his role as Tony Montana from the cult crime movie *Scarface*.

Terry spent a small fortune customising the home to his taste – £78,000 on remodelling his garden alone. Adams and his wife Ruth took dozens of luxury holidays – they favoured the Italian lakes – always travelling first class and staying at the world's most exclusive hotels. He indulged his passion for expensive watches and jewellery, motorbikes and cars. He bought a private yacht and sent his daughter Sky first to private school and later to stage school. For her eighteenth birthday, he bought her a £45,000 Mercedes sports car.

After the taxman came calling Adams hastily had false details made up showing that he worked as a jewellery designer and consultant. The tax returns he submitted showed him earning only modest sums stretching back for many years and he offered to settle his back bill for just £95,000.

He and Nahome quickly set up two sham companies, Skye and Clouds, to launder his money, provide him with a false income and pay his mortgage. 'We need to find ways to kosher you up,' Nahome told him. The only problem was, Adams made himself out to be earning so little, there was no way in the world he could afford to pay such a massive lump sum without causing suspicion that he was earning much more. It was, unbeknown to Adams, the beginning of the end.

Increasingly incensed by their inability to make progress against the gang, Scotland Yard opened up a new battlefront with the help of the security service, MI5, which had turned its attention to organised crime as the threat from the Eastern bloc subsided. Operation Trinity, launched soon after the tax probe, was staffed by a hand-picked group of detectives and agents and ensured that details of its operations were kept as quiet as possible.

(A rare clue as to how Terry and his brothers had managed to avoid police attention for so long came when it emerged that the family had bought a list of thirty-three police informers for £500 from Mark Herbert, a junior clerk with the Crown Prosecution

Service and the son of a retired Scotland Yard detective. Herbert, who also worked part-time as a bouncer, had helped the family stay one step ahead of the authorities selling them tips about forthcoming arrests and investigations.)

Terry usually insisted on giving personal approval to any schemes the brothers lent their names to, but around this time Tommy decided to branch out on his own. Working with two trusted friends from his schooldays, Michael Papamichael and Edward Wilkinson, Tommy set up a side operation to smuggle vast quantities of cannabis into the UK. Convinced he was being watched at every moment, Tommy insisted on holding all meetings related to the enterprise from the back of a black cab.

He had reckoned without the skill of the surveillance team that had been assigned to his case. They simply planted their bugs in the cab and soon had enough evidence to arrest and prosecute him.

In the days leading up to Tommy's 1998 trial, he and Terry were seen having a huge row in the visiting area of Belmarsh prison. Soon after the case opened, Tommy and his co-defendants all pleaded guilty. He was jailed for eight years.

The trial judge ordered Tommy to pay £1 million in confiscated proceeds of crime or face a further five years. Just days before the deadline expired, his wife turned up twice to the court, carrying £500,000 in cash inside a briefcase on each occasion.

Some were surprised the brothers allowed Tommy to go to prison without attempting to save him with bribery or intimidation. Their reason, it appears, is that he had to be punished for 'going behind his brothers' backs' and getting into difficulties because Terry had not been there to organise things properly.

Terry's anger continued even after his brother began his sentence, expressing fears that the pressure might turn him into an informer. More than that, he was furious that Tommy's carelessness had exposed the whole family operation to the authorities. He described Tommy as a 'jealous, evil cunt' and told one friend: 'When your so-called brother is saying he represents the family behind our back. Who gets us put into the newspapers. He's trying to get us all fucking done, so he can have his freedom ... worse than a fucking grass.'

What Terry had failed to realise was that the same police/MI5 operation that had planted bugs in Tommy's black cabs had also planted listening devices in his own house, disguising themselves as engineers when Terry had the mansion fitted out for Sky television. For the next two years, all his conversations were relayed, twenty-four hours a day, to Thames House, the security service HQ in Westminster. The list of visitors to his home read like a Who's Who of British organised crime.

But compared to Tommy, Terry Adams was a far tougher nut to crack. 'He was always careful to remain once-removed from the criminality, he could never be caught getting his hands dirty,' says Harry. 'People would also come to him with information, hoping to get into his good books. By the time they started bugging him, Terry had already taken a back seat from what was going on. He wanted to be able to live a normal life and was desperate to find a way to reinvent himself.'

For all his wealth and power Adams lived a life full of frustration. He longed to shop at Harrods but could not do so. He had no bank account, no credit cards and was increasingly at odds with a world in which paying for high value items with cold hard cash was no longer a sign of wealth but purely a sign of criminality. 'Harrods always look at cash,' he moaned to Ruth one night. 'And our cash is dirty.'

Terry Adams rarely held money himself. In fact much of his day-to-day existence was funded by his associates. Whenever the need arose for money, cash appeared.' Solly Nahome held £375,000 for him, while his brothers, Tommy and Patsy held £196,000 and £50,000 respectively.

After his brush with the Inland Revenue Terry redoubled his efforts to present a wholly legitimate front to the world. In November 1997 police recorded the following conversation between him and Solly Nahome.

TERRY ADAMS: So it's illegal?

SOLLY NAHOME: It's illegal afterwards.

ADAMS: Then it's an illegal transaction. You should have said straight away. I don't do anything illegal . . . No you don't do anything like that cos you're doing something illegal. Why are you doing something illegal when you don't need to, Sol? We're not, we do things straight now, Sol.

NAHOME: I spoke to you about it, you told me don't do it and that's the end of it . . . It ain't a lot of money anyway.

ADAMS: What is it?

NAHOME: Half a million dollars split three ways. [Inaudible] the aggravation.

ADAMS: [Inaudible] doing something illegal. We don't do anything illegal now, Sol. We do everything straight. All right. I'm not a criminal no more, Sol. I'm a straight person now. You've never been a criminal, Sol. You've always been . . .

NAHOME: Mr Big.

ADAMS: You've always been a straight person.

NAHOME: Well, no. I've been a straight person but I'm the adviser, aren't I?

ADAMS: All you've ever advised me is to go straight. I'm straight now. No, what I'm saying, Sol, you don't do anything illegal.

But while Adams claimed to have left criminality behind, he still relished the gangster life and was addicted to the violence that surrounded him. He continued to order punishment attacks and beatings and occasionally reminisced about his own exploits.

Speaking about a girl called Aleesha who had incurred his wrath he said: 'She's gotta be done. She's gotta have acid flung in her face.' In another conversation he is heard ordering punishment on a man in Marbella who deserves 'a seeing to . . . nothing naughty, no cutting so you can't get nicked for it.'

It was clear to those listening in that Terry got pleasure from describing his past experiences in full and gory detail.

While watching *Blind Date* on television with his brother Danny and his friend Paul Tiernan, Terry Adams suddenly starts ranting about a family associate.

ADAMS: Paul, all I'm saying to you mate, we're all straight. What we've done in our past is now straight – all right.

PAUL TIERNAN: It's history, fucking hell.

ADAMS: We all sit round and say anyone who has had it with a grass ... We've got to play fucking detectives. It's right, Dan, it's right. Right is right. Anyone who has it with a grass is a grass, on my daughter's life, Dan, when he comes out I'm gonna say that to him before I'll do what I'll do. I know what I'm gonna do. Dan, on my baby's life I'm gonna butt him. I gonna go to him, I know what I'm gonna do. I'm gonna smash him in the face with an iron bar. I'm gonna go up to him on my baby's life. I'm gonna do him with an iron bar. Let God know that, Dan. I'm gonna go up to him, say to him ...

DANNY ADAMS: What are you on mate? [laughs] You are mad.

ADAMS: Dan, I'm gonna go up to him and say to him on his doorstep, Dan. I'll do it on the pavement. I'm just gonna say, I'll do it in front of him. I'll do it in front of his kids. I'm gonna do it, Dan, Dan, wherever I get him. If I have my mood, Dan, I'll do him with an iron bar. I'm gonna go to him: 'I'm the cunt, I'm the cunt.' I am gonna fucking have him. If he goes down, Dan, I'm gonna put my foot there. You won't be with me. [He becomes animated] I'm gonna do them, Dan, I know that, I am gonna fucking do it.

DANNY ADAMS: Tel, I will be there, mate.

ADAMS: Me and Bobby Warren was in a car once, right, Dan. There was a geezer that was lying to us, Dan, right, on my baby's life. Dan, I've got something about me when things happen. When I hit someone I do them damage. And I went to the geezer. Stealing a hundred grand it was, Dan, or eighty grand, and I went crack. On my baby's life, Dan, his kneecap come right out there.

DANNY ADAMS: [laughs]

ADAMS: All white, Dan, all bone and . . . on my baby's life every time I do damage, Dan. If I have a fight I cut them with my knuckles.

Later that same month, in another conversation with Solly Nahome the talk turns to a dispute with an associate over a payment of £250,000 for use of the Adams name. Only in this case the person making use of the service has failed to hand over any cash. The Adams name was, in a sense, just like any business brand – and they protected it just as guardedly as any corporation.

Adams makes it very clear that the offender must be dealt with harshly.

ADAMS: Then you let Simon give the geezer a hiding, right? I don't give a fuck about the geezer . . . the geezer's gonna be stamped on. He's using the family name, the geezer's using the family name . . . And he's gotta be hurt, this fella. We ain't gonna be no one's cunts, Sol.

Later Gilbert Wynter, the Adams family's main enforcer, joins the conversation.

ADAMS: Just grab him . . . That's what I want, Gil. Gil, you do that for me, I'll love you for that, mate. Knock him out, put him on his arse . . . I want them hurt double, double, double bad. I mean it, Gil, you've got to liven him up, put the fear of God into him mate, [so] he knows it's only down to you that he's walking about and breathing fresh air.

WYNTER: I'll open him up like a bag of crisps.

As the months went by, especially in the aftermath of Tommy's conviction, Adams soon suspected he was being bugged and he and his wife Ruth mocked the police by faking the sounds of passionate sex for the microphones. He broke the news to his elderly mother.

[Flo Adams offers Terry Adams a hot drink]

ADAMS: Mum, I don't drink tea.

FLO: Oh sorry. What do you reckon you are getting on now, everything all right?

ADAMS: Who?

FLO: Better now.

ADAMS: Who with? I've got some news to tell you, Mum. Everything I do, Mum, right, I do straight.

FLO: Yes.

ADAMS: Right, they've got listening devices in this house, I know that, right.

FLO: I don't believe that.

ADAMS: Yeah, they've got listening devices in this house. Me and Ruth have a right giggle with them right, you understand.

FLO: Yes.

ADAMS: We have a right thing, you know, like, er . . .

FLO: Yeah, I know what you mean.

ADAMS: Dennis has had conversations with me people, things like that. 'Cause they do. We give 'em things to talk about.

FLO: Yeah. Ain't it terrible though, Tel.

ADAMS: Er . . .

FLO: That you're on tape.

On 27 November 1998 Solly Nahome arrived at the Finchley home he shared with his wife and daughter and noticed a helmeted man, who had been standing by a motorcycle, suddenly turn and head towards him. Knowing only too well what lay ahead, Nahome made a run for his front door. He never made it. The hitman pumped four bullets into his head and then made his getaway on the waiting Honda motorbike.

Nahome was key to the Adams' hidden fortune, organising 'front' companies and disguising financial arrangements. He is said to have invested and hidden more than £25 million of Terry's money.

For some time it was rumoured that the murder had been ordered by the Adams family who had discovered that Solly was skimming off some of the profits. But recordings of telephone calls made and received in the days following the killing show that Terry Adams was genuinely shocked by what had happened.

His murder seemed to indicate that a rival gang was trying to disrupt the family cashflow and that's just what happened. Nahome's death left the gang confused about where all its cash was stashed. Terry's wife Ruth was taped explaining to Nahome's widow: 'It's all over the fucking place.'

A second tragedy was just around the corner. Gilbert Wynter, once a rock in the organisation, disappeared among rumours of a major fallout with the family. He is, according to sources, either in hiding in the Caribbean, or holding up the Millennium Dome inside one of the pillars.

By 2003 the police were ready to arrest Adams. When they knocked on the door of his house, early on the morning of 30 April they walked into a luxurious home filled with £500,000 of antiques and paintings. In one of the bedrooms they discovered £48,000 of jewellery and in the loft, hidden away in a shoebox to use as pocket money when he fancied, £60,000 in cash.

But in the end the massive investigation could only scrape together enough evidence to put him on trial for what essentially amounted to laundering his own wages. Like Chicago gangster Al Capone before him, Adams was finally nailed for a financial crime after the police failed to amass sufficient evidence to send him down for his more bloodthirsty activities. Despite the many references to violence, the only useable evidence from the surveillance operation related to financial impropriety.

In May 2003 Terry Adams was charged with money laundering, tax evasion and handling stolen goods. He was released on £1 million bail – his wife brought the money to court in cash. And in February 2007 he pleaded guilty to conspiracy to launder £1.1 million. The judge said: 'Your plea demonstrates that you have a fertile, cunning and imaginative mind capable of sophisticated, complex and dishonest financial manipulation.'

After being charged Adams used every trick in the book to delay his trial as long as possible. First he sacked his legal team shortly before the trial was due to begin, forcing the judge to give him time to appoint and brief new counsel. Then he claimed to have an IQ too low to understand the allegations. He also said he was dyslexic and even consulted psychiatrists about his mental state.

In another delaying tactic, he demanded that thousands of hours of largely insignificant MI5 surveillance tapes be transcribed before the case could go ahead. Once this had been done at significant cost to the public, his lawyers said the tapes were no longer required. Then, just when it seemed Adams could do no more to postpone the inevitable, he sacked his legal team once again.

Finally, 1,378 days after he was charged, Adams admitted a specimen charge of money laundering after reaching a deal with the prosecution which involved dropping charges against his wife. He admitted conspiracy to conceal criminal property on the basis that he had not engaged in criminal activity to create money for the last six years and that he did not earn it from drugs trafficking.

Eight charges were left on file, including furnishing false information, making false statements, fraudulent trading and conspiracy to contravene the Criminal Justice Act. Adams also faced charges of mortgage and tax deception.

It was once the trial had finished that it was revealed that Adams, despite his undoubted wealth, had been on legal aid throughout his trial.

On 18 May 2007 he was ordered to pay £4.8 million in legal fees to three law firms who had initially represented him under the UK's free legal aid scheme. He was also required to pay £800,000 in prosecution costs. In May 2009 Adams was forced to put his beloved home on sale in order to pay his mounting bills.

In the end it was a two-tier approach that brought Adams down. Eager to present a legitimate front to the world, Adams had set up various companies to launder his ill-gotten gains, which paid him as a consultant, giving him a legitimate source of income. The problem was, Adams had not gone legit until the age of forty-five and up until that time he had never paid a penny of income tax. He didn't even have a National Insurance number. Adams simply couldn't have it both ways. He had no choice but to plead guilty, either to money laundering or tax evasion.

The other reason Adams pleaded guilty was for the sake of his wife, Ruth. Seriously ill with a stomach disorder during the run-up to her husband's case, she had been charged with eight counts of laundering and tax evasion, all of which were dropped as part of his agreement with the prosecution.

'The Adams would get whatever job they needed done and the other firm would have the prestige of saying that they were working for the Adams,' Harry tells me. 'And that was always worth a lot. It means that even if the heads of the family are all behind bars or out of the country on some kind of self-imposed exile, there are enough others around to keep their business going.

'Terry's got a stretch and to a lot of people that might sound like a long time. But Terry always knew the risks he was taking. By the time he gets out, he'll still be young enough and rich enough to enjoy himself. When you think about it, to have done what he has done and made as much as he has made but only to end up doing three years inside is pretty remarkable. You really have to take your hat off to him. As for me, I'm glad I walked away from it. It was fun for a while but I prefer to live my life without having to look over my shoulder the whole time.'

16
THE PLAYER

One month after the conviction of Terry Adams, another kingpin of British organised crime who had managed to evade conviction for most of his career finally came to the end of his run.

But unlike Adams, Brian 'the Milkman' Wright, one of the richest criminals in the country, had to endure the full force of the judicial system. Shortly before he was sentenced to thirty years at Woolwich Crown Court for conspiring to import millions of pounds worth of cocaine into Britain, the judge asked if he wanted to say anything in his defence. Wright, then sixty, shook his head. 'There is no mitigation,' he said softly, before being led down to the cells.

Wright's conviction brought to an end a criminal career in which he not only became one of Britain's most successful and sophisticated drug smugglers – he was called the Milkman because he always delivered – but also a leading horse-race fixer and a friend to the stars. He lived in the best villas and apartments in London and Spain. He drank champagne at the finest nightclubs. He entertained friends at his private boxes at Ascot and Newmarket. Wright was so confident that he could outsmart Customs that he even wagered an investigator £1 million for a £1 stake that he would never be caught.

Throughout the 1990s, Wright's gang literally swamped Britain with cocaine. In 1998 alone he is thought to have been responsible for shipping two tonnes of cocaine to Britain, leading one Customs officer to remark that the drugs were coming into the country 'faster than people could snort them!'

By the time of his arrest in Spain in 2005, Wright had smuggled cocaine worth at least £360 million into Great Britain and was said

GANG LAND

to have had his fingers in dozens of other equally lucrative pies. In 2004 he was said to be worth £600 million in the *Sunday Times* Rich List. Following his conviction, Senior Investigating Customs Officer Paul Seeley said: 'Brian Wright is twice as big as Terry Adams. This is the top, top dog.' The pair had worked together on occasion and Wright is said to have been one of the only people to be able to stand up to Terry and his brothers and get away with it – a true mark of his place in the organised-crime hierarchy.

Smuggling, though, was not the Milkman's only vice. He could often be seen in his boxes at Ascot or Newmarket, where he would regularly bet between £50,000 and £100,000 on a single race. One jockey who knew him in that period says he always carried a roll of notes 'that would choke a donkey'. It was an ideal way of laundering his drug earnings but Wright took things a step further. He bribed jockeys to throw races. The bungs took various forms – sometimes it was a cash payment of £5,000, sometimes cocaine or prostitutes, sometimes a night out at London nightclubs Annabel's or Tramp – but the result was always the same: Wright got the result he wanted.

'Sometimes, when we put money on a race, we knew what was going to be first, second and third,' said one associate. 'For some races there would be days or weeks worth of work that had gone into them.' More than twenty leading jockeys were accused of being associated with Wright.

The former borstal boy, who is almost illiterate, owned a plush villa in Spain's Sotto Grande which he named El Lechero – Spanish for the Milkman. He also rented several riverside apartments in central London, one at a cost of £20,000 per month. When the rest of his gang was rounded up in a massive police and Customs operation, Wright fled to northern Cyprus – which has no extradition treaty with Britain – and set up home in a luxury villa. His friends included Clint Eastwood, Jerry Hall, Frank Sinatra and leading jockey John Francome. He is also godfather to the son of comic Jim Davidson. None of these celebrities were in any way aware of Wright's criminal dealings.

286

Many of these high-profile associates supported Wright during the series of trials connected to the gang. Jim Davidson told one court: 'I still count myself as a good friend of Brian's. I have known him very well for nineteen or twenty years.' Davidson said the suggestion that Wright was involved in drug trafficking was 'laughable'.

Former National Hunt jockey Graham Bradley described Wright as one of his 'very best' friends. 'Like any professional gambler who is being honest, Brian will admit that he has his contacts and I was one. But the kind of money he was having on was always going to make people put two and two together and get six. When there was a breath of scandal within racing there was only one name that comes up: Brian Wright.

'One mistake he has made is being a success at gambling because that jealousy eats away at many people. Brian has never been shy of using his money for pleasure as well as punting.'

Wright had supply networks in Colombia, Mexico, Brazil and Panama, and shipped cocaine directly across the Atlantic. Wright controlled the shipments from his villa in Spain, but made frequent trips to Britain to oversee the operation.

Despite his well-known friends and lavish lifestyle, Wright operated outside the reach of the law for most of his adult life. He had no bank accounts and no verifiable home address. He paid for his rented Chelsea flat in cash. He preferred public phones to mobiles. When he conducted business in London, he booked a suite at the Conrad Hotel in Chelsea Harbour under an alias.

The authorities only started to close in on the Wright organisation in September 1996, when rough weather forced an oceangoing yacht called *Sea Mist* to find shelter in Cork harbour. The yacht had been heading for the south coast of England, where its cargo would have been offloaded onto a series of smaller, locally registered vessels and taken ashore.

This process, known as 'coopering' involves using the latest Global Positioning System technology to allow the yachts to meet several miles off the coast and pass the drugs from one to the other. While transatlantic vessels like *Sea Mist* are generally checked by Customs, smaller local craft are far less likely to arouse suspicion.

Instead of being able to dock 'clean' the *Sea Mist* came in fully loaded. When Irish Customs officers carried out a routine search of the vessel, they found 599 kilograms of cocaine concealed in a dumb waiter.

Packaged in bales and marked with the 10 of diamonds playing card, the drug was found to be 83 per cent pure and 'conservatively valued' at £50 million. After being 'coopered' to another vessel, the *Caista*, the drugs were to be taken to a safe house in King's Saltern Road, Lymington, Hampshire. But once the *Sea Mist* was raided, the rest of the gang were forced to hastily flee the property – leaving vital evidence of Brian Wright's involvement in his Channel 4 *Racing Diary*. The book contained contact numbers for several other members of the cartel as well as dozens of famous names in horse racing and TV.

The British and Irish authorities immediately realised they had uncovered part of a monumental smuggling business. Later that year, British Customs officers launched Operation Extend, specifically to curb Wright's smuggling activities.

Operation Extend spent two years working on the Wright gang, during which time they bugged his Chelsea flat, followed him to meetings, and monitored his son, Brian – a key member of the gang – along with his right-hand man Kevin Hanley.

They also observed Wright meeting with members of the gang and visiting pubs and hotels also known to be frequented by agents of the South American drug barons, including Brazilian economist Ronald Soares.

In autumn that year Wright was seen meeting Hanley and Brian Wright junior shortly before £30 million in cocaine was offloaded from a boat called the *Moonstreak*. It later emerged the smuggling ring was organising even bigger shipments of cocaine from two different cartels in Colombia in 1998.

This time three yachts, the *Cyan*, *Lucky Irish* and *Flex*, were sailed from Panama, Guadeloupe and Trinidad to the British coast near Poole, Dorset, and Salcombe, Devon, for coopering so the drugs could be stored at a safe house nearby before being taken to London for distribution.

American sailor Judith Parks helped cooper the drugs from the *Cyan* near Studland Bay in Dorset. She was paid £50,000 for helping to transfer the bricks of cocaine – marked with a picture of the famous American 'Uncle Sam' figure – to a safe house near Ringwood, Hampshire. With the drugs ashore, the gang began planning more and even bigger shipments of cocaine.

A bug recorded Ronald Soares telling another man: 'They want to double everything, crazy. England is flooded. They put 1100 kilos of cocaine, gets out very, very slowly, slowly. They are going to be selling until after Christmas.'

By September 1998 the net was closing in as Wright was arrested in connection with horse race corruption and doping. He was released on police bail without charge but two months later his right-hand man Kevin Hanley – who was responsible for drug distribution – was arrested with twenty-nine kilograms of cocaine and paperwork which tied him to other drug consignments. It meant Wright had lost the person responsible for moving, storing and distributing the network's haul of cocaine.

Without the assistance of Hanley, Wright was forced to break cover for the first time and meet directly with his South American counterparts.

The same month, Wright had a heart bypass operation at the private Wellington Hospital in London after suffering shoulder pains while watching a horse race on TV. Shortly afterwards he left Britain to spend Christmas in Spain, his recovery aided by the decision of the Crown Prosecution service not to charge him in relation to the horse doping case in December 1998.

But on 12 February 1999, Wright's son Brian Anthony Wright and son-in-law Paul Shannon were among fifteen people arrested in connection with the smuggling investigation. Other members of his gang were rounded up in the United States and the Caribbean.

Five days after his son's arrest, Wright senior paid £20,000 through his daughter Joanne for a private jet to take him and jockey Declan Murphy to northern Cyprus. He told the jury during his trial he had always intended to go to northern Cyprus to watch the Cheltenham Festival with a friend who lived on the island and claimed it had been his plan 'to retire'. But because the territory had no extradition he was effectively safe from arrest.

Even after BBC *Panorama* had uncovered his whereabouts, there was nothing the British police could do about it, and Wright continued to live a life of luxury in the Turkish half of the island. In 2005, however, either because he believed the authorities had struck a deal with Britain, or because he was bored, he moved to Spain. He was arrested in Marbella and returned to the UK.

Because of Wright's strong connection to Spain, I immediately made a call to Jake, the Marbella-based gang associate who had earlier helped me peek into the world of British and Irish criminals living in the Costa del Sol and on the Costa Blanca.

Jake readily confessed that he knew several people who had worked with Wright over the years, many of them had also worked with Terry Adams and several other leading figures in the underworld.

'What you have to understand,' Jake explained, 'is that even though these are totally separate organisations, they all work for one another. They all do the same things. Which is why the minute you probe into Wright's organisation, you realise there are strong links to the likes of the Adams family and so on.'

When I asked whether any of those people might talk to me, Jake sighed deeply.

'The problem is, the higher up the ladder you go, the less people are likely to talk. They won't even give you the time of day – they've got too much to lose. And if it looks as though you're actually going to be a threat to what they have going on, then you're going to end up with a bullet in your head. The people at the top, they like the fact that only a few people know who they are. The last thing they want is to attract any kind of attention to themselves. Anybody with a reputation, they're a target. As soon as your name gets out, you're fucked, you're useless.

'You only need to look at a few of the big names out there, the ones that crop up in all the books. Once upon a time they were good earners, some of them at least. Then they get known and they can't do shit. It's the same as if you get nicked. Once the police know who you are, they ain't going to forget what you did.

'Look at Terry Adams. The only reason he got away with such a light sentence is because he'd pretty much given up anything that was hands on. Once his brother started getting his mug plastered all over the papers and people started calling them the "A-Team", it was game over.

'Yeah, he made enough so he was able to retire and still live it up, and he'll be all right in the future, but at the end of the day he didn't have any choice. If he had kept at it, he'd been looking at coming out of prison in a box.

'Some of the stuff you see out there is a joke. I remember a couple of years ago watching some Channel Five documentary following around some gangster from up north. At one point the commentary said: "And now he's going to make an alliance with the local triads." And there's this bloke opening the door to his house and a couple of Chinese blokes come in, then they all sit down and start chatting.

'And all this is on film and I'm thinking: "Triads my fat hairy arse!" Some fucking secret society that is. What a load of bollocks. As if they'd go anywhere near a fucking camera. As if anyone would talk business with a reporter in the room.

'If you're extra, extra, extra lucky and you have the right contacts, one or two people might speak to you, especially if you don't fully identify them. People like me, for instance. But no one in a million years is ever going to sit down in front of a camera and talk to you about what they've got going on. Not unless they're stupid or they're lying. It's fine for the kids and the wanabees but you don't reach the top of this business by being on telly or talking to journalists.'

A rare exception to that rule is the man known as Horace Silver. Silver – a pen name taken from one of his musical heroes – has spent most of his life dicing with death. As a senior member of one of Britain's most successful criminal gangs, he has made tens of millions of pounds from drug trafficking, armed robbery, kidnapping and murder over the course of twenty years.

Although he worked closely with Adams and distributed drugs on behalf of Wright, he has evaded repeated police sting operations, served only a few months in prison and survived at least two attempts on his life. I met him in 2004 soon after he published his first novel. *Judas Pig* is the gripping tale of a career criminal who reaches the top of his profession before the ghosts of his past catch up with him and threaten to destroy him. What sets the book apart is that, while essentially a work of fiction, the key elements of the story are true. With all the main characters easily identifiable in the underworld, the book reveals for the first time who was responsible for at least five of London's unsolved gangland murders.

Silver has now retired from crime but the other members of his gang remain active. Like all the most successful criminals, they have avoided becoming household names and, like Silver, have never been convicted of any major crime. The book, which reveals the inner workings of the gangs and details the rip-offs, double crosses and many killings they have been involved in, sent shockwaves throughout the underworld.

'I haven't come to terms with some of the things I have done. I don't think I ever will,' Silver told me. 'At the time you can shut yourself off from it, and the drugs – I used a lot of cocaine – help deaden the pain. But I guess I wasn't much good as a gangster, because in the end I wasn't strong enough to cope with the reality of what I was involved in.

'Everything in the book actually happened. Sometimes I've changed a few dates or names because otherwise I'd be leading myself down the path to prison, but everything in the book is real.'

Silver chose to write the book as a novel, changing some names but keeping others the same, to distance himself from the current fashion for celebrity gangster autobiographies. 'Any of these gang-sters who have written books about their lives, they're failures. They've been caught and they've done lots of porridge and the stories they tell are no more relevant than Dick Turpin, because it all happened such a long time ago. Anyone who has made their money, they want to keep quiet. Look at [he mentions the names of three prominent and very active London criminals]. They haven't said a word and they never will.'

The central figure in the book, Silver's former partner in crime, is known simply as 'Danny'. In real life Danny is well known to police. He has stood in the dock on at least five occasions, three times for attempted murder and twice for murder. Each time he has walked free, usually after witnesses vanished, died or declared themselves to be suffering from amnesia.

One of the unsolved murders detailed in the book is that of Barry Dalton, whose body was found in his car on the outskirts of London's Alexandra Palace in September 1992. He had been shot in the head at point-blank range. At the time of his death, Dalton, married with five children, was described as the manager of a minicab firm but was in fact running protection rackets across the capital.

A former bare-knuckle prizefighter with connections to the IRA's southern command, Dalton had fallen out with the legen-dary Lenny 'The Guvnor' McLean. Dalton took his revenge by turning up at McLean's flat with a shotgun. 'McLean had just got out of the shower,' says Silver, 'and answered the door with a towel wrapped around him. He saw the gun and was trying to get away when he was shot in the arse. If Dalton had wanted to kill him, he would have. He was just mugging him off.'

The book explains how Dalton fell out with Danny's gang after trying to muscle in on some of their business interests. The killing was carried out by a hired hitman named Del Croxton. He had recently been released from prison after serving sixteen years for armed robbery. He was recruited because, as Silver puts it, 'it's always handy to have a couple of psychos around in case you have stuff that needs doing.'

A few months later Croxton was arrested after carrying out a second killing. Once inside he started to crack up. His partner had recently given birth to his first child and he feared he would never leave prison. His fragile state was worsened by his addiction to heroin. Someone in the gang arranged for Croxton to be supplied with heroin while in prison, but the drugs were far more potent than anything he had previously used. He overdosed in his cell and died with the needle still stuck in his vein.

Silver finally left the gang after falling out with Danny. Part of his reason for writing the book is to seek revenge on the man he once considered his friend but who later tried to have him killed. 'All gangsters hide behind a myth of themselves that they put forward, not only to the straight world but to the criminal world as well. I'm exposing Danny for what he really is.'

Silver is finding the transition from gangster to author difficult, but only because so many people confuse the reality with what they see in gangster films. 'The public have a very strong image of what gangsters are like, and it's tied up with the likes of Lenny McLean or Dave Courtney, but that's a long way from the truth. I did an interview with a journalist from one of the lads' mags and he asked me if I had any funny stories. I didn't know what to say. To me, the time I put a nonce case in a coma was fucking hilarious. I fell about laughing afterwards. We used to laugh when we tortured people, too. I don't think he understood. I think he wanted a tale about the time we went out to rob a bank, pulled our guns out and our trousers fell down around our ankles.

'The humour is there, but it's dark. And that's how it should be. These people go around pretending to be some kind of Robin Hood, but the truth is that they're scumbags, and I should know because I used to be a scumbag too.'

Silver's story illustrates another of Jake's points. The real identity of Silver's boss, a man every bit an equal of Terry Adams in both power and influence, is known to only a handful of people. With no actual convictions it is almost impossible for me to identify him fully without opening myself up to a potential libel suit. And that's just the way he likes it.

With that in mind it came as no surprise to find that, despite Brian Wright's legendary status as one of Britain's richest criminals, he actually worked in partnership with another individual whose name never emerged during his trials and who remained active until far more recently.

I learned about him from a highly placed source within the British criminal fraternity who quite literally risked death by speaking out about the inner workings of the organisation that once employed him. He will, of course, remain anonymous.

'Rick was Brian's partner. They were supposed to be equal, but Brian never got an equal split of it. If Rick brought in 600 kilos, he would tell Brian there were only 400 kilos and all that sort of nonsense. Everything Rick does is bent. I mean, Rick can't even lay in a bed straight. It was more like seventy/thirty partners.

'Rick is the top man though. As far as I'm concerned there are only two or three people in England of the same ilk as Rick. There is nobody more serious when it comes to importation. Yeah, there are loads of people bringing in fifty and thirty kilos at a time, but there's nobody brings it in like he does. He puts a whole new meaning on the word wholesale, Rick does.

'And to be honest with you if you said to Rick today can you bring 500 in of cocaine he'd just look down his nose cos he wants to bring more. He's like the craziest guy I've ever known, but he actually does do it.

'He never wants to do less than 500. Anything under 500 and he's not interested. Totally not interested, and we're not talking puff or cannabis, we're talking about cocaine. I mean, he does get involved in grass sometimes but that's always three tonnes or whatever but he doesn't like it. He'll do it if there's nothing else but the cocaine he likes because it's easy to sell and the money is there within days. It's not like the other stuff where it goes on for months. He doesn't like giving to someone for three weeks on credit and all this nonsense then just getting a few quid here and there. He likes the coke. Straight out and they've got the money and that's that.

'Rick was born over here but has spent most of his time in the States. Because of that he has major worldwide connections for cocaine. He also knows a lot of very serious American criminals.

'I've been to Mexico with Rick and met very, very serious people there. I mean absolutely frightening. To be honest with you, this sounds like this is a wind up but they said to me that they take twenty tonnes of cocaine by road through Mexico up to the American border with a Mexican army escort and have it picked up by the local sheriffs department. The lifestyles were incredible. One of them was looking to spend up to $50 million on property in Europe. Money was flowing like it was going out of fashion.

'I tried to get involved with some of the bigger jobs but it never worked out. It's hard when you're bringing stuff in from South America. We liked to hide it in fruit, but everything needs to fall into place. You need to have your connections at the airport and then it needs to be the right season. You can't hide it in melons if there aren't any melons around. You need to have the contacts to get the melons and hide the drugs inside.

'Sometimes we'd use the yachts. Rick was the one who started using the west coast of Ireland. Sometimes it would come into the airport. Rick had a facility where stuff would come in international and would get put on the belt for domestic. He used that a few times. He had loads of people at the airport.

'The only problem with Rick is that he is a very bad gambler. He once said to me that he thought he'd spent £40 million on gambling over the years. Most people who have got say two or three million want to retire. Rick, all he wants to do is spend the money and do the next load. At Cheltenham he lost £600,000 at the races over the four-day meeting. I've just never met anyone who could spend that kind of money. Not spend, lose. It's beyond imagination.

'But Rick doesn't care. He believes that every year he's got the right to bring in drugs four or five times. And there's nothing about him saying well I'm getting a bit old, the police are getting a bit clever, I'm going to do this and stop. He spends it. As soon as he gets it he spends it. Literally within weeks the money is gone. He's putting twenty thousand, thirty thousand on a horse. Not once a week but every day.

'Rick doesn't get many losses. He got more successes than losses. He always had 600 to 700 kilos coming in at least four or five times a year. You haven't got to be Einstein to work it out. You can't spend £40 million quid and not work unless you're doing something. It's a lot of money for someone who doesn't do a proper job of work.

'You walk round Harrods with him for a day and everybody in there knows him by his Christian name. He's been shopping there all his life. His house in Mayfair is fabulous. He's got another house in Canada. He's got a house in Athens. He's got a house in Greenwich Village. He's doing quite well.

'He's got a name of being very solid but also not to be trusted with money, so that was where Brian Wright came in. For the credibility side of the partnership. I've known Rick go to New York or Canada for a meeting on drugs, on an importation, and he's had to get Brian Wright to go over there and guarantee the money to the people.

'It's not that Rick's not trusted – he's trusted not to talk to the police or anything like that, but he's not trusted around a five-pound note and that's where Brian fitted into it. And equally, if there's any expenses needed, Brian was always quite happy to put it in. If they wanted a couple of hundred thousand dollars to show good faith or something, Brian Wright could always pull the money out whereas Rick has always got a problem with money because he spends it just like water.

'Brian's a bit cleverer. He doesn't spend all his money but Rick, he seems to have a disease. I once said to him why don't you have the load sent straight over to Ladbrokes and they could give him an account, that way he wouldn't have to be involved in selling it. He didn't find it funny, but it's so apt it's untrue. I've never known a guy to get hold of £2 million and spend it within weeks. Well, not even spend it. Lose it. He doesn't get anything for it. He just like puts it on a horse and gambles and it's gone. And then it's like, oh well, let's get on with the next load.

'He goes to the bookmakers every day. He likes to stand in there when it's all happening. He enjoys it. There's one bookmakers, when you come out of his flat and cross Piccadilly it's on the right-hand side, he uses it regularly, there's another one on Park Lane up some stairs from the Hilton. I mean, if I tell you he does £500 a week on the lottery, give you some idea what sort of gambler he is.

'He's fearless with other people's money. Another story he told me himself. He actually gambled $2 million of the mob's money. Lost it. They sent someone over to shoot him. Kill him. And he said to them, look, you can shoot me if you like, but it's far better that you give me six months and I pay the money back. So they did.

'Rick used to be connected to the Adams family. When Rick needed money to gamble, Tommy Adams would let him have twenty or thirty grand and the next day another twenty or thirty grand until he really got into him for a lot of money. Then they would put pressure on Rick, call him up there and actually say to him you owe us £500,000 and you've got to pay. So then Rick would bring a load of cocaine into the country to pay the Adams. But instead of taking the £500,000, the family would take back kilos to the value of the money. So if it was going for £20,000 a kilo, they'd take back twenty-five kilos. So they've got their money back plus they're earning out of the cocaine. It happened all the time. Tommy and Rick were together the day before Tommy got arrested and Tommy managed to get a message to Rick for him not to stay in the country.

'Brian used to rent out a suite at the Conrad for work. All of these people, when they've actually got a bit of work on, none of them work out of their houses. They all rent a property or stay in a hotel.

'Rick did the same. He also had his own fleet of taxis which he would use to help avoid surveillance. He would keep them stationed, one behind the other, at a convenient taxi rank. If he needed to go somewhere he would go for a walk around the block and then jump into the first taxi. Because any police officers following him were likely to be on foot too, they would be forced to jump into the second taxi in order to keep an eye on him. The second driver would then let Rick know if he was being followed. They were tame taxi drivers who he would pay for the week to do nothing but wait for him.

'Mostly he just does smuggling. He doesn't have time for much else. Rick and I were trying to arrange a scam involving a container. We wanted to throw it into the sea and claim the insurance. It was going to be empty, a container full of nothing, but we'd say there was all sorts. But the problem is that at the end of the day, you can't do that unless you're 100 per cent respectable. They won't pay out. So we gave up on it.

'What Rick does, he's a great believer that if he's got three lots of deals going on, he doesn't finish paying you for one deal. Then he starts paying you from the second deal. Then he gets into the third deal before he's paid for the first deal so he gets everybody totally confused and just keeps taking money and at the end of the day everybody ends up with nothing.

'Instead of doing it deal for deal and saying right, I've got a hundred grand to come, give me my hundred grand before I do anything, he's already pulling money out of a second deal before anyone's been paid for the first. You know there's nobody like Rick for being straight with money. I mean, really, once the casino's had it or the bookmaker, I mean that's the end of that and lets go on with the next load because I owe the Colombian a million quid.

'Rick lost it a bit when Kevin Hanley got arrested. Kevin was the UK connection. He knew everybody in the drugs business. His network went right around the country. I've seen him sell 660 kilos of cocaine in ten days. And he got all the money for it as well.

'Rick's always been a user of cocaine himself. He's on it all the time now. He can't even talk to anybody now. He just shouts. He's rude to everybody. He gets back from America and he texts thirty people and doesn't get one call. People are fed up to death of him. To be honest with you, I have actually been there and seen him do it to Colombians and people. I mean when you get kids of nineteen and twenty worth millions of pounds and you've got an old man of like nearly sixty insulting them, they don't seem too happy by it.

'And I mean a couple of times they've said to me if he keeps on we're just going to hit him, and by that they don't mean hit him, they mean kill him. So that really puts it into the pecking order.

'But for now they need him. Last time I saw Rick we were at the Hilton and he had these Colombians or Mexicans with him. One of them was called Louis and he wanted to send 200 kilograms of cocaine every month or every other month to Felixstowe.

'He had a plan. Instead of just sending one container, he was going to send three at a time but the drugs would be only in one pallet. He said the chances of being discovered are remote because you've got three containers, twenty pallets on each, that gives you a one in a fifty-nine chance of finding it. He said one container would look very suspect but to send three, Customs would look at that and think oh well, that's normal business. I mean, he was even prepared to send more than three if need be.

'He said he could do it from about four countries over there in South America. Colombia, Venezuela, Peru and Brazil. Louis was saying they have got three submarines and he was laughing. He said the Americans have got their inflatable boats in the Caribbean sea and they don't realise there are all these submarines full of drugs underneath. That's why they're winning the war, he said. That's why the price is dropping all over the world. Because we're winning the war.'

17

TOP MAN

The man known as 'The Pimpernel', a legendary figure in the world of British organised crime for the past four decades, was doing a superb job of living up to his nickname.

I had returned to the Spanish coastal city of Marbella and driven my tiny hire car to the base of the hills in the upmarket, eastern region known as El Real, along the edge of the enormous, beautifully manicured golf course and then onwards and upwards past rows and rows of spectacular villas in order to pay an unannounced visit to a man once described as a 'criminal superstar', only to discover that this famously elusive character was nowhere to be found.

Michael John Paul Green was born to Irish parents in London in June 1941, soon after the end of the waves of destruction that had devastated the city during the blitz, and came of age just at the start of what would come to be known as the swinging sixties. That same optimism and hedonism that swept through London at the time also seeped into the underworld, propelling the likes of the Krays and the Richardsons to new heights of wealth and power.

Fearless, ambitious and eager to make a name for himself, the young Green had picked up the first of a series of minor convictions at the age of fourteen and by the time the sixties were halfway through he had become a respected and experienced member of the criminal fraternity. After two more spells in prison, one for burglary, another for receiving stolen goods, Green became a member of the Wembley Mob, a loose-knit coalition of between ten and fifteen villains who specialised in armed robbery.

The mob was phenomenally successful: in the space of four years the gang made off with more than £1.3 million, including a raid on a Security Express van outside a bank in Ilford in February 1970 that contained £237,000 – at the time the biggest cash robbery ever to take place in the UK. Although the raid was a success, two of the bank's security guards who had passed information to the gang eventually broke down and confessed what they had done. That November, Green was sentenced to eighteen years for his part in the raid.

Released on licence in 1979, Green immediately joined forces with another former member of the Wembley Mob, Ronnie Dark, and became one of the first villains to see the money-making potential of large scale VAT fraud. The pair bought hundreds of gold Krugerrand coins – on which no VAT is payable – melted them down into ingots and sold the bars back to the bullion house, this time collecting the VAT. In the space of a year the gang is believed to have made at least £6 million.

When the authorities finally cottoned on to what was going on and moved in to arrest the gang, Green chose life on the run and fled to Spain. Although his sentence for the VAT fraud would have been relatively short, the fact that he had breeched the conditions of his release meant he would also have to serve out the remaining nine years of his term for the Ilford robbery.

Green arrived in Spain just as other expat Brits were taking their first tentative steps into the drug trade. Having already excelled in one field of criminality, Green had no difficulty adjusting to another and quickly became one of the leading figures in the marijuana trade. Soon, thanks to direct contacts with major players in the Colombian drug cartels, Green began trafficking in cocaine as well and his wealth soared into the stratosphere. He used his profits to buy property in Spain, France and Morocco as well as a Rolls-Royce, a Porsche convertible and a small fleet of watercraft.

He named his Spanish home 'Villa Annie' after his wife, Ann, an accomplished drug dealer in her own right and a well-connected gangland figure having previously been married to none other than

Jack 'The Hat' McVite, one of two men murdered by the Kray twins during the height of their reign.

By the mid-nineties the Spanish police were becoming increasingly alarmed about what was going on under their noses and launched a series of major operations aimed at busting open the British drug cartels based in the Costa del Sol. By then Green's operation was being referred to in law enforcement circles as 'El Pulpo' – the Octopus – because its tentacles seemed to reach everywhere.

Police swooped in February 1987 and seized £2 million worth of cannabis and made six arrests. Green was not among those taken into custody, though his cars and properties were among the assets confiscated. Having long been aware of the potential danger, Green had worked hard to distance himself from the source of his wealth and when he was finally arrested a month later, he spent only a few weeks in custody before being released when a magistrate decided there was insufficient evidence of his involvement to proceed with the case.

Just a few months later British police got their own lead on Green with the arrest in London of a major international drug trafficker named Nikolaus Chrastny. Caught red handed with £5 million of cocaine, Chrastny immediately agreed to turn supergrass and named Green, along with several other high-ranking villains, as one of his main conspirators. Unwilling to risk placing him in prison, police and Customs arranged to hold Chrastny in great secrecy in the custody suite of a police station – a procedure still carried out with supergrasses to this day.

During many hours of interviews Chrastny began singing like a bird. In between he whiled away the hours putting together plastic and plasticine model kits – items delivered to him as a special request when he complained of boredom. One morning when his handlers went to see him, they found only an empty cell. Closer inspection revealed that he had sawn through the bars and masked the damage using paint and plasticine.

Chrastny has not been seen since and has been heard of only once – a few days after his escape he called the front desk at Dewsbury police station and apologised for any inconvenience he had caused. Without him, there was no way the British police could proceed with a case against Green. The luck of the Pimpernel had saved him once again.

Now living in Morocco, Green continued to be heavily involved in drug trafficking. In 1990 a shipment of 1,100 kilos of cannabis and cocaine was seized by French customs. The bust was the result of a long-term undercover operation in which a French operative had won the trust of Green's gang and been present at several meetings in Paris where Green and others had finalised details of the shipment.

When the French raided Green's flat they found more drugs as well as significant amounts of gold bullion, but not the man himself. Based on the evidence that had already been gathered, an international warrant was issued for Green's arrest on drug trafficking charges. When he could not be located the case proceeded without him and in November 1991 a court in Lyon sentenced Green to seventeen years in his absence.

More failed law enforcement operations and more missed opportunities followed. In 1992 Dutch police seized 1,000 kilos of cannabis and a further 1,100 kilos of cocaine, all of which were destined for the UK market. The drugs had been found in a warehouse rented using one of Green's known aliases. In an adjoining lock-up they found gold bars and a selection of cars, again all registered to Green. Several arrests were made but the Pimpernel had somehow gotten wind of the operation and relocated to the USA.

Such was his reputation that Green was now being watched by the DEA and the FBI as well as being on the wanted lists of the British, Dutch and French authorities. Still living as ostentatiously as ever, agents watched, stunned, as he consorted with figures from the mafia, flew to and from Colombia to strike new drug deals and continued to coordinate the activities of his global network. He was finally arrested while lounging by the pool of a mansion in San Francisco formerly owned by none other than Rod Stewart.

He was found to be in possession of three fake British passports as well as his official Irish passport.

Although it seemed as though Green's number was finally up and that his luck had run out, he had suspected that he was about to be picked up and had already started making contingency plans, moving money around and isolating assets. Not being accused of committing a crime in the USA, Green resigned himself to being returned to Holland or the UK. But just as all hope of freedom seemed to have been lost, Green had the most extraordinary stroke of good fortune.

Wanted in France, Britain and Holland, a meeting was held to establish which case should take priority. The Dutch and British quickly agreed to drop their own action in favour of France, which, after all, had already convicted and sentenced Green. But then the undercover officer from the French case was arrested and charged with a criminal offence. The credibility of the case against Green was suddenly tainted. After spending more than $100,000 on lawyers to argue his case, Green was released. He even managed to get compensation against the Dutch authorities for the time he had spent on remand when their case also fell apart.

Green struck a deal with the Americans who seized hundreds of thousands of dollars worth of his cash but returned the rest – more than half a million dollars – back to him. They planned to deport him to London but when the plane he was travelling on touched down in Ireland, Green simply got off and, using his genuine Irish passport, decided to stay.

He was soon back in business. He purchased a penthouse flat in the centre of Dublin and a palatial home on the outskirts of the city. Set in four acres of grounds near Kilcock, County Kildare, Maple Falls featured stables, a snooker room, an indoor swimming pool, a gymnasium and its own sauna. There were also tennis courts, a pond filled with thousands of pounds worth of Koi carp and a fully equipped outdoor bar. The house soon became the venue for regular raucous parties for Green's gangland contacts from across the world. Among the guests known to have attended were Terry Adams and 'Bob Coombes'.

Green's neighbours had no complaints about the comings and goings – the only thing they thought was a little odd was that, despite his obvious wealth, Green could regularly be seen in the call box a few hundred yards down the road from his home. It was from this same phone box that Green continued to coordinate his global drug empire, arranging for hundreds of kilos of cocaine to be smuggled from Spain to the UK and Ireland.

Just when it seemed that life for the Pimpernel could not get any better, disaster struck. Early one April morning in 1995, Green was driving his Bentley Turbo after a night of heavy drinking in Dublin and jumped a red light at nearly 100 miles per hour, ploughing into a local taxi and killing the driver, father-of-nine Joseph White. Green's immediate reaction was to restart his car and drive away. When the Bentley failed to restart he staggered away from the scene of the accident, only to be arrested an hour or so later.

Released on bail of £50,000 and having pleaded guilty to charges of failing to provide a sample of blood or urine and leaving the scene of an accident, Green was relieved to escape with a fine of £950 for dangerous driving and causing Mr White's death. He was also banned from driving for two years. The relief lasted only until the following year when an inquest was held into the taxi driver's death and Green feared a massive civil action from the man's widow if he was found guilty of unlawful killing.

To tip the balance of the scales of justice in his favour Green arranged for some additional witnesses to give evidence to the authorities dealing with the inquest hoping they would cast his actions on the night in a slightly more positive light. By the time the inquest ended, Green's luck was holding up as well as ever and he ended up walking away without having to pay a penny in compensation.

Up until the time of the inquest Green had managed to maintain a low profile in Ireland, but within weeks of the verdict a massive exposé of his life and times had been splashed across four pages of the *Sunday World* newspaper under the banner headline: 'Mr Big'. Although rocked by the unwanted attention, Green soon brushed it off and, after spending a few months travelling to allow the fuss to die down, got back to the serious business of making money. Green had always assumed that the Garda were fully aware of his presence but what the newspaper coverage showed was that, other than the incident with the taxi, there was no evidence of him being involved in anything criminal in Ireland.

More drug shipments followed, some successful, some not – a large shipment of Thai marijuana Green was supplying to the Adams family was seized by Customs in the South of England – but overall the profits continued to flow into his coffers. Within a year everything seemed to have returned to normal and Green began expanding the scope of his operations, striking deals with new suppliers and opening up new transit routes in order to stay one step ahead of the authorities.

The only cloud on the horizon was the formation of the Criminal Assets Bureau (CAB) in Dublin in the aftermath of the murder of *Sunday Independent* investigative journalist Veronica Guerin by leading figures from the drugs underworld in June 1996.

Comprised of personnel from the Gardai, Customs and social services, the CAB was the first unit of its kind anywhere in Europe. New legislation was introduced giving the squad sweeping powers to seize cash and property from anyone suspected of making money from criminal activity. Soon after the bureau was established Green confessed to friends that he was extremely worried about the potential implications.

His concerns only grew when the CAB seized the assets of leading Dublin gangster John Gilligan, once the leading suspect in the Guerin murder. Veronica Guerin had turned up at his house to confront him about his lavish lifestyle and he had brutally assaulted her. He later turned up at her house and threatened to rape her son and kill her if she dared to write anything about him. He was ultimately tried and acquitted of the reporter's murder but convicted of his part in a massive cannabis shipment.

In early 1998 another of Green's shipments of cocaine and cannabis was intercepted on the way to the UK. Instead of seizing the drugs there and then, Customs decided to allow the consignment to continue on its way so they could find its final destination. Within the space of a month Customs had raided the epicentre of Green's UK operation, recovering 2.9 tonnes of cannabis, sixteen kilos of cocaine and around £800,000 in cash.

Customs also arrested Green's right-hand man in London, a sleazy character who, it transpired, had actually been working as a police informant during the entire time he had been running the Pimpernel's affairs. (Such situations are not at all unusual. Anecdotal evidence suggests that a significant number of high-ranking villains become official or unofficial informants as a way of gaining an upper hand on their rivals and as an insurance policy against possible prosecution.)

The informant had kept extensive records of his business dealings with Green as well as dozens of other leading crime figures. As news of the man's arrest began to spread throughout the criminal community people started to panic. Green and his mistress promptly packed their bags and left Ireland, travelling the world, staying at top hotels for several months, all on a string of fake identities, before ending up in Spain.

Once there, a secret conference was held between representatives of some of the gangsters the informant had been working for including members of the Adams family. The meeting ended with the decision to put out a contract on the man's head. The price started out as £1 million but as the scale of his betrayal became increasingly clear, the amount rose to £4 million and included his wife and children.

By 1999 the CAB, using information from the informant, moved against Green's properties in Ireland, seizing Maple Falls and his penthouse flat in Dublin. Shortly afterwards the Crown Prosecution Service issued an arrest warrant for Green on drug trafficking and money laundering charges. After a tip-off Green was tracked down to the Ritz Hotel in Barcelona and arrested.

With extradition to the UK looming over him, it finally seemed to be the beginning of the end for the Pimpernel.

The informant had given evidence in dozens of cases and thirty-four out of the forty-nine people had been arrested as a result of his testimony so it seemed inevitable that Green was going to have to come to the UK to face the music. But once again luck was on his side. Following a legal challenge by several defendants, the courts decided they could no longer rely on the informant's testimony and all remaining cases – including that against Green – were dropped. Green was a free man once more, just in time for his sixtieth birthday. He remains in Spain to this day.

As I stood outside his lavish villa, it was clear that Green continues to live an extremely luxurious lifestyle. Although many of his assets have been seized by numerous law enforcement authorities around the world, he is understood to have hidden plenty of cash and valuables safely away.

During one recent court case it emerged that Green had kept a box containing £1 million in Swiss francs buried beneath a flower box in one of his previous properties. Similar stashes are said to exist all over Europe and beyond. A much-circulated rumour around the more sleazy bars of the Costas is that Green has up to £10 million buried in the hills overlooking Marbella but, having partaken of too much of his own product, is no longer able to remember exactly where some of the money is.

Despite this, Green is believed to have more than enough to keep him in the five-star lifestyle for many, many years to come. Now well into his sixties, Green is said to be tired of running and unwilling to spend his last days behind bars, far away from the girlfriends, grandchildren and numerous luxurious creature comforts he has become so accustomed to. If he is still involved in criminality, it is likely that this is more as a figurehead, rather than a fully active participant.

That said, the fact that Green has managed to remain at liberty and enjoy most of his ill-gotten gains for so many years while supposedly remaining fully active in the drug business is all the more remarkable when you consider the fate of others who have operated at the very highest levels of British criminality and attempted to do the same.

Take the case of one of the few genuine Mr Bigs whose name and face are well known to the public at large: Curtis 'Cocky' Warren. Once Interpol's 'Target One' and Europe's most wanted man, Warren is thought to have amassed a hidden fortune estimated at between £180 million and £300 million, thanks to having direct links to the top of the Colombian drug cartels.

The gangster had walked free from a trial at Newcastle Crown Court in 1993, when he was accused of smuggling 1,000 kilograms of cocaine into the UK, hidden inside lead ingots and at the time worth £250 million on the streets. So detailed was Warren's knowledge of the law enforcement teams ranged against him that he actually knew the length of the longest drill bit that Customs held. This meant he could hide the drugs deep enough inside the ingots so that they could not be discovered. Although he was caught, the trial collapsed and Warren walked free after it emerged one of his co-conspirators, Brian Charrington, was a paid informant for Customs officers.

During his peak the former street dealer from Toxteth, Liverpool, was believed to be putting more than £1 million a week into various money laundering schemes. He even appeared on the *Sunday Times* Rich List in 1997 when he was listed as a property developer worth £40 million. Eventually justice caught up with Warren and in 1997 he was convicted in Holland of smuggling 400 kilos of cocaine, 100 kilos of heroin, 1050 kilos of cannabis and 50 kilos of ecstasy. The value of the cocaine alone was at least £75 million. Warren was also convicted of possession of firearms and jailed for thirteen years. Two years later he was further convicted of the manslaughter of a fellow inmate and had a further four years added to his sentence.

Warren was held in one of Holland's most secure jails and spent six years in solitary confinement. The Dutch authorities obtained an asset seizure order against Warren worth £6 million but have never been able to trace anything more than £180,000.

The cash is said to be laundered through properties across the UK as well as hotels and nightclubs throughout Europe.

On his release from jail in June 2007, Warren was refused a passport by the British, Irish and Portuguese governments. Armed Dutch police escorted him on to a ferry and stayed with him until he walked ashore at Harwich in Essex. From that moment officers from the Serious Organised Crime Agency followed his every move as part of a 'lifetime offender management' programme.

'Serious organised criminals don't suddenly stop just because they've been caught once,' Bill Hughes, the director-general of SOCA, said. 'That's why, when a criminal comes on to SOCA's radar, they stay there for life. Curtis Warren was a career criminal for whom prison was a temporary setback. He was already planning his next operation from inside prison and, when he was released, we were waiting, watching, and listening.'

Just sixteen days after his release, Warren stepped off an early afternoon flight from Manchester to Jersey Airport. Sources close to 'Cocky' said he spent that time visiting family, friends and associates and getting reacquainted with a Liverpool he had not seen for more than twelve years, a city that had changed beyond all recognition.

Collecting his bags from the airport conveyor belts Warren – said to have hundreds of millions of pounds stashed away in bank accounts that only he knows the location of and has access numbers for – had little idea his new-found freedom would last only another twenty days and end with his being jailed for thirteen years for his part in a plot to flood the island with cannabis.

Warren got his nickname – short for the Cocky Watchman – because of his uncanny ability to sense danger in the air. 'I've got the sixth sense, haven't I?' he would brag to friends. That sixth sense must have been dulled by ten years in a Dutch jail. Cocky seems to have had no inkling that SOCA, the Dutch police, the cops in Jersey and just about everyone else were on his case twenty-four hours a day.

He had headed for Jersey under the pretence of seeing his girlfriend, Kimberley Lockley – a Norris Green mum-of-one who left

Liverpool fifteen years ago to pursue TV and modelling jobs before getting involved in the Jersey finance sector. But he was picked up from the arrivals terminal by Liverpool-born John Welsh – a small time cannabis dealer on the Channel Island.

The SOCA team contacted the States of Jersey police to warn them that Warren was on his way and all the red flags went up. In the three weeks that followed, the island's police rode rough-shod over their own laws and international relations as they gathered evidence against Warren and his gang.

An Abuse of Process hearing held before Jersey's Royal Court saw the chief of police, the country's top prosecutor and the tight-knit drugs squad called to the witness stand as Warren tried to have the case against him thrown out.

Over four days they admitted breach after breach of foreign laws and, more tellingly, knowing exactly what they were doing as they did it. Jersey Police originally claimed Warren, Welsh and the four other defendants had hatched a plot that would see them bring around £300,000 of cannabis into the island. On the first day of the three-week trial the value of the drugs shot up to £1 million.

To do the deal police claimed Welsh originally planned to drive his Jersey-registered Volkswagen Golf on to the ferry at St Helier and off at St Malo, in Brittany, France.

Acting to the letter of the law, officers sent requests to the French, Belgian and Dutch authorities asking for permission to have a tracking device and listening bug in the car as it passed over foreign soil. SOCA operatives were set to listen in and record anything that was said in the car while Jersey officers tracked its movements. But within a day the French and the Dutch authorities came back saying they would allow the car to be tracked but no listening device was to be activated within their borders.

The Belgian police gave permission for a Jersey car to be bugged but not one from outside the island. Then, a day before the run was due, drugs squad officers said the plan changed without warning. Now, instead of driving on to a ferry in Jersey, Welsh, a friend of Warren's for more than twenty years who had already done a stretch in prison for drugs, would walk on and pick up a hire car at the other end.

A red Citroën C1 was waiting for Welsh at Alamo Car Hire on the St Malo port and he planned to drive 524 miles through northern France, across the top of Belgium and into Holland. He was supposed to drive to Amsterdam, buy the drugs from associates of Warren and then bring them back to the French coast.

Here the packages – 180 kilos worth – would be put on a speed-boat *The Skiptide* and both passenger and cargo would be raced back across the water to Jersey. That same day two Jersey detectives were dispatched to France with tracking and audio devices to be put on the hire car – despite them being told by all three countries bugs were banned. They left with the strict instructions to lie to the French police if they queried what the two devices were. Senior officers told Detective Constable Lawrence Courtness and Detective Constable Rachael Hart to tell anyone who asked the second system – the bug – was merely a back-up to the tracker.

Then, when Welsh picked up the C1 on 18 July and began his journey, Jersey's drugs squad was listening in all the way. Recordings were so crystal clear officers could hear his Tom-Tom satellite navigation system telling him what roads and turns to take. But though Welsh got to the Dutch capital he never went through with the deal.

Instead, three of the other defendants failed to turn up with their half of the cash and the Dutch dealers refused to let the shipment go without full payment.

An angry Welsh was then heard on the phone during the eight-hour trip back ringing the others and telling them they would have to go back next week with their slice of the cash and pick up the cargo. At St Malo he dropped the hire car off and got a ferry home. As he drove back police realised they had a major problem. High-level discussions went on between the drugs squad chief and his team, top officers and legal advisers from the Law Officers Department as Welsh headed back from Holland.

Police were told it would be better for them in court to wait, let the other co-conspirators go and try to make the deal again and then pick them up with some hard evidence. But fearing they had blown their chance and relations with their foreign counterparts by using tracking and bugging devices for which they had no authority, they chose to pounce. An email from Supt Shaun Du Val, then head of the operations management team, to his Chief Officer Graham Power reads: 'Re: Floss. Things don't half change quick. There is a strong chance foreign forces might not cooperate next week. Some have sussed the kit they were opposed to and would leave us with big gaps.'

Rounding up the alleged main players, the police went all out on an allegation of conspiring to import drugs, rather than wait and catch suspects with something incriminating. The officers involved later admitted they took the chance of getting the evidence through the court. Detective Inspector Gary Pashley, one of the men running the investigation code-named 'KoalaÚFloss', told the court: 'This was the best chance we had. This was a matter of national security, island security and economic well-being and I made the decision I thought was right.

'I didn't hear him be specifically told to "lie" but knew that DC Lawrence Courtness was told that if he was asked what the second device was, he was to just say it was a back-up. Even if they [the other authorities] only agreed to a tracking device, the operational decision had been taken earlier that we would proceed with the audio device anyway.'

Police said they were acting after taking advice from the Law Officers Department – Jersey's equivalent of the CPS. Crown Advocate Matthew Jowitt was said to have advised the officers it was unlikely any court would rule evidence collected in such a way was inadmissible and couldn't be used. This turned out to be absolutely correct.

In his ruling on the matter the jury heard that Sir Richard blasted the police conduct as 'reprehensible' and 'unlawful'. But he said the tactics did not amount to an abuse of process and allowed the evidence into the trial where it would prove crucial.

During his trial Warren denied being involved in the drug deal and left it to his barrister to try and prove his innocence via a series of outlandish theories.

Ordinarily, a defendant's previous convictions cannot be aired in open court because of the risk of prejudicing the jury. But Warren's barrister Stephen Baker chose to reveal his client's criminal past, claiming his notoriety meant that the authorities had set him up in an attempt to claim a famous scalp.

Mr Baker also claimed that his client was such a 'sophisticated' criminal that he would never have bothered to get involved in such a small-time scam, which was badly planned and would net him just £1 million. When recorded calls of Warren apparently discussing the drug deal were played to the jury, Mr Baker claimed his client was buying guns for protection. The jury heard a recording of Warren saying: 'If we get twenty or thirty pieces for ourselves, I will be happy.' The prosecution claimed 'pieces' was code for drugs; Baker said it referred to guns.

Ultimately Warren paid the price for being such a well-known criminal and such a high-profile target. The authorities on Jersey and beyond pulled out all the stops to ensure he would be convicted no matter what.

It was a similar story with Turkish drugs baron Abdullah Baybasin, who ruled his £10 billion heroin empire with violence and intimidation. Despite being wheelchair-bound since the mid-1980s, the middle-aged father of one headed a Kurdish and Turkish crime syndicate and was considered to be one of Britain's most powerful gangsters. At one point his gang was said to control around 90 per cent of all heroin smuggled into the UK.

Baybasin coordinated a massive drug-smuggling ring, ran extortion rackets and forced other criminals to pay him a 'tax' for permission to operate. He was linked to more than a dozen brutal murders.

The gangster, known as 'Uncle', came to England from Turkey in 1997 to claim asylum. Although unable to walk since he was hit in the spine during a shoot-out in an Amsterdam bar, he managed to establish himself in north London and recruited young Kurds to form a gang called the Bombacilars, the bombers. Armed members would force their way into shops and small businesses and demand money.

On one occasion, twenty of them, armed with samurai swords, metal bars, pool cues and a gun, forced their way into a Turkish café in Hackney, north-east London. One man had his index finger chopped off by the gang and shots were fired.

For years, Baybasin had ensured he was never in the same room as even the smallest quantity of drugs in case of a police raid. But in March 2001 he became too closely involved in a deal, and that began his downfall. Detectives hid a tiny video camera and microphones in the office behind a Green Lanes sports club from which Baybasin was operating. The watchers say it was like spying on scenes from *The Godfather*.

'People were clearly in awe of him,' one says. 'Baybasin would turn up two or three times a week. People would come and kiss his hand. When he spoke, it would be in a soft whisper so only the people closest to him could hear.'

Their cameras recorded shopkeepers and local businessmen being brought into the room and beaten until they agreed to pay protection. 'You could hear people being kicked and punched. The violence erupted out of nowhere.'

Guns were distributed, petrol bombs were assembled and punishments for those who had refused to pay were discussed. Police had footage of one of the gang members being stripped and threatened with a machete over a breach of discipline. Fellow criminals did not escape Baybasin's attentions. Human traffickers had to pay £1,000 for each person smuggled. Pimps and drug dealers would also hand over money.

Much of their fear stemmed from Baybasin's family connections and the reputation of his elder brother, Huseyin, who is in prison in the Netherlands.

Better known as 'the Emperor', Huseyin began his criminal life selling black-market cigarettes in Istanbul. Then he moved into hashish trafficking, then heroin. As his business grew and the money began to roll in, Huseyin bought business and property interests in Britain, including a seaside hotel in Brighton and foreign exchange bureaus.

He also owned dozens of beach resorts, electrical shops and car-hire businesses along Turkey's southern coast. In 1984, he was arrested in London with a load of heroin and sentenced to twelve years. But after just three years he was transferred to Turkey and immediately released, prompting allegations of high-level Turkish corruption.

In 2001, in Amsterdam, 'the Emperor' was convicted on charges of conspiracy to murder, kidnapping and drug smuggling and sentenced to twenty years, later increased to life. Abdullah moved in.

Like many senior gangsters, Abdullah was also an informant for Customs and Excise, which allowed him to sabotage rivals and operate with protection. This fell apart when the now-defunct National Crime Squad began investigating.

By the time of his arrest, police estimate he was controlling 90 per cent of Britain's heroin trade as well as earning hundreds of thousands of pounds from blackmail and extortion.

Angry members of the Green Lanes community got together and decided to fight back. In November 2002 a battle broke out between forty men armed with guns, knives and baseball bats outside a café owned by a relative of Baybasin, the Dostlar Social Club in Green Lanes. Twenty men were injured and an innocent man, Alisan Dogan, a forty-three-year-old Kurdish cleaner, was knifed to death.

Once the dust had settled and Abdullah was safely behind bars, it seemed as though the fighting was over. In fact it was only on hold.

In 2009 a new wave of violence broke out among Britain's Turkish community. In October 2009 the feud's most audacious killing took place. Oktay Erbasli, a prominent member of the Tottenham Boys, was waiting at traffic lights at a busy junction in his Range Rover when a motorcycle pulled alongside him. A hitman linked to the Bombacilar gang opened fire, killing the twenty-three-year-old, but missing his five-year-old stepson seated beside him. Within the tit-for-tat mentality of gangland retribution, reprisals are inevitable. In Erbasli's case it came within seventy-two hours: Cem Duzgun, twenty-one, had been playing snooker in a Clapton social club with friends when two hooded men approached at 10.50 p.m. and opened fire with a semi-automatic weapon. He died instantly.

This new wave of violence is being linked directly to the jailing for twenty-two years of Baybasin, something that destabilised the gangs' natural order, creating a power struggle now filled by the dozens of young men affiliated to the Bombacilar and Tottenham Boys. The ongoing battles are said to be being orchestrated by members of rival clans striving to reach the top spot.

For a time if you were talking about the Mr Bigs of British organised crime, they simply didn't come any bigger than the likes of Green, Warren and Baybasin. Now that crown has been passed on to a new generation of gangsters who are set to battle it out among themselves in years to come in order to secure the top spot. Among the best of the contenders is an outfit so violent, so ruthless and so bloodthirsty that it seems unlikely that anything will be able to stop their relentless pursuit of complete and utter domination of the British underworld.

18

THE NEXT GENERATION

She was a hopeless alcoholic, he was a desperate heroin addict and they fell in love after meeting at a DSS office in the East End of London in the summer of 2003. It wasn't exactly Shakespearian, but Anne McCarthy and Christopher Jacobs were star-crossed lovers all the same.

By October, Anne's husband Kenneth was becoming increasingly irate about the fact that his wife was choosing to spend more and more nights away from home in the arms of her new lover. When he spotted her out shopping in Hoxton market one autumn afternoon, he promptly frogmarched her back to the ramshackle house in Bethnal Green that the couple shared with two of their six children. Jacobs tried to 'rescue' Anne, but Kenneth threw him out into the street.

The forced reconciliation lasted only a week before Anne disappeared once more, leaving her husband in no doubt whatsoever about where she was heading. That night a furious Kenneth drank fifteen pints of beer, pulled on a balaclava and smashed his way into Jacobs' flat, hell bent on revenge. Heading straight for the bedroom, he pushed his booze-sodden, drug-addled, half-naked wife out of the door, pulled out a knife and began brutally and systematically attacking his love rival.

Kenneth had always been an extremely violent man and was well practised in the art of inflicting pain. He picked up his first conviction in 1974 at the age of seventeen and served a two-year sentence for wounding with intent. He was convicted for assault and ABH in 1982 and then again in 1997. Little wonder then that Jacobs didn't stand a chance. By the time a dazed and confused Anne McCarthy found her way back to the bedroom, Kenneth was gone and her lover was sitting on a sofa, bleeding from dozens of stab wounds to his face and neck. Jacobs never regained consciousness and choked to death on his own blood before an ambulance could reach him.

Kenneth swiftly returned home where, despite his heavily inebriated state, he had the presence of mind to wash the blood out of his clothes and shave off his moustache in a bid to disguise his appearance. The police arrived in the early hours of the following morning and arrested him on suspicion of murder. Questioned about his movements, Kenneth claimed to have no knowledge of the attack on Jacobs and told the officers that though he had gone to the flat looking for his wife, he had been unable to find her and spent the rest of the night at a pub.

Released on police bail pending further inquiries, Kenneth was supposed to report back to the station a month later. The following morning he fled to his native Ireland and went on the lam. In the weeks that followed he made legal history, becoming the first person to be arrested and extradited to the UK under a new EU-wide warrant. In September 2006 Kenneth pleaded guilty to manslaughter, a plea that was readily accepted by the Crown after the prosecution agreed there were difficulties in establishing the absolute truth of what happened as 'all the witnesses were drunk or high on drugs at the time of the killing'.

The brutal murder of Christopher Jacobs received barely any news coverage in the UK and at first glance seems to have precious little to do with the upper echelons of the world of international organised crime. But first impressions can be extremely deceptive.

Kenneth Dundon, a former traveller hailing from Limerick, met his future wife, Anne McCarthy in 1971. The couple moved to London and got married in Hackney in 1982 – Anne kept her maiden name – before going on to have six children, five boys and a girl. Despite a somewhat unsettled, unconventional upbringing, one of their sons turned out to be a model citizen. The other four, however, took after their father in all the worst possible ways.

From an early age Wayne, John, Dessie and Ger Dundon were constantly in trouble with the police and noted for their predilection for extreme violence. On one occasion, Wayne beat his own mother so severely that she had to be hospitalised for three weeks. A few years later, while still a teenager, he carried out a series of robberies on the elderly, beating one wheelchair-bound pensioner and his ninety-year-old wife in a bid to make them give up their valuables. Sentenced to four years, he was considered so dangerous that when he was released he was deported from the UK and banned for life.

Wayne and his brothers promptly upped sticks and moved to their ancestral home of Limerick, Ireland's rugby capital and an increasingly popular tourist destination. There the Dundons started hanging out with members of their extended family including their cousins, Larry, James and Anthony McCarthy. It was a match made in heaven. The McCarthys had a wealth of local knowledge and contacts, the Dundons brought with them a level of viciousness hitherto unknown on the streets of Limerick.

Soon after that, the entire group made a collective decision to pursue a life of crime, starting out with armed robbery and protection before moving up into the drug trade. Right from the start the gang made it clear that their ultimate goal was nothing less than complete and utter domination of the underworld. True to their word, the gang's influence quickly spread from their base on the Hyde Road, first across the run-down Southside estates of Prospect and Ballinacurra-Weston and then beyond.

Today the McCarthy–Dundon gang forms the nucleus of a multi-million-pound drug trafficking and organised-crime network with tentacles in London, Birmingham, Bradford, Dublin, Belfast and Spain to name but a few. Almost everyone who has ever dared to stand in their way has been ruthlessly eliminated. So much blood has been spilled during the vicious battles for supremacy that over the past decade Limerick, a tiny yet sophisticated and occasionally stunning city with a population of just 80,000, has one of the highest per-capita gang-related murder rates of anywhere in Western Europe.

The fact that my journey through the British underworld in search of 'Mr Big', a journey which started some 320-odd pages ago, ends with the McCarthy–Dundons should not be taken as a sign that they are in any way criminal masterminds. Far from it. The four Dundon boys are known to be barely literate, leading detractors to dub them the 'Dum Dum Dundons'. There is undoubtedly a serious lack of common sense applied to some of their activities – John Dundon once loudly threatened to kill the chief witness in a court case against his brother while inside the actual courtroom, standing next to the wife of the witness and surrounded by several police officers and court officials – but the wealth, influence and sheer ambition of the McCarthy–Dundons speaks for itself.

When officers from the Serious and Organised Crime Agency were asked to get involved in an undercover operation involving the gang, they were initially sceptical about just how much of a threat a small outfit from southern Ireland could really be. That scepticism did not last long. Most gangs buy one or two guns at a time. When the McCarthy–Dundons met up with covert officers posing as underworld armourers, they placed an order for two RPG rocket launchers, two Uzi sub-machine guns, five AK-47 assault rifles, a further fifteen semi-automatic rifles and ten semi-automatic handguns.

Such a request might easily have been dismissed as bravado were it not for the fact that the gang already had access to many such weapons – along with numerous hand grenades, pipe bombs and booby traps – and had shown time and time again that they would not hesitate to make use of them. Even against their own.

When notorious hard man John Creamer, another cousin of the Dundons, turned up to collect his share of the proceeds of an armed robbery the gang had organised, they decided he was no longer part of their team and should be executed instead. Armed with a Mac-10 machine gun, a sixteen-year-old member of the gang shot his former colleague fourteen times. Remarkably Creamer survived and was visited in hospital by the youth that had tried to kill him. After that, Creamer refused to name his attacker or cooperate with the Garda in any way. He moved to London and lived the rest of his life in fear, eventually dying of a drug overdose.

THE NEXT GENERATION

The Dundons in particular have a complete lack of respect for both the police and the courts. When two Garda attempted to arrest Dessie Dundon he brutally attacked them and called out to his brother, Wayne, 'Get me a knife so I can stab this fucker.' Wayne waded in, not with a knife but with a concrete block, which he used to crush the arm and the shoulder of one of the policemen. The officer has never been able to return to active duty. Two years later, Wayne was being interviewed under caution in a police station when he lashed out again, breaking the nose of one Garda and the jaw of another. The whole thing was captured on CCTV.

At Limerick Crown Court in February 2005, after failing to win back a bulletproof vest that had been confiscated by the police, Wayne Dundon pulled down his trousers and underwear and mooned Judge Terrance O'Sullivan. 'See that, Your Honour,' he said, slapping his bare behind, 'That's what the Dundons think of you and the Garda. Fuck you, Your Honour.'

Two things in particular mark the McCarthy–Dundons out as a potentially significant force in the future of international organised crime. The first is the fact that they have youth very much on their side. Terry Adams is less than a decade away from getting his pension, Michael 'the Pimpernel' Green is nearly seventy and even Curtis 'Cocky' Warren is now the wrong side of forty-five. By comparison, at the time of writing, the oldest of the Dundon boys is thirty-two. The youngest, Ger, is just twenty-three.

A second, equally important factor is that the bloodshed in Limerick is every bit as much about family pride as it is about profits from the drug trade. In the words of one local detective: 'It's not professional, it's personal.' In that sense the violence between the McCarthy–Dundons and their rivals has more in common with the feud between the Hells Angels and the Outlaws – the two sides simply abhor one another. But while biker gangs have an increasingly mature membership, the feuding families in Limerick are producing new generations reared on pure hate who are thirsty for revenge almost from the moment they are born. 'When I grow up I'm going to get a gun and kill them all,' the ten-year-old son of one of the leading figures in the feud was heard to say of a rival family. 'And I won't stop until they're all dead.'

Prior to the emergence of the McCarthy–Dundons, the drug trade in Limerick was dominated by a gang led by brothers Christy and Kieran Keane. Ruthless and extremely violent, the pair were also involved in protection rackets, vehicle theft and gun running. They had close links with paramilitary groups including the IRA and INLA, as well as criminal gangs in Dublin and Belfast. Although they were more than capable of looking after themselves, the Keanes preferred to leave much of their 'heavy' work to their enforcer, Eddie Ryan.

A one-time armed robber, Ryan had stabbed a man to death during a fight outside a cinema at the tender age of seventeen and served time for manslaughter. As a result he had just the kind of hard-man reputation that the Keanes were looking for. With Ryan on board keeping dealers and debtors in check, the Keane operation quickly went from strength to strength.

The bond between the three men became stronger still in early 1993 when a nephew of the Keanes knocked down and killed a woman, Kathleen O'Shea, who had stumbled in front of his bread van. Though police fully exonerated the driver, the family of O'Shea, who were low ranking criminals, were furious and threatened to kill those responsible. Eager to smooth things over, Christy Keane paid for the woman's funeral and offered the family compensation.

For a short time things quietened down but just before Christmas, Patrick, O'Shea's common-law husband, turned up mob-handed at Christy Keane's home and demanded more money. Christy came to the door with his nephew, Owen Treacy and refused to hand over another penny. In the scuffle that followed, Patrick was stabbed through the heart and died instantly. Christy Keane was arrested and charged with murder after three eyewitnesses said they had seen him wielding the knife.

Patrick's funeral took place a few days later and afterwards his family held a wake in a caravan close to the graveyard. By then the Keane gang had decided that enough was enough. Livid about the disruption to their drug business and the arrest of Christy, they decided that the only way to resolve the matter was to strike a decisive, devastating blow against Patrick's remaining family. Just after 10.30 p.m., Eddie Ryan and an accomplice – most likely Kieran Keane – armed themselves with a shotgun and pistol, burst through the door of the caravan and began firing at the mourners. They were completely oblivious to the fact that two young children were sleeping in bunks at the back of the vehicle. When the gunsmoke had cleared one man, Patrick's brother, was dead while another, along with two women, were left seriously injured. Miraculously the two children escaped unharmed but the message had been received loud and clear – anyone speaking out against the Keanes would be signing their own death warrant.

The Garda arrested Eddie Ryan, Kieran Keane and others in connection with this second murder but there simply wasn't enough evidence for them to proceed with a prosecution. When Christy's own case came to court in March 1995, the three witnesses all developed temporary amnesia. Christy was acquitted and walked away a free man.

Having quite literally gotten away with not one but two murders, the Keane gang quickly got back to the business of making money. As the drug trade expanded, so their profits soared. At one point the gang were making so much money that they were forced to store the cash inside wheelie bins. It was around this time that Eddie Ryan came to believe that he should be receiving a far greater share of those profits for himself. He opted to set up his own, independent drugs-distribution network, much to the annoyance of Christy and Kieran.

The rift between the one-time friends slowly widened. When a row broke out between Eddie's niece and one of Christy's relatives, both sides decided the only way to sort things out would be to bring the two teenage girls together for a prearranged fight. After half an hour of vicious punching, kicking, gouging and head-butting, Samantha Ryan was declared the winner and the other girl went away with part of her ear missing where her opponent had bitten it off.

That should have been the end of the matter but three months later, Christy's sister-in-law Anne bumped into Samantha Ryan in the street one afternoon. A fight broke out and Anne Keane was knocked to the ground, punched and then slashed in the face with a Stanley blade.

That night several shots were fired through the front window of Samantha Ryan's home. Her father, John, called his brother Eddie and urged him to do something. When John met Eddie a few minutes later to drive him to Christy Keane's house, Eddie had armed himself with a shotgun.

The Keanes ran their empire from the same streets they had grown up in: a poverty-stricken district known as St Mary's Park on the northern tip of King's Island in the centre of Limerick. Surrounded by water and wasteland, there is only one road into and out of the area, meaning that strangers are easily spotted. As the Ryan brothers drove towards Christy's home, a member of the rival gang was waiting for them with a gun of his own. He began firing as soon as he saw them, hitting their car twice and then shattering their rear window as John and Eddie made a hasty retreat.

A few days later, Eddie Ryan ambushed Christy Keane as the latter sat in a car waiting to collect his son from school. Ryan pulled out a 9mm pistol from under his jacket and pointed it at his former partner-in-crime's head. The gun jammed and Keane drove off before Ryan could clear the blockage. Both sides had seen their share of good fortune but there was no way it could last. The only question was whether a Ryan or a Keane would be the first to die.

Eddie Ryan lay low in the countryside for a couple of days but on Sunday 12 November 2000, he returned to Limerick for a family funeral. Afterwards he attended the wake at the Moose Bar in Cathedral Place close to the city centre, with his son. Just before 10 p.m., seconds after Ryan's son headed off to the toilet, two gunmen appeared in the entrance of the bar. Both wore balaclavas over their faces but when one of them called out to Ryan:

'Ya bastard, come out ya bastard', there was no mistaking Kieran Keane's voice.

Ryan, who had his back to the entrance, barely had time to turn around before the first rounds were fired. Of that first volley of fourteen shots, eleven found their target and Ryan collapsed in a pool of blood. Seven bullets had torn through his back, shredding his lungs and severing his spinal chord. Two more bullets were in his shoulder, one in each hip and one in his left arm. A mother and daughter drinking in the pub at the time were also hit and seriously injured in the fusillade. They were lucky to survive.

It didn't take the Garda long to draw up a list of potential suspects and within the space of a few days several men had been taken into custody, including Kieran Keane and gang associates Philip Collopy and Paul Coffey. Almost as soon as he was questioned Coffey broke down naming Kieran Keane and Collopy as the gunmen. He himself, he explained, had been driving the getaway car. Charged with murder, he initially agreed to become a witness against the others, only to change his mind a few days later and retract his statement in the face of a campaign of extreme intimidation launched against his family. Coffey would later be sentenced to fifteen years in prison for Ryan's manslaughter. No one else has ever been charged in relation to the murder of Eddie Ryan.

In the weeks and months that followed Ryan's murder, the Limerick underworld exploded with a series of tit-for-tat gun and petrol bomb attacks. The house of Eddie's brother, John, suffered more than thirty such incidents alone. But then the Ryans had an amazing stroke of luck.

On a Tuesday morning in August 2001, three Garda on foot patrol who were chasing a bag snatcher lost their quarry on the outskirts of St Mary's Park. Just as they were about to leave the area, they spotted a man walking across a nearby patch of waste ground with a heavy coal sack slung over one shoulder. The officers quickly moved in to investigate, making full use of the element of surprise. The man turned out to be Christy Keane, the bag turned out to contain twenty kilos of cannabis worth around €250,000 and, having been caught red-handed, Keane was soon languishing on remand. With no witnesses to intimidate and no evidence to compromise, Keane could do nothing but wait to face the music. One of the most powerful gang leaders in Limerick was taken out of the game in a manner that was little short of embarrassing for a kingpin of his stature.

It was at this time, against this backdrop of continuing violence and with the opposition at its weakest, that the Dundons and the McCarthys chose to join the fray. They had spent the previous year acquiring weapons, carrying out armed robberies and recruiting enforcers and hitmen from all across the UK, all before agreeing to focus their attention on the area that offered the most lucrative returns of all. The gang had also prepared themselves well for the battles to come, posing as a 'sports team' to travel to Florida en masse in order to receive advanced weapons training at a top shooting range.

Keen to expand their fledgling drug operation as rapidly as possible, the McCarthy–Dundons identified Doc's, a city-centre nightclub and bar popular with both students and tourists, as a potential gold mine. If they were able to peddle their wares inside, they could earn at least €30,000 per week from this one venue alone. The only thing standing in their way was the club's vehemently anti-drugs head of security, Brian Fitzgerald. As soon as their intentions became clear, Fitzgerald barred John and Dessie Dundon and Larry McCarthy from the club for life.

A short time later a shotgun was fired through the front room of Fitzgerald's home, narrowly missing the man's wife and children. The next day Larry McCarthy and John Dundon walked up to Fitzgerald outside Doc's. Dundon made a gun gesture with his hand: 'Fitz, you're going to get it soon,' he hissed. McCarthy slowly drew his finger along his throat. Both men were arrested, charged with making threats and remanded in custody, but this only made the remaining McCarthy–Dundons even more furious with Fitzgerald. At first the bouncer was determined to make a stand but then McCarthy was released on a technicality and John Dundon also found himself at liberty, albeit unofficially.

THE NEXT GENERATION

While returning to prison from a court appearance in the back of a Garda-escorted taxi, Dundon simply arranged for a friend to open the door from the outside (child locks had been fitted inside) allowing him to make a run for it.

With two of his key tormentors both at large, Fitzgerald found the pressure too much and agreed to withdraw his complaint. Fitzgerald might have believed it was all over from that moment but the gang had other ideas. Larry McCarthy in particular was concerned that Fitzgerald might change his mind. He was on licence from a previous prison sentence and any conviction, no matter how minor, would result in him spending at least four years behind bars. The gang members got together for a quick conference and came to an agreement: the only way to guarantee Fitzgerald's silence would be to kill him.

In a complex and well-planned operation, a Birmingham-born gangster, James Martin Cahill, was brought in as the trigger man and offered a fee of €10,000 to carry out the execution. The deed was set to be done on 29 November 2002, a day that also happened to be Cahill's twenty-eighth birthday.

Having been shown Fitzgerald's house in Brookhaven and then driven by Dessie Dundon to Doc's so that he could get a clear look at his target, Cahill and his getaway driver, Gary Campion, returned to Fitzgerald's home and hid themselves in bushes to wait for their target to arrive. As soon as Fitzgerald stepped out of his car, Cahill rushed forward and shot him twice in the chest. The powerfully built security man was knocked down but incredibly managed to get up and make a run for it, banging on the doors of several neighbouring houses for help before collapsing. At that point Cahill walked up to Fitzgerald and finished him off with a shot to the head at point-blank range.

The Garda launched a massive investigation into the murder of Brian Fitzgerald, a killing that sent shockwaves of revulsion throughout the entire Limerick community. However, despite their suspicions, the police were unable to find any evidence which they could use to prosecute any members of the gang. Far from being disturbed by their actions or concerned about the increased level of police attention they had brought upon themselves, the McCarthy–Dundons seemed to have developed a taste for murder and waited only a few weeks before they struck again.

This time their target was thirty-nine-year-old car dealer Sean Poland. With no criminal record and no aspirations to be part of the underworld, Poland had unknowingly sold a car to a member of the gang soon after the Fitzgerald murder. The vehicle was more than satisfactory, but the gang member decided to rob Poland and get his money back all the same. Five members of the gang raided his house in the early hours of New Year's Day 2002, shooting him in the chest then tying up and terrorising his wife until she revealed where they kept their cash. By the time his wife managed to free herself, Poland had bled to death.

Shortly after Poland's murder Christy Keane was finally sentenced to ten years in relation to the cannabis he had been caught with the previous year. In his absence, the feud between the rival families seemed only to intensify. When Kieran Keane ran into the widow Mary Ryan outside a courthouse he couldn't help taunting her about Eddie's death. The argument grew until Keane bellowed: 'I got your husband, now I'm going to get you,' before launching a head butt into the woman's face. Keane was arrested and jailed for three months but even with both Keane brothers behind bars, the war went on.

Eddie Ryan's son, Kieran, got into a fight with Christy Keane's son, Liam, a battle that ended with Liam being stabbed in the back. Having made a statement to the Garda to that effect, Liam Keane found his faculties failing him when the case came to court. Asked to identify the man who had stabbed him, Liam Keane looked around the courtroom, his gaze sweeping over Kieran Ryan who was sitting just a few feet away from him, then told the court that his attacker did not appear to be present. The judge had no choice but to acquit Kieran, freeing the pair to continue their feud in private.

Later that same Thursday night Kieran Ryan and his brother Eddie Jnr were walking along Moylish Road with a friend when a van pulled up along side them and two armed, masked men jumped out and grabbed them. The friend managed to escape and went straight to the Garda, who immediately launched a massive manhunt amid fears the brothers had been abducted as part of the ongoing feud.

The search effort grew quickly – by the following morning a helicopter had been drafted in to help and by the Sunday, sixty soldiers from a local barracks were brought in to cover even more ground. When asked about her sons a grief-stricken Mary Ryan broke down in front of the cameras: 'I know my boys are dead,' she sobbed, before putting a widow's curse on the kidnappers. By the following Tuesday, with no word or sign of the brothers, the chief superintendent vowed to search on but admitted he believed the brothers were almost certainly dead.

But nothing was quite as it seemed. During the two years since they had established themselves in Limerick, the McCarthy–Dundons had not sided with one or other of the two main warring factions. They had, however, previously helped to supply guns for the Keane family so it seemed only natural that when Kieran Keane decided he needed help bringing the feud to a conclusive end, he called in the help of the newest and the meanest kids on the block.

Kieran Keane is believed to have offered members of the McCarthy–Dundon gang in excess of €60,000 to murder Eddie and Kieran Ryan. He feared that at some point in the future, the boys would attempt to kill him. On the Wednesday following the abduction Keane was told the contact had been 'filled' and that he should meet with the gang in order to see proof that the Ryans were dead. He should also bring the fee.

But it was a trap. Keane had been double-crossed. Behind his back McCarthy–Dundons had negotiated a more lucrative contract with the Ryans in order to cancel the existing contract and instead kill Kieran Keane.

Keane, along with his nephew Owen Treacy, arrived at the house in the Garryowen area of the city later that evening and were immediately ambushed by Dessie Dundon, Anthony McCarthy and several others. They had their hands tied behind their backs, hoods placed over their heads and were driven to the outskirts of the city in the boot of a Nissan Micra. On several occasions they were told to phone Philip Collopy – the second gunman in the Eddie Ryan shooting – and his brother to lure them into the trap as well. Keane and Treacy refused, despite being brutally beaten and tortured in a bid to make them comply.

Eventually the pair were made to kneel on the ground in a quiet road in an area called Drumbanna. Their hoods were removed and then one of the gang, David 'Frog Eyes' Stanners, stabbed Kieran Keane in the side of the face several times before shooting him once in the back of the head with a handgun. Stanners and another man then began to attack a terrified Treacy who had just seen his uncle murdered before his very eyes. Treacy was stabbed a total of seventeen times and collapsed in a pool of blood as the gang made their escape.

In fact, although he was seriously injured, Treacy was only playing dead. Once the coast was clear he somehow managed to get to his feet and stumble to a nearby house to call for help.

A few hours later, the Ryan boys turned up at a police station, totally unharmed. The consensus is that the abduction was a ruse, staged purely to get Keane to lower his guard. That night the Ryans called the Keanes to let them know they were throwing a party to celebrate.

Treacy's survival would prove problematic for those that had tried to kill him. He made a miraculous recovery and gave evidence against five members of the gang including Dessie Dundon, Anthony McCarthy, James McCarthy and two further associates. All were jailed for life as a result of his evidence. After the trial Treacy refused to go into witness protection, deciding instead to return to the Keane stronghold of St Mary's Park where he remains to this day.

It was a major setback for the gang – particularly for the Dundon boys – but they refused to allow it to interfere in any way with their illegal activities. Drug deals continued to be struck, various businessmen continued to be intimidated and family members on both sides of the feud continued to die.

THE NEXT GENERATION

In July 2003 John Ryan, brother of Eddie Ryan, was shot dead by a pillion passenger on a passing motorbike as he worked on the patio of his home at Canon Green Park, an area he had moved to believing it to be safer having suffered repeated gun and petrol bomb attacks at his previous home. That night the Keanes phoned the Ryans to let them know they were having a party of their own.

The two suspects for the attack on Ryan were teenage members of the Keane gang aged just fifteen and sixteen at the time of the shooting. Other members of the Keane family were arrested and questioned about the murder including the then fourteen-year-old Joseph, Kieran's son. When he was searched, he was found to be holding a handwritten note in which he had scrawled the following: 'People who set up and killed my father, all will be dead by the time I am thirty-two, now I am fourteen. That's a promise, boys.' This was followed by a list of names of all the main players in the McCarthy–Dundon gang and several others.

The young Keane had chosen his timeline because some of those on the list were in prison serving long sentences. The last of them would not be released until he had reached the age of thirty-two. He had ended the note with the words: 'I love you, Mam.' (Four years later at the age of nineteen, Joseph Keane would be jailed after kicking a man to death having mistaken him for a gang rival.)

By now John Dundon, on the run since escaping from his taxi, had been captured and sent to prison for a short time on a charge of threatening a prison officer. He was free in time to attend court to see five members of his gang, including his brother Dessie being tried for the murder of Kieran Keane. The trial began in November 2003 and Owen Treacy was still giving evidence when John Dundon approached his wife, Donna Treacy, and said in a loud voice: 'I swear on my baby's life that when this is over I am going to kill Owen Treacy.' He was arrested immediately and subsequently jailed for four years.

Wayne Dundon also had trouble controlling his temper. Shortly before Christmas the following year he decided to spend the evening at a pub called Brannigan's Bar with his wife and then fourteen-year-old sister Annabel. The doorman, nineteen-year-old Ryan Lee explained first to Dundon's wife and then to the man himself that a minor was not allowed in the pub at that time of night. A brief argument followed and ended when Dundon made his fingers into the shape of a gun, pointed at Lee and said: 'Fuck you, you're dead.'

Half an hour later a man on a motorcycle arrived outside the pub and entered, still wearing his full-face helmet. He walked the entire length of the bar until he found Ryan Lee, produced a hand-gun and fired a single shot at close range through the barman's left knee. The gunman tried to leave but the front of the bar was locked, forcing him to go back the way he had come in. For good measure, as he passed Lee who was rolling around on the floor in agony, he fired another shot, this time hitting him in the right hip.

As the gunman left, Lee's uncle, Steve Collins, who was also the owner of Brannigan's, went after him. The gunman turned and fired a single shot, narrowly missing his target. Collins realised he had no choice but to let the man go.

Arrested two days later, Wayne Dundon was charged with making threats to kill but because it could not be proved that he was the gunman, was not charged in connection with the shooting. Ryan Lee and his family were placed under armed police protec-tion but still received numerous threats via friends and family and Brannigan's was forced to close following an arson attack.

The threats continued right up to the night before the May 2005 trial when a letter was slipped through the door of Lee's girlfriend's home. Addressed to his uncle, Steve Collins, who was due to give evidence, it read: 'Steve, if you think it's over, think again. Look at all the people that are dead. Look, if you want to call it quits you know what to do. If not, we will attack you, your staff and your businesses . . . it's up to you.'

In court the next day both Ryan Lee and Steve Collins stood their ground and were rewarded with Dundon being jailed for the maximum term of ten years, though his term was later reduced to seven on appeal.

The gang was forced to tangle with the judicial system again when James Cahill, the hitman in the Brian Fitzgerald murder, began suffering from vivid nightmares and flashbacks of the many violent incidents he had been involved in during his life. Increasingly paranoid that members of the McCarthy–Dundon gang were planning to have him killed he started hearing voices in his head that told him he would only find peace if he confessed to his past crimes.

In October 2007, Dessie and John Dundon, Gary Campion and a fourth gang member, Anthony Kelly, went on trial under heavy security at Cloverhill Court in Dublin for the murder of Brian Fitzgerald. During the course of his evidence James Cahill admitted to a host of increasingly disturbing previous crimes including abusing at least six children in Ireland and the UK and having sex with a dog. Cahill initially insisted that John Dundon had been present when Fitzgerald had been pointed out to him but during his evidence claimed he could not remember. The judge directed the jury to acquit John Dundon and continue the case against the remaining three.

An appalling witness by any standards, Cahill admitted that he was still hearing voices, even while giving evidence, and that those same voices had told him to attack a prison guard. During his summing up, the judge reminded the jury that they could only accept the parts of Cahill's testimony that could be corroborated. On 15 November the jury returned unanimous verdicts finding Kelly and Dessie Dundon not guilty. Only Gary Campion, whose distinctive monobrow had been spotted by eyewitnesses in the aftermath of the murder, was found guilty.

The two years prior to the Fitzgerald murder trial had seen a further half-dozen gang related killings, many of them credited to the McCarthy–Dundon gang and the violence didn't stop there. The fact that the gang could be equally as ruthless with its own members as with its enemies was reinforced in April the following year when twenty-year-old James Cronin was taken along to his first 'hit'. He was driven by an armed gang sent out to hunt down and kill Mark Moloney, a friend of the Keanes. Having shot Moloney dead in a drive-by shooting the team drove back to a safe house and celebrated in the traditional manner by throwing a party. As the night wore on and drink and drugs took their hold, Cronin became increasingly paranoid. Those around him became paranoid too. They feared that if he were ever arrested, he would confess to everything before his feet had even seen the inside of a cell.

Two days later Cronin was asked by senior figures in the McCarthy–Dundon gang to help them move some weapons to a new arms dump in Limerick. When they arrived at a secret hide-out, Cronin was told to dig a hole near a railway line close to the Hyde Road. Little did he know he was digging his own grave. As soon as he'd finished, James Cronin was shot in the back of the head and dumped in the hole.

In November 2008 rugby player Shane Geoghegan was murdered in what turned out to be a case of mistaken identity. Unconnected to the feud or to the underworld in any way, Geoghegan bore an unfortunate resemblance to a known drug dealer who had moved to a new area of the city close to where Geoghegan lived in the belief he would be safe there. The killing of an innocent led to an outpouring of rage throughout the city. More than 2,000 people attended Geoghegan's funeral and thousands more demanded new legislation to crack down on the gangs. But the McCarthy–Dundons seemed completely unfazed by what they had done.

In February 2009 Christy Keane was released from prison having served his time for the cannabis charge and tension in the city rose to an all-time high. Keane immediately returned to St Mary's Park and has rarely been seen, but the hatred between the two rival families is as powerful as ever. That same month Christy's twenty-four-year-old son, Liam, began a ten-year sentence after being caught in a car holding a loaded 9mm handgun and wearing latex gloves. The gun had been discharged fourteen times in a shooting two weeks earlier and the Garda believed Liam Keane was on his way to another drive-by attack.

In March Philip Collopy, suspected of being the second gunman in the shooting of Eddie Ryan, was himself shot dead. At first it was assumed that he had been a victim of the McCarthy–Dundon gang but the matter was quickly resolved after one of his associates handed over remarkable footage of the shooting that had been taken on a mobile phone. Collopy, twenty-nine, and high on drink and drugs, had been showing his friends the best place to put a gun if you wanted to execute someone by shooting them in the head. He had taken the magazine out of his 9mm Glock pistol but had failed to check whether there had been a round in the chamber. Collopy placed the gun against his temple, pulled the trigger and died instantly.

The following month, in April 2009, a chilling threat made five years earlier by the McCarthy–Dundon gang was made brutally real. Father-of-two Roy Collins was refilling one of the fruit machines in the casino section of his family's pub at the Roxborough shopping centre when a man in a mask walked in, shot him several times in the back and then walked out.

Like Geoghegan, Collins had no link to the underworld and was not part of a gang. He was marked for execution for one reason alone: his father, who was in the next room at the time of the shooting, was Steve Collins, former owner of Brannigan's Pub and uncle of Ryan Lee, the man responsible for putting Wayne Dundon behind bars.

Following another outpouring of outrage across Ireland in the aftermath of this fresh atrocity, new laws are set to be introduced making gang membership itself a crime and for the first time allowing the use of evidence gained via electronic surveillance to be used in trials. To prevent jury tampering, the new law proposes gang cases be held without a jury, a measure previously reserved purely for trials involving terrorists.

In the meantime, the feud between the Keanes and the McCarthy–Dundons continues and has of late embraced the same technology beloved of youth street gangs in London. In June 2009 a video was uploaded to YouTube featuring John and Ger Dundon posing next to a top-of-the-range AMG Mercedes. 'Christy, if you're looking for me, I'm somewhere in Europe, but I know where you are,' says

John Dundon, going on to demonstrate a variety of ways in which he might attempt to shoot Christy Keane during a drive-by attack. Towards the end of the video Ger Dundon calls out: 'See you soon, motherfucker.'

Ger Dundon's appearance in the video is particularly interesting. The youngest member of the clan, he has so far managed to avoid spending any extended periods behind bars, despite having amassed an astonishing eighty-four convictions by the age of twenty-two. His first came in March 2002 when, at the age of fifteen, he received a three-year suspended sentence after being caught with drugs worth €30,000 while working as a courier for the gang.

Since then he has mostly kept out of the limelight. He is known to spend a great deal of time abroad and was in Spain in the company of Paddy Doyle just days before the notorious Dublin gangster was shot dead on the Costa del Sol.

A prime target for rival gangs, Ger is said to have a €1 million contract on his life. He received a nine-month sentence in August 2008 after he attempted to use a false passport, in the name of Terence Ruth, in Cork Airport to board a European-bound flight. Dundon said he was going to Amsterdam for a few days as he had been advised by the Garda in Limerick that his life was in imminent danger.

During a recent court appearance Ger Dundon pulled up outside the building in an armoured 4x4 then, using an external PA system built into the front grille of the car, summoned his associates. About fifteen men appeared, all wearing body armour, and gathered around the car door so that Ger could safely get out. The group then moved as one, with Ger in the middle, towards the court entrance. Disqualified from driving on numerous occasions and currently the subject of a fifteen-year ban, Dundon continues to drive numerous bulletproof vehicles as he claims it is not safe for him to travel any other way.

Some sources within the Limerick underworld claim Ger Dundon plans to take over the running of the gang while others say he is simply waiting for Wayne, due for release from prison in the first half of 2010, to return. Either way, I decide the only way to find out what is going on is to head to Limerick and ask him myself.

By the time I arrive at Shannon Airport, pick up my hire car, and take the road towards the centre of Limerick, I am already trembling with anticipation. As I get closer to my destination I start to feel a little queasy and it doesn't get any better. By the time I enter the suburbs there's a knot in my stomach so tight it feels as though I'm going to throw up. Although I've investigated organised crime in cities all over the UK I know that I'm in for a very different experience.

In places like London, Birmingham and Bristol, even Cardiff and Glasgow, I've always been able to blend in and rely on a certain degree of anonymity. That simply isn't going to happen in Limerick. It's not just that the city, despite being the third largest in Ireland, is relatively small, it's that the communities where the gangs are based are smaller still. Moyross, a stronghold of many of the McCarthy–Dundon gang, is essentially a giant cul-de-sac. Like St Mary's Park there is only one road in and out of the development and no passing traffic. Although the centre of Limerick is considered safe and tourist friendly, the areas that are home to gang activity are considered all but out of bounds for anyone not living there. Even Garda patrols are regularly attacked in these areas. These are the kind of places where everybody knows absolutely everybody else and strangers are treated with suspicion. Blending into the background, even momentarily, simply isn't an option. Whatever I do, I'm going to stick out like a sore thumb.

There is also the fact that crime journalists in Ireland play for far higher stakes than those in the rest of the UK. As well as Veronica Guerin's murder in 1996, in September 2001, north of the border, *Sunday World* reporter Martin O'Hagan was shot dead by a loyalist drugs gang after penning similar exposés.

The feelings of unease remain as I get closer to my goal. I first decide to drive through St Mary's Park, just to get a feel for the place. Almost as soon as I enter the estate a kind of silent jungle tele-graph seems to sound. Wherever you are, a burnt-out house is never more than a stone's throw away. There are piles of rotting rubbish everywhere and virtually every property has been vandalised in some way. With groups of youths wandering aimlessly around in the midst of what should be a school day, you can literally feel the lawlessness in the air. Unlike inner-city estates where families are moved into high-rise blocks, these sprawling developments consist of rows and rows of low-rise buildings, twisting and curving around one another under a big grey sky for as far as the eye can see.

There's not much wealth on display, even in the form of flashy cars. Since the launch of the Criminal Assets Bureau, gangsters know that anything of value that they can't prove they bought legitimately will be taken off them. Ger Dundon has even lost both of his bulletproof cars, reckoned to be worth around €40,000 each, to the agency. It means that even the top kingpins are forced to live alongside some of the poorest members of their community. That said, the Keane gang is said to have millions of euros stashed away in accounts abroad and, thanks to making generous offers to their neighbours, is said to own the majority of properties in St Mary's Park. With the whole area scheduled for demolition at some point in the future, this could prove to be a nice little earner for the gang.

In the meantime, as I drive through, suspicions are high and eyes are following me everywhere. As I reach the bottom of the estate and curl round the ring road to head back out, it seems busier than ever with several residents looking out of windows, standing on the pavement or even standing in the middle of the road, forcing me to slow down or swerve as I drive by. I'm left with the distinct feeling that if I stop or even slow down too much, especially close to the area where Christy Keane and Owen Treacy are holed up, I might be in for an incredibly uncomfortable time. I speed up a little and make my way out of the area. It is only when I leave that I realise I've been holding my breath for the past few minutes.

A little later that afternoon I learn that both Ger and John Dundon, the only two brothers at liberty at the time of my visit, are out of the country. For a moment I am disappointed, but the more I think about it, the more I realise that it's probably for the best.

My contact, a local community worker who has tried without success to set up a meeting, wholeheartedly agrees. 'The biggest danger,' he explains, 'is that you're a stranger and that you've got an English accent. Both gangs have hired hitmen from the UK before now. If you go wandering through St Mary's Park trying to get face to face with Christy Keane, or head down the Hyde Road and go knocking on the door of the Dundons', you're going to get your fucking head blown off. This isn't some James Bond film, they're not the kind of cartoon villains who are going to sit down and tell you how it all works, they'll just take you out the back and shoot you. End of story.'

With the vicious murder of Roy Collins, the McCarthy–Dundons had let it be known that they were by far the dominant gang in Limerick, big enough to challenge the state itself, and that their quest for underworld domination remained their chief agenda. With Christy Keane – now a grandfather – seemingly under self-imposed house arrest and too old to pose a serious threat, they could finally reign supreme. Or so they thought.

In October 2009, four months after the Dundons posted their YouTube video, the Keane gang replied with one of their own. Filmed in the grounds of their home base of St Mary's Park the film shows a young man in a hoodie performing a minute-long rap during which John Dundon is warned that he will be shot six times until he does not breathe anymore. The man then shows a picture of an Uzi sub-machine gun printed on the back of his top and says: 'This is what you are getting, you are getting that in the fucking head, you fucking rat.'

Although they cannot be identified, it is clear that those in the Keane video are quite young, in their early twenties at most. With so many of the leading gangsters dead, behind bars or barricaded in their homes for safety's sake, the average age of those on 'active duty' has been getting lower and lower. Children are increasingly being used as drug or gun couriers and see gang members as role models. In one case a fourteen-year-old described as a 'foot soldier' for the McCarthy–Dundon gang was caught after firing eight rounds from a handgun into a house on St Mary's Park. Apprehended while driving a getaway car, he was found to be wearing a bulletproof vest. Another fourteen-year-old was caught with a shotgun and twelve cartridges. He told officers he needed protection as he was in danger of being shot or killed.

In his book *Outliers*, the author Malcolm Gladwell examines the reasons behind why some people go on to huge success and others fail despite their best efforts. Much of it comes down to simply being in the right place at the right time. This is why, the book demonstrates, the vast majority of Canadian hockey players are born in the first three months of the year (the cut-off date for new enrolments favours the most physically mature), why the world leaders in computing are all born within a year of each other (they all entered college at the start of the computer boom and were given unlimited access to programming terminals). According to Gladwell, success is not just about raw talent or hard work, it is also about opportunity and being in the right place at the right time.

The likes of Ger Dundon and the youths on both sides of the feud are, it is safe to say, perfectly placed to move up to the highest levels of organised crime should they choose to do so. A key figure from the gang is now based permanently in the UK and is in charge of co-ordinating the smuggling of ever increasing loads of cocaine shipped from Spain to the west coast of Ireland. The real threat for the future comes from this new generation growing up in a world where extremes of brutality and viciousness are the norm.

The kingpins of today are bad enough; from the look of things, the kingpins of tomorrow are going to be far worse.

ACKNOWLEDGEMENTS

For reasons of extreme shyness, sub judice, conditions imposed by the probation service and a general sense of concern about what might happen to me if I were to antagonise them, the vast majority of those I have spoken to in the course of researching this book would prefer not to be named. You all know who you are, and I am eternally grateful for you assistance.

For reasons that have nothing to do with the former but possibly a little to do with the latter, I would like to thank Debs and the boys, and everyone at United Agents, especially Caroline Dawnay and Olivia Hunt. Thanks too to the hardworking team at Hodder, in particular my editor Rupert Lancaster and his assistant Laura Macaulay.